AN HONEST ANGLER

AN HONEST ANGLER

The Best of
Sparse Grey Hackle

Edited by Patricia Miller Sherwood

The Lyons Press

Printed in the United States of America
10 9 8 7 6 5 4 3 2 1
Design by John Gray

Library of Congress Cataloging-in-Publication Data
Hackle, Sparse Grey, 1892–1983
    An honest angler: the best of Sparse Grey Hackle / edited by
Patricia Miller Sherwood.
        p.   cm.
    Includes bibliographical references (p.   ).
    ISBN 1-55821-624-3
    1. Fishing—Anecdotes.   2. Fishing—Humor.   I. Sherwood, Patricia Miller.
II. Title.
SH441 H124 1998   97-30931
799.1—dc21   CIP

"Introduction" first appeared in Simplified Fly Fishing *by S. R. Slaymaker II, published by Harper & Row, New York, Evanston and London, 1969.*

"A Drink of Water," "Chance Meetings," "Down the Great River," "Murder," "Night Fishing," "Nocturne," "Rain on the Brodhead," "The Angler Breeched," "The Indomitable," "The Lotus Eaters," "The Perfect Angler," and "The Young Conservationist" first appeared in Fishless Days, Angling Nights.

"The First Camping Trip" is a portion of a piece that first appeared in Fishless Days, Angling Nights.

"A Fey Day" and "A Fisherman's Fauna" first appeared in Fishless Days.

"Father of the Flyrod" and "Me and Those Canoes" first appeared in Sports Illustrated *magazine. "Father of the Flyrod" also appeared in varying forms in other publications.*

"Houseboats . . . Bah!," "Old Timer Puts Oar In," and "Sartorial Splendor" first appeared in The New York Times.

"The Darbees" first appeared as the introduction to Catskill Flytier *by Harry Darbee and Austin M. Francis, published by J. B. Lippincott Company, Philadelphia and New York, 1977.*

"Only Yesterday" first appeared as the introduction to Great Fishing Tackle Catalogs of the Golden Age *by Samuel Melner and Hermann Kessler, The Lyons Press, New York, 1972.*

"The Remembering Machine" first appeared as the introduction to The Pleasures of Flyfishing *by V. S. Hidy, Winchester Press, New York, 1972.*

All of Donald Stillman's "Rod & Gun" columns originally appeared in The New York Herald Tribune.

All of Red Smith's columns originally appeared in The New York Herald Tribune.

To those who went before . . . and those who come after: Mother and Dad, who made life's pathway clear, and my daughters, Amy, Pamela, and Holly, who make it a joy.

"I shall stay him no longer than to wish him a rainy evening to read this following Discourse; and that (if he be an honest angler) the East wind may never blow when he goes a-Fishing."

—Izaak Walton
The Compleat Angler

Table of Contents

Acknowledgments

To Bill and Jeanne, my dear brother and sister, eternal thanks for your unsparing confidence and love. And to Mikie, too, who would if she could.

But most of all, to Nick. There really are no words. "Thank you" is a phrase of limitation—it cannot be intensified, it can only be multiplied. So, as the number of stars in the sky, fish in the waters, sand grains on the beach, I repeat "thank you" for myself and for Dad, making it almighty strong and absolutely heartfelt.

Foreword

I didn't know my father very well. Although he had a fund of anecdotes of his earlier life—anecdotes that became all too familiar—they left great gaps. Between those few well-polished tales was a lifetime of highs and lows and successes and failures and feelings.

Although Dad was a marathon talker, his stories were meant to entertain, not reveal. So I knew the skeleton of his life, but not the meat and blood and heart. And besides, I'd heard it all before. Often. So if there were any revelations, they slid right past the uncaring imperceptions of my youth.

What's more, like all good storytellers—and he was a talented raconteur—Dad's stories were, well, embroidered. Sometimes to the point where you could hardly have recognized the circumstances even if you'd been there. So we children tended to discount a good part of what we heard as being the product of an exceptional imagination.

In truth, anyone who wants to know Sparse Grey Hackle really has only to read his stories. Every one of them reveals a time of life, a frame of mind, a facet of a multifaceted personality. He was his own best biographer.

Nonetheless, here are the bare facts:

Alfred Waterbury Miller was born November 27, 1892. He was raised in Brooklyn, New York, of poor but honest parents, and spent dreaming summers on his grandfather's farm in upstate New York.

He and his cousin Frank Miller very early took to camping and canoeing and other manly evidences of the rugged outdoor life. They explored New York's harbors and bays, sweating through the subway system to get

1

to the water, and then disporting themselves like the outdoorsmen Dad so admired.

While a student at The Commercial High School in Brooklyn he was an active—nay, voluble—member of the debating squad and, in fact, became the extemporaneous debating champion of the Greater New York Interscholastic League. Even then he talked a lot.

He was also a member of the track team; I get the impression he wasn't exactly the star of the team, but he often talked about his running days, which we kids all thought hilarious in view of his decided embonpoint in his later years. In fact, he was both skinny and agile in his youth, though those days seemed practically prehistoric to us.

Once graduated he went to work, as all right-thinking young men did. And about that time he joined the National Guard Field Artillery. For some reason—I think part patriotism, part the urge to swan about in a uniform, and part the romantic notion of riding a horse—he was impelled to submit to the discipline and, you should pardon the expression, horseplay of the military. I think he must have been a good soldier; he certainly loved it.

Dad was restless; he wanted more than a secretary's job in an insurance company. So he enrolled at Colgate University . . . and left again fairly quickly "at the earnest request of the Dean." His preparation at a commercial high school simply wasn't adequate, he had to work to support himself while he was there, and I suspect he may not have had quite the application to study required. His rosy mental picture came bump up against hard reality—he'd entered college hoping to become a chemist because he "wanted to know what things were made of" (an interesting early display of his wide-ranging curiosity). Unfortunately, chemists needed math, and Dad was on very shaky ground when it came to math, particularly since he'd never had any higher mathematics in high school.

(While at Colgate he acquired a sobriquet that stayed with him all his life. Because of his sober and pontifical manner, he was nicknamed Deacon; my mother always called him "Deac," as did many of his friends and all his grandchildren. Even the license plates on his car read DEAC.)

Washing out of Colgate was probably a very good thing; he went from there to being private secretary to C. W. Barron, owner of *The Wall Street Journal* and the Boston News Bureau—his introduction to the financial world. The Commercial High School may not have been much for calculus and algebra, but it was fierce on shorthand and grammar and typing and paying attention and all the things that make good secretaries and, incidentally, good reporters.

Mr. Barron's usual procedure was to keep a secretary for a year or two and then transfer him (secretaries were always men then) to one of his other enterprises. It was a prime opportunity for the young men, and a constant stream of well-trained staff members for Barron. So after a while he transferred Dad to the Boston News Bureau, where he began gathering and writing financial news, and writing his first daily column on the gossip of the money world.

Then along came the "Mexican War" and trouble on the Texas border. Well, Dad couldn't sit still while there was action happening somewhere; he got a leave of absence and rejoined the old Brooklyn Battery—a move which provided endless inspiration for funny stories and lengthy reminiscences. I knew it well.

There was that in Dad that loved the military. By the time the Texas border could get along without him, he was needed in Europe. The First World War was in full, horrible blaze and he desperately wanted to be part of it. No one would have him—he had terrible eyesight, being very nearsighted, and simply could not pass an eye test, though he tried every branch of the service he could find, including, I believe, the Canadian Army. Somehow or other he faked reading the eye chart and wangled duty as an ambulance driver, the fact that he couldn't drive notwithstanding.

That time in France marked him forever. He was lucky; he was on the fringes of the war, and he was a grown man compared to most of the troops. Still, the color and smell and feel of it were fresh to him always. The first evidences of his writing for the pleasure of it show up then . . . all I have left is a couple of poems, but the passion to put it down had clearly started to burst out.

Once discharged he returned to the Boston News Bureau, where he met the beautiful and charming Louisa Brewster. Soon afterward he was transferred to *The Wall Street Journal* . . . so he swept Miss Brewster off to New York and settled down to domestic life. (It may be of interest to note that he took his blushing bride fishing for their honeymoon. She became considerably better at it than he was.)

Dad loved the newspaper business—he loved knowing all the people, from printers to copyboys to editors in chief. He loved nosing out the gossip and rumors and secret deals that seethed around Wall Street then, as now. He loved the pressure of getting it right, reporting it correctly, and doing it on time, written clean and ready to set.

While at the *Journal* he met Ernest van Dyke, whom he said was the finest reporter the *Journal* ever had. Some years later, van Dyke invited Dad to become a partner in his small (read "one-man") financial public relations firm. Even after "Van" died, the firm remained E. C. van Dyke & Co.—for years at 55 Liberty Street. (One of the things I most admired about my father was his ability to pick up the two New York morning papers at the Darien railroad station and read them cover to cover during his morning commute—into Grand Central, across the terminal floor to the downtown IRT entrance, onto the subway, and out at the right stop—without lifting his gaze from the paper. He never missed a step, ran into anyone, or stumbled on a stair.)

Ernest van Dyke also fished . . . a sport which Dad had been quietly but avidly pursuing since he and Cousin Frank fished the then-clean waters of Jamaica Bay and the Hudson River. So van Dyke introduced Dad to The Anglers' Club of New York—the beginning of a long, sometimes contentious, and very valuable connection for Dad. He began writing little bits for its *Bulletin* and went on to become the editor—a position he held for many years, moaning and complaining about it all the time.

Sometime in the 1930s or '40s one of his beloved Catskill streams was in danger of being polluted. So Dad charged into battle, writing furious articles about it. He thought it the better part of valor to remain anonymous in this regard, so he coined the name "Sparse Grey Hackle." It was to become probably the most famous nom de plume in angling history.

That same choleric and exacting temperament was a very large part of his personality. At various times and for various reasons he severed a very profitable connection with a major magazine, demanded the return of his book manuscript from his first publisher (Crown) and was only dissuaded from throwing it to the winds by the tact and guile of his editor, resigned not once but a number of times from his beloved Anglers' Club, didn't speak to his own father for seven years, and cut off communication with his recalcitrant youngest daughter (me) for some months. It seems he got more cussed and more contentious as time went by, but, for some reason, his writing grew richer and deeper and more elegant.

On the other hand, he was a staunch and generous friend and had an enormous correspondence, much of which has been lost. He kept no carbons of his letters; he said he'd be forced out of his office by the volume. I believe it. Of the relatively few copies I have, many are six pages or more of single-spaced typewritten copy, full of the warmth, knowledge, curiosity, humor, and essence of Sparse Grey Hackle. Many of his correspondents he never met, and they ranged from Supreme Court justices to worn-tweed Scotsmen to one of America's great fly tyers.

And he had made friends among the newspaper sporting columnists as well; they were often very grateful for one of those yellow copy-paper letters from Sparse, just the right size to fill a column and sparkling with wit and wisdom. (One regretful column was entitled "A Sad Day for Columnists," referring to the fact that Sparse had discovered he could be *paid* for his work.)

As his name spread, through his appearance in the "huntin', fishin', shootin'" columns of some of America's finest sportswriters, national magazines and prestigious newspapers commissioned pieces to entertain their readers. These articles and stories appeared in publications ranging from *Sports Illustrated* to *The New York Times*.

In 1954 The Anglers' Club of New York privately printed Dad's first book, *Fishless Days*. And in 1971, his 79th year, *Fishless Days, Angling Nights* was published. (It was timed to be a fiftieth wedding anniversary surprise for my mother, "Momma.") The book's success absolutely stunned Dad—he had not expected it to sell out even the first printing. To this day, it is still in print.

Dad died on November 11—Armistice Day—1983, just a little short of his ninety-first birthday. He would have liked the symbolism of the date.

Now I believe the time is right to offer a fresh look at a timeless sportsman—an occasion to gather together "the best of Sparse Grey Hackle." Almost everything I deemed most worthy is included: choice letters, selected columns from New York's newspapers, original material, as well as those pieces which have proven themselves—favorite stories from prior books, articles from great sporting magazines, and special pieces done as a courtesy to other fishing authors.

The bright threads of Sparse's words create a magic carpet on which you can journey from tiny silver streams to the mighty Mississippi . . . from dusty Texas plains to cool Adirondack woods . . . from a Paris at war to the peaceful Catskills.

Not everything is here; true devotees may find their favorites missing. But with luck there will be new joys hidden away in this, the best of Sparse Grey Hackle.

—Patricia Miller Sherwood
Summer 1997

Who is Sparse Grey Hackle?

O ver the last thirty-five years discussions of various aspects of angling have appeared under the pen name of Sparse Grey Hackle. And for approximately that length of time readers have demanded: "Who does Sparse Grey Hackle think he is?" I can answer that query.

It was on a June evening, back in the old days, that my friend Everett Garrison and I entered the barroom of the Antrim Lodge, where were gathered the innumerable fishermen who were spending the mayfly season at Roscoe, New York, trout-fishing capital of the Catskills. We found the low-ceilinged basement already jammed with men in hobnailed shoes and waders who were either guarding their drinks with both hands or fighting their way through the crowd to the bar. A roar of conversation battled with the crash of the jukebox, and a blanket of tobacco smoke veiled the lights.

"This is hopeless. Let's go see Harry and Elsie and get a drink from them," I suggested. The reply came, not from Garry, but from a stranger beside me, a fat man with a red face and scanty white hair.

"The Darbees are fishing the East Branch and likely won't be home until midnight, but I'll be glad to give you a drink if you'll come upstairs to my room," he said.

He was a fisherman, by his tweeds and the wood-duck flank feather in his hatband; an old-timer if he knew Harry and Elsie Darbee, whom I call the best fly tyers in the world, that well; and sober, although he had enough alcohol on his breath to take the varnish off a rod.

We accepted and went upstairs, where the stranger took a bottle from a whole case of Scotch and poured for us. The conversation turned to fishing, and finally Garry mentioned Old Bill, the twelve-pound brown trout that lived for years under the old covered bridge at Arena.

"A mere minnow," said our new-found friend. This nettled Garry, for of course a twelve-pound brown is an enormous fish.

"Yes?" he replied. "What's the biggest fish *you* ever caught?"

"I caught the biggest brown trout in the world. He weighed at least fifty pounds and he was well over five feet long," was the answer.

I curbed my natural reaction. After all, I was drinking the man's liquor.

"Didn't you weigh and measure him?" I asked when I could control my voice.

"He's still in the river," said the stranger. He paused to open a fresh bottle, poured himself a tumblerful, and began:

"I am a big-fish fisherman; anyone in Roscoe will tell you that Sparse Grey Hackle has never been known to take a trout under three pounds. As you probably know, everything about the time, place, and method of taking big trout is completely different from taking the ordinary stream fish. So the big-fish fishermen are a clannish, secretive group, and each one has his own distinctive method. My method is to think like a fish.

"About this time last year I got to wondering why no one catches trout in the Mountain Pool, so I put myself in the place of a fish and asked myself why I avoided such a fine pool. The answer was obvious: I was afraid. And what was there about that pool that I, a fish, need fear? Only one thing—a bigger fish. Big fish drive away the smaller ones.

"I reflected that no one had ever taken even a five-pound trout from the Mountain Pool, which could only mean that there must be a trout in there big enough to chase a five-pounder away. I resolved to get him.

"So next day at dawn I drove down to the Mountain Pool with all my tackle, my lunch of bread and cheese, and a case of Scotch. I put a couple of bottles in the seat of my waders so I wouldn't have to be running back to the car all the time. Then I rigged my big nine-foot rod and went to work.

"I fished with everything from dry flies to minnows without moving a fish, and then I tore my waders on the barbed-wire fence that Guy Bury built across the tail of the pool to keep his cows from straying. So I went back to the car and patched the waders, spilling a little pool of rubber cement in the process. While I was waiting for the patch to dry, a shower came up.

"As I sat huddled in my slicker I noticed the bugs on the ground; they were rolling in the rubber cement and then running around in the rain having a fine time. They were, you might say, wearing raincoats.

"This gave me an idea, one that would occur only to a man who thinks like a fish. I went back in the bushes and caught one of those huge moths, coated it with rubber cement, and stuck it onto my hook. Then I threw it in at the head of the pool and fed out line to let it float downstream naturally.

"The moth fluttered along the surface, rising a few inches and then dropping back. About halfway down the pool, there was a sucking sound and the moth disappeared in a swirl as big as a washtub!

"I struck as hard as I dared; there was a terrific convulsion in the water; I began to reel . . . The next thing I knew I was in six feet of water and the line was reeled in right up to the leader knot. The fish was so big that I had reeled myself out to him instead of drawing him in to me! Gentlemen, I give you my word he was over five feet long and weighed fifty pounds if he weighed an ounce.

"In this emergency I began to think like a fish. What would I do if I were that big and I had a fisherman where he had me? I would chew the living hell out of him! Since I had no desire to be simultaneously the most famous and the deadest fisherman on the Beaverkill, I got out my knife and cut the line. But the fish got around between me and the shore, and I was having a terrible time with him when someone grabbed me by the collar and hoisted me ashore.

"It was Keegan, the state trooper who patrols Route 17 below Roscoe, where it runs beside the river. I was grateful to him for saving my life but exasperated because he had not even seen the big fish and intimated that I had been drinking. In fact, he threatened to run me in if I drank any more that day.

"When he left I went back to my car for my lunch and a couple more bottles. I dipped my bread in the whiskey—I wasn't drinking the liquor, I was eating it, see?—and sat down to think like a fish. This was no ordinary fish, so it followed that he would not be interested in an ordinary lure. I put my mind to work to invent an extraordinary lure, and I did.

"I was starting on my second loaf of bread when I saw minnows breaking water in the shallows as if something was chasing them. So I soaked a slice of bread in whiskey and let it float down the current. I figured that that old trout hadn't had a drink in years and would be eager for one. And I was right. As soon as he smelled the whiskey he took up his feeding position and—socko! I could hear his teeth clash. I took a bite of bread and poured whiskey into my mouth on top of it, which is a handier way to eat Scotch, and then I soaked another slice and put it on my hook.

"The big trout hit it furiously but he just stole my bait. He stole the next three slices, too. Then I noticed that he was weaving around in the current. He missed the next slice completely, floated downstream on his side, and began to swim in circles. And every little while he would open his mouth and emit a string of bubbles and a sound like 'Hup!'

"Then I sent him down a slice of bread with *two* hooks in it, and when he gulped I struck, hard. The rod bent down to the water. The reel began to screech and then to smoke, and in another instant the bearings burned out, the spool jammed, and the line broke. I thought I had lost the big fish but in a moment I saw him chasing minnows, upside down, with my line trailing behind him. I grabbed it and tied it to my wrist. It almost cost me my life.

"He started downstream like a torpedo, towing me behind him. He went through the barbed-wire fence like a bat out of hell, but I hit it with a bang that uprooted the posts. Tangled as I was in the wire, I could not get to my feet, so I started rolling to get ashore.

"The drunken trout lunged at me with his mouth open—and what teeth he had!—but just as he was about to bite me he said, 'Hup!' so he hit me with his mouth closed. Even so, the point of his great undershot jaw cut a gash in my leg. He charged again, but again he hupped at the last moment, so all I got was another gash. Again and again he attacked but each time he would 'Hup!' and have to close his mouth. My legs were covered with gashes by the time Keegan hauled me ashore.

"Again he had failed to see the big fish; he said my cuts were from rolling in the barbed wire. I think he was going to pinch me, but just then an old Model A Ford went down the road.

"'There's that damned deer poacher!' shouted Keegan and ran for his car.

"When I awoke it was dusk and I felt terrible, but I got out the Alka-Seltzer and a couple more bottles of Scotch and began thinking like a fish. The big fellow must be feeling terrible, too, I decided. So I rigged my big salmon rod, and when I heard him splashing in the shallows across the pool, I put a few Alka-Seltzer tablets onto the hook and cast into the darkness. There was a splash and a haul on my line, and this time I struck with both hands and then began pulling and horsing as hard as I could to bring this big fish over to my side.

"You never heard such a commotion in your life! The fish didn't swim around much but sort of floundered and yelled. I suppose you think a trout can't yell. Well, this one did, and swore, too!

"I hauled that fish almost across the river by main strength. Then the line went slack. The fish came toward me, half out of the water. Something hit me in the eye and on the nose, and began battering me, and all the while the fish was assaulting me it was shrieking and cursing.

"I went down in the water. When I scrambled up I was astounded to see Johnny Woodruff in front of me. Was I surprised, and was I mad!

"'What are you doing in my pool?' I yelled. 'I just had the world's biggest trout on and you come along and make me lose him! Where are your stream manners? Get the hell out of here!'

"But Johnny was madder than I was. You know what he accused me of? He said he had been night-fishing on the other side when I cast across him, hooked him in the neck, and tried to drown him.

"He started for me again, and believe me, I was glad to see Keegan for the third time. I thought fast, this time not like a fish but like a state trooper. I hauled out my remaining bottle.

"'You need a drink after chasing that poacher,'" I said.

"'I been after him all summer; he's selling deer,' said Keegan, mentioning the worst sin in the Catskills. 'I got the goods on him at last. I slapped the cuffs on him and turned him over to Roy Steenrod (the game protector at that time) to take down to Liberty.' And with that he poured down a drink big enough to keep his radiator from freezing all winter.

"'If you're wounded you had better guard against infection,' I advised Johnny. He took the bottle and sterilized his whole interior.

"'And in these wet clothes I must take precautions against pneumonia,' I concluded, and took all the precautions there were left in the bottle.

"While we were walking back to the car for another bottle I told them about the fifty-pound trout, but they only laughed. They wouldn't believe me! They wouldn't be—"

The speaker's voice had been dropping lower and lower, and now it stopped. A snore sounded.

Garry and I looked at each other, and tiptoed away.

The foregoing narrative is unreliable as to details, names, and places, and contains some misleading although technically correct statements—Sparse Grey Hackle never took a trout *over* three pounds, either! But it faithfully portrays the faulty observation and fallacious reasoning from unjustified assumptions to unwarranted conclusions that characterize the ordinary fisherman and cause him to "think like a fish." *A fish does not think at all!*

In other words, Sparse Grey Hackle is just an ordinary angler, even as you and I.

Letter to Al Severeid

April 11, 1972

. . . It is that Stillman and I were old friends, and I got my first "exposure" to publication writing pieces for his column in the Herald-Tribune, "Rod and Gun." In fact, I invented the pen name Sparse Grey Hackle to use in that column (and elsewhere) in a crusade against the town of Roscoe for running its sewer into the bottom of the Junction Pool.

I didn't waste time talking about pollution killing fish. I kept sending out publicity releases to small towns in the area, talking about typhoid fever. That's a very dirty word in resort country and I figured I might turn up floating in the river with my head caved in if they found out who was doing it. Hence the pen name. Nobody found out who it was for seven or eight years.

The Perfect Angler

I never saw him; if anyone else ever did, it has not been reported. I don't believe he exists. But if he did, what would his attributes be?

If we accept the little girl's statement that piano playing is easy—"You just press down on those black and white things"—and apply it to trout fishing, all it involves is:

1) finding a fish

2) deceiving it into taking an imitation of its food

3) hooking, playing, and landing it.

The first requirement is the most important; my guess is that finding a fish is anywhere from 50 percent to 80 percent of catching it. Overwhelmingly, the reason why so many experienced and well-equipped fishermen catch so few trout is that most of the time they aren't fishing over fish.

Bill Kelly, a research aquatic biologist and a skillful, experienced angler, says I should specify a *feeding* fish. If he means a big fish, I agree. "To catch a five-pounder, you must be there when he's feeding," Ed Hewitt once told me. And experts like Herman Christian agree that a good hatch of big flies must be on for about half an hour before the larger fish, over sixteen inches, will come on the feed.

Also, if Bill means the rich Pennsylvania limestone streams or the lush British chalkstreams, I agree. But most of our eastern trout waters are hungry streams in which the smaller fish, up to maybe twelve inches, tend to harbor between hatches close enough to a feed lane to seize anything edible that may come riding down the current.

Anyway, finding a fish is the problem; the rest is patience.

Fish-finding is done by sight; by knowing the kinds of places in which fish harbor or feed; or by the simple hammer-and-chisel process of fishing one stretch so often that eventually one learns where the fish are, without knowing or caring why. The first method is the rarest, the second the most difficult, and the third the easiest but most limited.

Really fine fishing eyesight is a gift of the gods, the rarest and most enviable attribute a fisherman can possess, and I have never known a truly great angler who did not have it. Edward R. Hewitt had the eyes of an eagle, right up to his death; so did George M. L. LaBranche. And Ray Bergman's ability to see fish was so instinctive that he never could understand why everyone couldn't do it.

The hawk-eyed angler sees not only the fish themselves but the faint, fleeting signs of their presence—the tiny dimple in the slow water next the bank, which indicates a big fish sucking down little flies; the tiny black object momentarily protruded above the surface, which is the neb of a good, quietly feeding fish; the slight ruffling of the shallows by a school of minnows fleeing from the bogeyman.

George LaBranche claimed in *The Dry Fly and Fast Water* that the knack of seeing fish under water can be learned by practice, but I am inclined to believe that either one is born with sharp eyes or one is not. On the other hand, there is a mysterious mental aspect of eyesight; sometimes it seems to be a quality separate from mere keenness of sight—visual acuity. Resolving power, the ability to see what we look at, seems to be a mental as well as a physical attribute. How else can we account for the almost-incredible ability of the great British angler-writer G. E. M. Skues to discern whether trout were nymphing immediately *under,* or taking spent flies *in,* the surface film, when we know that he was virtually blind in one eye and had to aid the other with a monocle? Of course, knowledge plays a part. "The little brown wink under water," as Skues called it, means a feeding fish to the initiate but nothing at all to the tyro, just as the Pullman-plush patch in yonder bush, eighteen inches above the ground, means a deer in summer coat to the woodsman but is never noticed by the city yokel looking sixteen hands high for a hat rack spread of antlers.

The second method of finding fish, by learning to be "a judge of water," is to my way of thinking the highest attainment in this aspect of angling. Anyone who is willing to do the work can make himself a fair judge of water; like piano playing, a little of it is a simple thing to acquire. But mastery of the art is granted to but few, and a lifetime is not too long to achieve perfection.

It is remarkable what a good judge of water can do. Gene Russell, who learned the angler's trade on hard-plugged public streams around New York City, doesn't even set up a rod when he gets out of his car to fish a new piece of water. He just saunters along the bank for half a mile or so, smoking a pipe and looking; then he saunters back and either drives away or gets out his rod and goes to one, two, or maybe three places which he has mentally marked down during his stroll.

What did he see? Maybe it was a tiny patch of watercress on the opposite bank, or perhaps moisture on a rocky face above the stream; either would indicate a seepage of cold spring water below which a fish is apt to be lying in hot weather. Maybe it was a big stone in the current—not any stone, but one so faced and undercut that it creates an eddy of quiet water in front of it in which a trout can rest at ease while the stream brings him his vittles. Maybe it was a smallish trout exposing himself where no trout ought to be, on a clean sand bottom in brilliant sunlight. If there is a good lie nearby, the chances are that a bigger fish has driven the little fellow out of it; he wants to go back but daren't.

Maybe Gene saw a long stretch of shallow, brawling water, the natural feeding grounds of the trout, without any cover for a sizable fish anywhere along it except one hollow about as big as a bathtub. Maybe such a fish is using it for an advanced base.

More likely, Gene didn't really *see* all this, for an experienced, capable angler's stream sense becomes a part of his subconscious. Probably all he *saw* were a few places that seemed to say: Try me.

The third method of fish-finding, that of learning a piece of water by experience, is, of course, a limited one, and yet it is remarkable how many miles of water an industrious and wide-ranging fisherman can learn by heart. I once heard the late John Alden Knight and a man named Crane, of Deposit, New York, testing each other's knowledge of some ten miles of excellent fly-rod bass water on the West Branch of the Delaware between Deposit and Hancock. They checked each other stone by stone on every pool and disagreed but once—as to whether there were four or five stones at the head of the Cat Pool. They finally agreed that there were five, but that there never was a bass behind the first one.

Still, the angler who depends on experience to know the stream is like the applicant for admission to the bar who had read nothing but the laws of the state. "Young man," thundered the judge, "someday the legislature may repeal everything you know." The stream is continually repealing much of what the local angler has learned; after every big storm, with its attendant filling of old holes and digging of new ones, he has to learn the water anew.

Thus far we have been able to follow a firm path. But it ends on the shores of an illimitable sea of controversy when we come to the second requirement of angling: to deceive the fish into taking an imitation of its food. Fortunately, it is not necessary for us to wet much more than the soles of our shoes in this sea.

First, let us consider a few fundamentals. The trout is a very primitive creature with only two primary instincts. One is the spawning urge; it comes during the closed season so we need not consider it. The other is self-preservation. It cannot be emphasized too strongly that the trout spends all its time at the business of staying alive.

Unfortunately for the trout, its internal economy is such that it is never very far ahead of starvation; and the larder of the stream is not in the safest but in the most dangerous, i.e., exposed, places. The whole "food chain"— plankton, insects, minnows—lives in the fast, shallow places where there is lots of sunlight and quickly changing water. So when a fish gets hungry enough, it has to risk itself out where the food is. Aside from food, it has only two other requirements: oxygen (as you know, it is dissolved in the water) and cover—protection from its enemies and shelter from such elements as floods and ice. Obviously, the only instinct of the trout to which the fisherman can appeal is its appetite; the only lure which will interest it is an imitation of its food.

Trout eat about every living thing that they can catch and swallow, but in the main they feed on smaller fish and the various life forms of water insects. There is something in the composition of water insects that makes them preferred by the trout to any other form of food. But a big fish, which eats more, in proportion to its weight, than a man, just doesn't have the time or the energy to collect its nourishment one insect at a time, so it is forced to feed considerably on minnows, frogs, crawfish, and other sizable mouthfuls. But it is the glory of the brown trout that he never entirely ceases to feed on insects, no matter how big he grows, so that the fly fisherman always has a chance—not a good one, but a chance—of setting his hook in the biggest fish in the stream. For the purpose of this article we shall assume that "food" means stream insects in their several life forms.

So to catch a trout the angler must deceive it into taking an imitation of some form of stream insect. There is a lot of dynamite in those two simple words *deceive* and *imitation,* for they are the keys to the most uncompromising and violent disagreements in the whole world of sport.

Let us consider imitation first. The trout, being essentially a very simple creature, does not go through elevated mental processes in feeding but depends upon its reflexes; it has more automatic controls built into it than a guided missile. (They work a lot better, too.) It reacts to the approach in, or on, the current of an insect larva or winged fly according to the triggering of these automatic controls, varying with the circumstances. So imitation can only mean: whatever deceives the reflexes, the automatic controls, of the fish, *according to the circumstances.*

That is an important qualification. An invitation to dinner doesn't look anything like a dinner, but, under different circumstances, each may bring a hungry man a-running. The angler may use a replica of the natural insect, complete even to its eyes, like Halford, or depend mostly on where he casts his fly and how it floats, like LaBranche, to deceive the fish. But if he does deceive the fish, that's all that counts; who will say he is wrong? For the purpose of our hypothetical perfect angler it is sufficient to say, as regards imitation, that he knows how to imitate the natural food of the trout so well that the fish is deceived under every circumstance.

This involves a great knowledge of both aquatic biology and stream entomology and a great skill in expressing this knowledge in the concrete form of artificial flies. Our perfect angler must have the technical knowledge of such authorities as the late Dr. James G. Needham and his son Dr. Paul R. Needham (*Life of Inland Waters* and numerous other works, jointly or severally), and the late Dr. Ann Haven Morgan (*Field Book of Ponds and Streams,* and others). And like Theodore Gordon, who was probably the first man to fish the dry fly in America, our perfect angler must have a large practical knowledge of stream insects and the ability to construct imitations of them.

Imitation of the fish's food, the stream insect, is only a part of deceiving it; the rest is presentation, which involves stalking—getting into casting position without alarming the fish—and casting, including also fishing out the cast.

Stalking is another of the fundamentals upon which one may judge the quality of an angler. The real expert is always willing to credit the fish with the inordinate wariness which it always manifests, and he is willing to take the trouble to stalk as he should, even if it is no more than taking pains to scare the little fish in the tail of the pool downstream, out of the way, rather than upstream where they will alarm the bigger ones.

The great Skues was well into his eighties, an enfeebled old man, when he wrote to a friend that he "found it increasingly difficult to adopt an attitude of becoming reverence to the fish." British chalkstreams usually can't be waded, and, typically, their banks are bare except for a few bushes to which the angler creeps and behind which he kneels to cast. Skues was finding it "increasingly difficult" to do so; but he was kneeling, nevertheless.

Over on what used to be the "railroad" side of Cairns's Pool on the lower Beaverkill, there was a magnificently deep, boulder-lined run that was just right for big fish. Every day during the season, literally scores of fishermen flogged that run, carelessly and ineffectually, from the shallow, "road" side. It couldn't be fished properly from that side and they knew it; they just wouldn't bother to do it right.

But for an expert like Harry Darbee it was not too much trouble to cross the stream above the pool, walk along the railroad track, slither down a dauntingly steep and loose embankment, and then work from one to another of the huge rough rocks that protected the railroad fill from floods. With the stream on his left, his casting arm had to contend with an abominable mess of high bushes, low-strung telegraph wires, poles, and the embankment itself, and most fishermen said it wasn't worth it. But I saw Harry perched like a chamois on one steep-faced boulder after another, holding his rod across his body and making niggling backhanded casts to every good spot within reach.

Seldom indeed will one see the average fisherman crawling to reach the right spot, or kneeling in the stream to reduce his visibility; but Ray Bergman used to wear out the knees of his waders before any other portion, and Otto v. Kienbusch not only fished but progressed upstream on his knees along a quarter mile of the flat, gravel-bottomed, fish-infested upper Nissequogue on Long Island. Otto was one of the few who could get into the big browns in that stretch.

Every dry-fly man knows that there are ways of casting a curve or loop in his line so as to allow his fly a natural float when he is fishing across varied currents. But Ray Bergman was speaking an important truth when he told me: "Curves are too hard to throw and succeed too seldom for you to bother with them. For every fish there is one place from which you can cast to him with a straight line and still get a free float. Figure out where it is and go there even if it means walking back a hundred yards to cross the stream and come up the other side." My lady wife, who can fish like an otter, heeded well this advice. Although she learned her fishing from a whole galaxy of expert casters and anglers, she has never even tried to cast a curve. She wades around until she finds the right place and then makes the short straight cast which, too often for the comfort of my ego, takes a fish.

Having stalked the fish the angler must now cast, and here all hell breaks loose, for there is more misconception, disagreement, and prevarication about casting than any other part of the sport. For one thing, practically no fisherman knows how far he really can cast, a fact which once nearly broke up one of the older Beaverkill clubs.

The clubhouse is right on the bank, and at noon the members come in for lunch and discuss the morning's fishing at the table. One low miscreant got tired of listening to these tales. Secretly he drove two stakes in the bank, a measured sixty feet apart. Next lunchtime, the first member to voice a standard fish-story remark—"I made a medium cast, about sixty feet"—was challenged by the miscreant. Bets were made, and the whole party repaired to the riverside, where an appalling thing was quickly discovered. The storyteller couldn't cast sixty feet, and, what is worse, none of the others could, either. Since it is obviously impossible to tell a fish story without mentioning a sixty-foot cast, the members lunched in gloomy silence until at last they rebelled, chucked the beggar out, and went back to making sixty-foot casts at the luncheon table.

As a matter of fact, long casting is not of much use in trout fishing, at least not in the East. Few, indeed, are the times when an angler really has to make a cast longer than forty-five feet, and fewer still the times when such a cast raises *and hooks* a fish. But if distance is not necessary to the angler's cast, control—the ability to cast accurately and delicately—is. Accuracy is a prime necessity when obstacles make it difficult to reach the fish. When deep water, overhanging trees, or the lack of room for a backcast forbid the use of that best of all fish-getters, the short straight cast, the angler must resort to high art flavored with black magic—the skillful manipulation of rod and line that so defies analysis and classification that it is called, simply, tip work.

George LaBranche likely may have been the greatest of them all at this, his forte. His preference was for smallish water, and the limitations imposed by so restricted an environment required him to perform blackest magic with the tip. It is a revelation to watch the tip work of an artist like Guy Jenkins, whose almost imperceptible manipulations seem to endow the fly with independent ability to guide its own flight among bushes and brambles and still achieve a perfect float.

Delicacy is the other half of control. The average fisherman cherishes the delusion that his casts place the fly on the water as delicately as an alighting insect. But if he casts on stillwater so that he can walk down for a close look at his fly, he probably will be distressed, as I have been, to see that it is awash *in,* rather than riding high *on,* the surface film. The reason, I think, is that most fishermen still believe in that ancient chestnut which one fishing writer has copied from another ever since the dry fly became popular. It is that the caster should check his line while his fly is three or four feet above the water and "allow the fly to flutter down onto the water like an alighting insect."

This is so much bilge, tosh, sheep-dip, and hogwash. Even without a line or leader attached to it, an artificial fly cannot be dropped onto the water "as delicately as a natural insect alighting" or anywhere near it anymore than you could do the same thing with a seaplane. Every winged creature uses its wings, and uses them a lot, in effecting a landing; a flying duck can make a beautiful three-pointer, but a shot duck can hit the water so hard he bounces. The instant and universal popularity which fan-wing flies and long-hackled spiders achieved in the 1920s was due to the fact that their larger sail area permits them to parachute down slower and more gently than an ordinary fly when they are checked high in the air and allowed to drop.

George LaBranche had the most delicate presentation of any angler whom I have ever observed. In his books, George speaks repeatedly of checking the fly in the air to get a delicate delivery, but what he did was really more than that. He made each cast, short or long, with a deliberate powerful stroke; checked the line hard so that the fly whipped down until it was only an inch above the water, with its headway killed; and then seemed to lower it gently, through that remaining inch, onto the water. On short casts, he could put his fly on the surface before line or leader touched the water.

To sum up presentation: In this, as in imitation, our synthetic perfect angler must meet one test—the exacting standards of the trout. He must be able to stalk and cast so well that he always deceives the fish.

The final angling requirement—hooking, playing, and landing the fish—is universally slighted both in practice and in literature, in spite of the axiom that a sale does the store no good until it is rung up on the cash register.

The average fisherman's record on big fish is brief and dismal. He loses practically all of them that rise to his fly, and on the average it takes him less than five seconds apiece to do so. He hits them too hard and holds them too tight; that's the whole story.

Striking and playing a fish correctly is a matter of iron self-discipline and rigid control of one's reflexes. One of the greatest examples of it that I know is Tappen Fairchild's conquest of "Grandpa," a four-and-a-quarter-pound brown trout that each year in late summer was driven by the warming of the upper Neversink to take refuge in a little ten-foot feeder stream that is always forty-six degrees Fahrenheit.

There was just one pool, about fifty feet in diameter, in this little spring brook, and in it this veritable whale lived, nervous and wary because of its restricted, dangerous quarters.

Tappen studied that fish for most of two seasons. He was a very tall man, and he had arthritis, but whenever he found time, he *crawled* to the edge of the pool and *knelt* behind a bush in order to study, hour after hour, the feeding and harboring habits of this fish. He found that its lie was under a submerged, fallen tree on the other side, and that, when feeding, it worked around the pool, vacuum-cleaning occasional nymphs off the sandy bottom.

The trout was patrolling like that when Tappen finally went after it. Of course, laying a line anywhere near the fish, no matter how gently, would have sent it flying in panic. So Tappen cast a small nymph on 3X gut and let it sink to the bottom while the fish was at the other end of the pool. Imagine the mounting tension as he watched this enormous fish turn and start feeding back toward him. The faintest movement of rod, line, or lure would have sent it bolting off, but Tappen knelt like a bronze statue while the fish approached the nymph, inspected it, picked it up, started away with it, and by its own movement pulled it into the corner of its mouth and hooked itself!

The fish lashed the pool into foam when it felt the iron and darted irresistibly in among the sunken tree branches. Tappen backed off into the meadow so as to be out of sight, pointed his rod at the fish, and with his left hand gave a couple of very delicate, gentle pulls on the line. The fish quietly swam out the same way it had gone in.

To top it off, Tappen had lent someone his net. So he had to play his fish until it was broad on its side and completely exhausted, and then crowd it against his leg while he gilled it with his middle finger and thumb, thus completing a perfect demonstration of angling technique.

The tactics of playing a fish, like those of warfare, depend almost entirely on the "terrain," and it is difficult to establish doctrine on them, but there are a few principles on which knowledgeable anglers seem to be fairly well agreed.

Holding a fish hard when it is first hooked lets it break off.

"Let him go; tear line off the reel and throw it at him; don't put any pressure on him at all. He won't go far—maybe fifty yards," Ed Hewitt used to say. "Don't try to check that first run."

The time-honored adjurations "Keep the tip up" and "Don't give any slack line" should not be observed strictly. They may be wrong or they may be right; it depends on the circumstances.

In order to breathe with any facility, a fish must face the current; even when migrating downstream it lets the current carry it tail first so it can breathe readily. So when a fish starts to take line downstream, it won't go far at any one time. Try to lead it into slacker water at the side of the stream. When a fish gets below the angler, it can hang in the current, breathing comfortably and doing no work to maintain its position. In this situation it is simply recuperating; unless the angler can get below it and put it to work, his chances of losing it are good.

A fish going straight away from the angler with the leader over its shoulder is like a horse in harness—in the best position for pulling. If it is held hard, it may easily break off. But a fish swims as a snake crawls through the grass, by moving its head from side to side and using its broad body surfaces against the current. A light sideways pull will so hamper this serpentine movement that it will quickly abandon its effort and turn aside. Where there is room, it is possible to keep an active fish turning almost continuously in a figure-eight pattern and thus prevent it from dashing downstream or into a hole.

It takes long to tire a fish by swimming; the angler seeks to drown it by maintaining steady upward pressure so as to tire its jaw muscles and force its mouth open. A fish has to close its mouth to squeeze water through its gills; when it can no longer do so, it quickly drowns.

The harder a fish is held, the harder it fights; if pressure is released entirely it will stop fighting and swim around aimlessly or rest on the bottom. A fish that is held too hard tends to sound, or go to the bottom, and sulk, jerking its head like a bulldog. This is hard on tackle and the hold of the hook; lightening the pressure will encourage the fish to come up and make an active, hence tiring, fight.

After the first five seconds of hooking and fighting his fish, the angler's greatest chance of losing it is through trying to net it before it is completely exhausted and broad on its side. Usually he unfurls his net immediately after hooking the fish. As soon as he can drag the still-vigorous trout within range he extends his rod hand far behind him, assumes a

position like a fencer lunging, and extends the net at arm's length like a
tennis player trying to stop a low shot. In this position the angler goes to
work with his net like a man chopping down a tree, and unless his fish is
well hooked and his leader sturdy, he's going to lose his prize.

Charlie Wetzel is the best netter I ever saw. He uses one of those big
"snowshoe" nets, and he doesn't even get it out until the fish is on its side
and completely tuckered. Standing erect, facing upstream with his elbows
at his sides and his rod held just back of vertical, he sinks the net deep and
draws the fish over it. Slowly, gently, he raises the rim of the net, tilting it
from side to side to free the meshes from the fish's fins. Then he quietly,
deliberately lifts the fish out of water, and it lies in the net as if hypnotized
until Charlie grasps the upper meshes to hold it shut. It doesn't go into its
final flurry until too late.

To sum up, we must require our hypothetical perfect angler always to
hook his fish perfectly, in the corner of the mouth; to maintain utter,
absolute control over his own reflexes; and to play and net the fish without committing an error.

Now we have constructed the perfect angler, but he's dead. To bring him
to life we must infuse him with the spirit of a great angler. That is *not* the
relaxed, gentle, lackadaisical spirit which delights in birds, flowers, wild
animals, clouds, and the sweet clash of running waters. I have known great
anglers who were thus benign, but it was not the spirit of their formative
years, the thing that made them great, but a luxury which they could afford
after fishing had ceased to challenge them. Ed Hewitt pinpointed it when
he said: "First a man tries to catch the most fish, then the largest fish, and
finally the most difficult fish." After that, the birds and flowers.

The spirit which makes the great angler is compounded of terrifically
intense concentration and a ferocious, predatory urge to conquer and cap-
ture. What less would drive Dick Jarmel, a well-known Beaverkill fisherman, to risk a bad battering and possible drowning by working his way for
fifty yards along the retaining wall of the Acid Factory Pool, holding his
rod crosswise in his mouth and clinging with fingertips and toes to rough

projections of stones, simply to get to *the* spot from which the run can be fished effectively during high water?

Or impel Tom Collins (Ed Hewitt once called him the best fisherman ever) to climb down the face of a cliff, swing across a cleft on a rope affixed to a branch, and shinny down a convenient tree, all to get to a secret spot on a secret stream, down in a gorge? Tom had the heft of a grizzly as well as the strength and endurance of one, and he risked a broken neck and stove-in ribs time after time, as a matter of course I laugh when I hear a doctor approving fishing as light recreation for a heart patient without finding out what sort of fishing it will be. He thinks of his man as soaking a worm while he dozes on the bank; he would be shocked to see, as I so often have, the hard-case angler coming in at eventide limp and sweat-soaked from prowling and galloping along the stream all day.

The furious urge of the great fisherman expresses itself in an intense competitive spirit. Some anglers conceal it very well, but it is there nevertheless, so strong that it can even bias their devotion to the truth. I still grin privately at what happened long ago when two really great anglers, who must remain nameless here, met by chance on a certain pool. They got into a discussion of wet fly versus dry fly and set up an informal competition, each fishing the pool in turn. I've heard the story from each of them, and you'd never guess that they were both talking about the same event. The only thing they agreed on was the name of the pool.

Ed Hewitt and George LaBranche were always tilting at each other. When both of them were aged men, Ed and I went up to George's office to surprise him one day. The two really dear old friends fell upon each other, and then George asked Ed what was new. Nothing, said Ed, except that he had another grandchild.

"How many grandchildren have you?" asked George.

Ed fell for it. "Eight."

"That's one thing I can beat you at," crowed George. "I have twelve."

Ed's eyes darted about as he sought furiously to redeem his defeat. "How many great-grandchildren have you?" he demanded.

This time George was under the guns. "Five."

"Hah!" cried Ed triumphantly. "I have twenty-one!"

George's secretary looked shocked and beckoned me into the hall.

"Mr. LaBranche doesn't have twelve grandchildren!" she whispered.

"That's all right," I reassured her. "Ed doesn't have twenty-one great-grandchildren, either. They're just trying to beat each other."

Some twenty-five years ago I met on the stream a then-well-known fishing writer, the late Albert C. Barrell, who, it developed, had fished a lot with LaBranche on the Konkapot in Massachusetts.

"George is a duelist," he explained. "The fish is his antagonist, his adversary. He'll return it to the water after he has conquered it, but he attacks it as furiously as if he was fighting for his life."

Here, then, out of the zeal and the skills of many experts, we have synthesized the perfect angler. In the flesh this perfect dry-fly fisherman does not exist, and it is doubtless a good thing that he does not, for surely he would be intolerable to all us imperfect anglers.

Letter to Howard Schuck

July 13, 1972

. . . Ah well, I have long maintained that the true fun, thrill and excitement of fishing was learning about it; that when one became a master, with all the knowledge and skill he needed . . . he was on his way out of any continuation of his interest in fishing.

I've known a few like that, too. Charlie Fox and Vince Marinaro, and their merry men of the Letort, disdain the "big fish" of that river (and it has some real whoppers), but I remember a group sitting on the famous "deacon's bench" on Charlie's water, taking turns trying to catch a 6-inch brook trout that was disporting itself in midstream before them. They didn't any of them put it down; but it was a couple of hours (give or take an hour) before one finally hooked it. Whereupon he pulled off one boot, filled it with water, put the live fish in it, and drove swiftly to some small feeder that they were trying to restock with "surface-feeding" wild fish.

. . .

In the clubhouse (onetime CCC Camp) of the Union County (Pa.) Sportsmen's Association, there hangs in the beer bar an incredible brown trout, stated on the brass plate to be 37 pounds. It was the ugliest, homeliest-looking fish I ever saw; resembled nothing so much as an old-fashioned leather dress-suit case. It had lived for many years behind a broken board in the lagging of a rearing pond at the Bellfont Hatchery. One day they decided to drain the pond and repair some other broken spots.

When the water was about all out of the pond, this incredible monster came wriggling out of his hiding place and my information is that at first

29

sight, everybody turned and ran like hell. I don't blame them. It was killed with a pitchfork, or some such a thing.

. . .

When Eisenhower was president, George Murnane, who knew him, had been the lessee of the lower Connell water, which included the Junction Pool at that time. George invited Ike up to fish, got an acceptance, and forthwith judiciously stocked the stretch with 2½-pound brook trout. Then Ike had to cancel, so no one ever heard about the big fish. A few of them persisted in that water for a number of years afterward . . .

While they lasted they gave rise to some tall tales. Edgar Wandless had a cottage next to Stan Berry's, and one day he was fishing to the docking pool in front of a neighboring cottage. He hooked an enormous fish and played it to a standstill, right in front of the docking. He was just reaching for it with the net when a voice above and behind him shouted loudly: "Wow! J—— C——!" There was a man standing on top of the docking above and behind Edgar, who didn't know he was there.

Of course, Edgar did just what you and I would have done—gave a start and a tremendous jerk and, of course, broke off his fish. Right up to the time of his death, years later, Edgar's wattles would turn crimson and his voice would quiver with fury when he told of this dastardly deed. Unfortunately, the docking stood six feet above the water and there was no way up the bank and out of the stream for fifty yards either way, so the kibitzer escaped the punch in the nose Edgar always earnestly stated he otherwise would have given him.

Introduction to
Simplified Fly Fishing

So you're a bait fisherman and you want to graduate to flies. Or you're not even a fisherman; or you fish with worms—

What! You've never fished with worms? You go dig some, right this minute, and start learning a number of things you ought to know before you begin fooling around with flies.

Particularly, the worm will teach you two vital things: where fish are and how water runs. Where fish may be in the stream and at what depth varies more or less continually. So you need to search the water from side to side and top to bottom as well as from end to end to find out where the fish are. Usually you can search more water faster and more dependably with a worm than with a fly; there are a lot of different flies, and sometimes you have to experiment a good while before you find the right one.

Besides showing you where the fish are, the worm will show you how currents run. No stream moves at a single pace, bank to bank and top to bottom. Friction against the sides and bottom, the narrowing and widening of the streambed, obstructions, and even small stones speed up, slow down, divert, and disturb the stream flow so that every part of it moves at a different speed. So if you want your lure to come to the fish naturally (and that's the way they want it), you've got to know how water runs— how to read the stream. A floating fly is fine for gauging surface currents, but beneath the surface a worm works best; not only is it easier for you to control the depth at which it runs, but you can see it under water better than most wet flies.

Once you have learned where fish are and how water runs, you will know where to look and how to handle your lure, and you won't need worms anymore. Then you can take up fly fishing, which is more fun.

Now about books; you don't learn fishing from a book—you learn it
from a fish. But books help you by interpreting what the fish is trying to
tell you. However, you can't learn from one book, even this very good one;
read every fishing book, good or bad, that you can get hold of. Put them
all in together and let them eat each other up. You'll end by realizing that
a book is just the reflection of one man's mind and personality, and there
is a tremendous difference in men; that there are a lot of different ways of
doing the same thing, and some or all of them may be right; and that there
is more than one side to every question. In the end you must draw your
own conclusions on the basis of your own experience. This will give you
perspective, and perspective is the handmaiden of judgment.

There is another reason for reading all the books, the curious one that
no matter how trivial, worthless, or even wrong a book may be, you can
almost always find in it some one thing that you won't find in any other.
Usually that marks the point where the author stopped repeating what
other writers before him had said, and dipped into his own experience to
record something he had observed himself.

As to this present book, it is tailored to cover the transition of an experienced fisherman into an experienced *fly* fisherman. It was written by a
skillful and experienced angler, and offhand I don't recall any other of its
precise kind. So read it studiously and reread it often; it will do you good.

Letter to Lewis Hull

September 21, 1951

. . . This is my last night on the range; Momma will be home on the week-end. I have been roaming around in alleys and kennels, drinking beer with copyreaders, foreign correspondents, sports columnists and other riffraff, watching that goddam machine that winds wire around bundles of newspapers, chewing the fat with cops and doormen, sitting around with guys on the lobster trick, and sleeping on trains. Wasting my youth and consuming my substance! I am getting gaunt, hollow-eyed, pallid and hectic. Shall have to walk around the reservoir and cast for bass this week-end in order to restore the tissues and rejuvenate the system.

Wish you were around to side me on these expeditions. There was a first-class bum lost in you when you embraced education and industry.

As ever

Sparse, The Man About Town

Letter to Howard Walden

December 20, 1952

You established your quality with me long ago, in <u>Upstream and Down.</u> But when I finished <u>Big Stony</u> one Sunday night two or three months ago, I was so moved that I dug out the old portable and relieved myself of the most incoherent, intemperate and overwrought screed that I ever perpetrated. When I read it over, I cursed myself even more energetically than usual for not being able to say what I meant, and put it in its proper place, the fireplace.

I have intended ever since to tell you what I thought of the book and of your writing as exemplified in it; and I still intend to do it but the transition from emotional stimulation to logical expression is not far enough along for me to do it yet.

I have been telling intending authors ever since to read these books and convince themselves that they ought not to insult the English language and the sport of angling until they can get into your class. It is unpalatable medicine—I know because I take it myself—but it's good for what ails most would-be authors.

I have been reading a few of the "classics" recently; spent my new-suit money on about 20 standard fishing books like J. W. Hill's three, Haig-Brown's best two or three, Sheringham, Plunket Greene, Francis, etc. etc. It has been a delightful experience and an educational one too. <u>Big Stony</u> was in that lot and foremost of them all in a number of aspects—for graphic imagery, for the subtle, unerring choice of words, for character-drawing, and for a certain singing, intense, joyful quality which is based on an illimitable love for and appreciation of angling and of the living water. Ah hell, I still can't tell you what I mean. But I could take you through the book line by line and even word by word and show you how beautifully right, how fine, how true to the mark it is. I can't do it but I can appreciate it; I suppose that is like saying that I can't make whiskey but like to drink it!

. . .

Coming in on the train today I was reading an old back copy of American Rifleman and found this passage:

"If you've ever hunted when you really needed meat, you'll know it's tough going. You're overstrung, you creep and sneak and send the scent of murder far ahead of you." <u>Saga of a Springfield,</u> Gerald Averill.

Perceptive and graphic, eh? So easy to read and so goddam hard to write!

Letter to Dana Lamb

March 31, 1965

. . . The sentence which evoked my nausea was a . . . gem, a perfect specimen of writing, for a man who is paid by the word.

"I cast my dry fly again out upon the surface of the pool."

The beggar had already told the reader that he was fishing with a dry fly; did he now need to reassure reader that he had not surreptitiously changed to a wet? Out with "dry fly."

Unless the fly buried its point in the caster's neck, any cast he made was bound to be "out," so out with "out."

Where in hell would he lay a dry fly except on the surface—on the bottom, mayhap? Out with "upon the surface."

And finally, perhaps you and I cast as often into the trees or onto the bank as we do onto the water, but a man writing as an expert scarcely needs to reiterate that he is fishing on water and not land or trees. Out with "of the pool."

So finally, and properly, the sentence read: "I cast again."

One need not lose effectiveness by imparting a certain terseness to his writing; more likely, he will gain it when his thought is not smothered in qualifying clauses, explanatory phrases, and elaboration which merely slows down the pace of the story.

Letter to Richard Rossbach

October 15, 1965

. . . I note that your verse is true fishing verse. I have always maintained that the distinctive characteristic of a fisherman's verse is the extra foot which he always throws in. If my count is correct, you threw in two.

When I finish with this, my next chore will be to return to their author a set of verses entitled "In Defense of Salvelinus Fontinalis" and beginning "Oh, where are the brookies of yesteryear. . . ."

The work of an editor is extremely varied.

Letter to Dana Lamb

August 16, 1972

 . . . My high-school English teacher, debate coach, and cherished friend, the late Wallace Teall Stock, never was able to hammer into me much of writing skill, but he did teach me to respect and admire and enjoy the wonderful English language, and particularly to have some comprehension and appreciation of the weight, connotation, origin and meaning of words, and some enjoyment of their beauty. . . .

Letter to Frank Woolner

December 4, 1972

. . . It's the human heart . . . that makes literature endure. The best how-to-do-it is ephemeral stuff. Cane succeeds greenheart, glass succeeds cane; silk displaces horsehair and is displaced by nylon. Hot tips and great secrets of flytying, casting, etc. become common property.

But the boy with glass rod and spinning reel is blood-descended from the barefoot boy with the cut pole and can of worms. He's the eternal part of the sport.

Letter to Nick Lyons

April 2, 1973

I thought of you yesterday. I was hunting through some old files and found a letter from my beloved debate coach and English teacher, the one who taught me reverence for the English language and just a little of his own passion for the weight, derivation, denotation, connotation, precise meaning, and skilful use of words.

He wrote and privately printed a little book of verse, and one piece that I particularly liked he dedicated: "To Alfred Miller, stout in friendship." I wrote to thank him, and express amusement at his play on the word "stout" for in my previous letter I had admitted that I was becoming "stout, nay positively corpulent."

There was just one line in the letter referring to that, and I'm going to have it engraved and jewelled on fine gold.

"'Stout' is half as long as 'stalwart' and twice as strong," was all he said. How'd you like to have a stable of authors like that!!!!!

Letter to Nick Lyons

April 17, 1978

. . . Do not worry that you haven't the time to do the amount of writing you would wish to do. Some of the best writing in almost every field of English expression has been wrung out of hard-pushed people who used fragments of time between household chores, composed their stateliest rhythms amid the squalling of infants, or the crash of trolley cars, or the needling of a persistent telephone. Don't pick apart, fiddle with, polish or tease what you have written until you have taken all of the life, vividness and spontaneity out of it. There is a lot to be said in favor of the newspaper man's traditional requirement to "get it up" before a close deadline and send it down the tube without even re-reading it. If it's so close to presstime that the copy desk can't start removing the doll's arms and legs one at a time to let the sawdust run out, you just may find on Page 1 something that will hit you a punch in the eye and hold you until you read the whole piece. Yes, it'll have a little roughness; yes, another word might have been more accurate here and there; but yes, the piece <u>marched</u> and yes, it was alive and vigorous.

I don't know anything about English, let alone the writing thereof, but I have learned from experience, from abrasive contact, from osmosis. And I am firm on the opinion that after you have shined the piece a little and corrected the misspellings—if it doesn't tell you it's ready, throw it away and start a new attempt. I admit that one or two of my own old favorites—"The Indomitable" and "Nocturne," for instance—were rewritten or touched up ten times or more before they saw type the first time . . . and I guess as many additional tinkerings and patchings before they wound up in the anthologies, but that was done over a period of 30 or 40 years. . .

. . . my big desk had an enormous double file drawer . . . and whenever I wasn't busy I'd write for it, or reread what was already in there . . . I knew I couldn't sell the fishing magazines of that era . . . So at nominal cost, I had the luxury of writing for myself; to please, interest, amuse or instruct me.

Entomology Class

It may be that Mr. Sparse Grey Hackle is the kindest man in the world, and then again, maybe he is the meanest. He almost never forgets to send along a letter at the very time a guy needs a piece to travel on, yet what he writes is not necessarily calculated to send the guy away with mind at rest and heart full of *gemutlichkeit*.

For example:

"This is the time of year when I begin to think about fishing and you begin to think about going South to the baseball training camps. So it is natural that when I think of you and your compatriots in the sportswriting field, I do so in terms of the angler.

"Thus I am impressed with the way in which you, as a group, resemble the water insect which is the principal food of the trout and which we imitate with our artificial flies. [So far okay: He has only called us bugs, an acceptable if not flattering comparison—Ed.]

The Editor Emerges

"The insect hatches from the egg reposing on the stream bottom as a sluggish, crawling worm which the fisherman calls a nymph, but which in the newspaper world is called a copyboy. This static creature eats all the time and so grows bigger and bigger until finally it rises to the surface, splits its shell, and emerges as winged insect.

"Fishermen call this a dun, but to newspaper men it is a reporter or an editor. At this stage its wings are covered with a thick skin, its body is tubby and opaque, and when first hatched it is nearly incapable of flight.

The scientific name for it is subimago, which means 'less than perfect.' I think it is particularly appropriate for both the insect and the newspaper man.

"I do not mean to call any specific editor an imperfect insect except, perhaps, when he advocates spoiling the sport of a million anglers by running Route 17 down the bed of the Beaverkill River, just because he doesn't like to fish himself. No, I draw no such inference as regards newspaper men, either in general or in particular; it is just a figure of speech.

The Perfect Being

"In the course of time the fly which is called the dun sheds its thick skin and then that beautiful creature—the spinner, the imago, the perfect insect, or, to continue the metaphor, the sports columnist—emerges in all glory.

"He is transparent: I mean, it is easy to see through him. He is full of gas. He spends his time with others of his kind, dancing up and down in the sunlight and not doing a lick of work. He is the imago, the perfect one. Eventually he flies far away and lays an egg. The metaphor is perfect.

"Do not consider that there is anything personal in the foregoing. It merely arises from my bitter realization that while I am shoveling snow off 150 feet of driveway and jamming quarters into the New Haven Railroad's parking meters with numb fingers, the columnists will be sipping Scotch, rye, bourbon, gin, rum, vodka, and other varieties of nectar, dancing up and down in the sunlight on diaphanous wings, and not doing a lick of work.

"Try not to lay an egg."

Mr. Miller

Through all the years when communications from Sparse Grey Hackle have appeared here, people have asked repeatedly whether he is a real person or an imaginary correspondent. He is indeed real.

He is a bald, portly, courtly gentleman of wide learning, a skilled but sedentary angler, a boon companion, and a man of monstrous evil. When he isn't fishing or writing letters, he does things in Wall Street. His name is Alfred Waterbury Miller. He is deeply sinful and he ought to be suppressed but not, please God, while a guy needs help.

(Red Smith's column, February 15, 1962.)

One Silk Stocking

A t the very outset of his letter, Mr. Hackle states the case clearly enough. "What I need," he writes, "is a light-black silk stocking."

Black and Blue and Transparent

Now, Sparse is no dope. He knows perfectly well that the reader is going to squint narrowly at that opening, go through it again to be sure, and say, "A light-black stocking? Silk? Gossakes, why?"

"Because," he writes, "there is this particular trout stream insect. All the other insects, which start as crawlers on the stream's back, one day rise to the surface, burst their shucks, and emerge as winged creatures. They take their time about it, yawning and stretching and hanging out their new wings to dry in the sun, while they ride the shuck like a raft down the current. This much aggrandizes the trout, which gulp the beggars, shuck and all.

"But there is one fly with a gimmick of his own. He hatches on the way up through the water. And he does not laze around. He comes hellity-hooping out of the chute like Smoky Yunick [beats me—Ed.], blower screaming and engine bellowing, and goes through the surface like Colonel Glenn through Mach l.

"Trout don't have great luck fielding this hot one, but as a diet they prefer him to all others, so a good imitation is bound to be a fish-catching fly. The trouble is, he is almost impossible to imitate.

"He is as transparent as a columnist's expense account but withal has a delicate smoky tint of blackness like the haze sportswriters see before their eyes in the morning. And when the light hits just right, he is as blue as the atmosphere in the train hauling horse players home from Big A.

Trophy from a Saloon

"A genius too modest to be named has discovered that this critter can be superbly imitated with a certain kind of lady's silk stocking—I mean a lady's certain kind of silk stocking—the sort you can't see, but which looks as if the lady had not washed her legs.

"It is what my Pennsylvania Dutch friends call light-black, and thinner than an angler's alibi. We had one; a friend of mine got it from a lady who took it off in a night club and discarded it because it had developed a run. But we used it up, and, as my friend neglected to ask the lady's name, he can't go back for the other one.

"I have some small renown for being able to spring husbands for fishing trips. I do it by getting the lady so mad at me she forgets her spouse long enough for the poor wretch to stuff his tackle into my car, whereupon the pair of us lam like stickup men departing the supermarket.

Now Is the Time for All Good Ladies

"However, it is quite difficult to get a silk stocking off a lady who is sore at you, and besides, I might become a victim of uxcrial tension if the news got around.

"You know things that are hidden from other men, old buddy, and you get around a lot. How about getting us a sheer, light-black stocking that looks blue when the light hits it right? If you come across, we'll give you a chance to fish with the end product in our company, no questions asked."

(Red Smith's column, May 16, 1962.)

Letter to Harry Darbee

February 2, 1951

. . . the behavior of fish with the fly . . . is the <u>basic behavior of the fish.</u> In other words, this is the way the fish feeds when he is not handicapped by scarcity of food, rough water, turbidity, competition with other fish, etc. In other words, the fish always acts this way, as nearly as he can.

Frankly, that is just a guess, but it seems rather logical.

Now the next question in my mind is—how much like that does the fish act in "freestone" streams, without our realizing it? M. seems to think considerable; he told me in correspondence a year or so ago that if I would fish the broken water with long floats and not pick up until I had to, I would get a lot of fish that I otherwise would miss without even knowing they had been about to take.

What I am coming to believe is that the whole question of imitation is governed by <u>the speed of the current.</u> What I mean is this: the faster the current, the farther ahead of the fly the fish must rise. As he rises, the width of his window diminishes. I believe that in really fast water, the fish may have to rise so far ahead of the fly that <u>he never has it in his window</u> until the very instant he is about to take it. By that time his "feeding reflex" has already pulled the trigger and even if he recognizes the fraud at the last instant, he can't keep himself from taking it. Maybe that is why we get so many lightly hooked fish, so many splashing last-minute refusals—fish trying to keep from taking a fly they recognized as fraudulent, almost too late.

If you add broken water to fast water, the actual size and visibility of the fish's window must be a matter of much doubt.

So maybe the exact imitationists (leaving aside their differences of opinion about what is "exact") are OK when the fly is taken in the window, and maybe the "action" and "light pattern" boys are just as OK while the fly is outside the window.

It seems to me more and more as if the flats are the school of the stream—the place for the fisherman to learn presentation and to test the attractiveness of his patterns. It seems to me more and more that George LaBranche's marvelously delicate and precise casting is the sine qua non of the LaBranche theory of fishing.

Everybody is saying "it won't be long now" until fishing starts but to me it is the longest time of the year. It is only some 70 or 80 days, but they are ten to twelve times as long as the days in the rest of the year. The shortest days are those when I am fishing with you, and the shortest day of the year is the one when I fish with Elsie—when I get to fish with Elsie. I am not forgetting that the last time she fished with me, she took up with a stranger on the stream and left me flatter than the low end of Dow's Eddy.

. . . Incidentally, I have a date to teach Kerlee how to tie flies.

What are you laughing at, you goddam lug? Don't you realize how experts are created? It is not skill of the tying fingers, the casting wrist, the wading legs or the fishing mind that makes experts—the mouth is the organ which does that job. In spite of the fact that I have always taken pains to tell everybody that I am a lousy fisherman and tier and know nothing about it, I can muster quite a corporals' guard of boobs who have never seen me fish (even some who have, but none who ever saw me catch a fish) who will maintain that I am an expert. I would laugh if it were not so sad. . . .

So if you have any sense, you will cut out this damn flytying and start just talking about it . . .

The Darbees

There's a lot more to fly tying than just lashing feathers onto hooks. Roosters, for instance: Harry and Elsie Darbee have raised dry-fly hackles ever since they started their business. One must be fond of music to dwell among roosters, for these gamecocks all salute the dawn, and, since each has its own idea of time, the first challenge rings out soon after midnight and the last as the sun tops the trees. I love to listen to them, and many and many's the night I have done it in the Darbees' spare bedroom after a long day of fishing the Beaverkill and a longer evening of angling tales and talk.

One midnight I remember it was not a rooster's defiance but panic in the hen coops that shattered the silence. It took Harry and me a few moments to surface from the depths of sleep, but Elsie turned out like a fireman on call, leaped into overalls and moccasins, and departed running with a .22 rifle in one hand and a flashlight in the other.

The fowl were in pandemonium when she reached the coops. Gripping the flashlight beneath the gun barrel, she shined a pair of eyes, fired a single shot between them, and slew an enormous raccoon. Panic still resounded at the other end of the row. She ran there, shined another pair of eyes, fired once again, and racked up another gigantic 'coon.

By the time Harry and I got downstairs, here came Elsie lugging almost 80 pounds of dead 'coon. With her flashing eyes and bold stride, this tall, comely woman reminded me of the dauntless wives of the old frontier who stood in the cabin doorway, ax in hand, and exacted the full penalty from any Indian who dared try to enter.

I mention this incident not to glorify the Pioneer Mother, as I named her that night, but to remind you that there's a lot more to fly tying than lashing feathers onto hooks.

Besides roosters, there are dams. Of all the classic Catskill trout streams that were the first home of the brown trout in America—Schoharie, Esopus, Mongaup, Rondout, Neversink, East and West Branches of the Delaware, Beaverkill, and Willowemoc—only the last two have not been dammed, bulldozed, and, for the most part, diverted into the plumbing of New York City.

Those two streams were saved by a boy from Roscoe and a girl from Willowemoc, both in the Catskills. Without a war chest, an organization, or any experience to back them up, these country kids declared war on the city of New York and won. Just country kids, but through their tiny shop flowed, during six months of the year, a flood tide of city people of every kind and degree. The kids talked to them, and when *they* raised their voices, the city engineers filed away their plans for those two streams. (The plans are not dead, just delayed. *Vigilante!*)

Besides roosters and dams, there's spraying. So far as I know, Harry and Elsie were the first to take effective steps toward setting afoot resistance to the drenching of the Catskills with lethal DDT sprayed from aircraft by one federal agency or another to combat the gypsy moth. It killed the gypsy moths, all right; it also took incalculable bird life, eliminated from the area the honeybees upon which so many plants depend for fertilization, and indiscriminately killed off both stream and land insects to such an extent that it was years before the standard stream insect hatches regained their normal size and order of emergence. To this day, the grasshopper has not returned to its former abundance.

This fight was a triumph of initiative, ingenuity, improvisation, and on-the-spot organization. There were (and are) a substantial number of ichthyologists, biologists, entomologists, ecologists, and other specialties in the fisheries sciences at Cornell University in Ithaca, New York. They were aware of what was about to happen and were perturbed by it. When

Harry, who knew them all, called for volunteers, these qualified scientists responded nobly. They were deployed in squads at various Neversink pools by the time the first spray plane flew its pattern down the valley.

Fifteen minutes later, they witnessed a tremendous rise of fish to the dying insects dropping into the stream. Fifteen minutes after *that,* the backwaters and eddies were filled with incredible numbers of fine brown trout writhing and dying of DDT. Scores of specimens were gathered and preserved as Exhibit A in a movement that quickly curtailed the Catskill spraying program.

Finally, there are highways. The Darbees lost their bitterest fight, an effort to prevent the state from running a limited-access, multi-laned race-course down the lower Willowemoc and lower Beaverkill. It was a savage fight, from which both the state and the Darbees bear scars. The Darbees lost, but they delayed the actual construction of that stretch for seven long years, and a lot of politicians, tame engineers, contractors, and highway department placemen knew they had been in a fight.

The Darbees' fly and tackle shop is in their home on Old Route 17 about midway between Roscoe and Livingston Manor. I hate to make so trite a comparison, but really, it puts me more in mind of the Mermaid Tavern of Shakespeare, Ben Jonson, and their peers than any other meeting place I ever heard of. Fishermen come in for their needs, remain to tell their experiences, get into conversations, and finally constitute a voluble, vociferous, constantly changing, nonstop seminar, with the participants standing crowded together and all talking at once.

Here the choicest angling spirits of the age come, along with innumerable run-of-the-mill fishermen, eager novices, and such hopeless dubs as I. The front room is crowded with Harry and Elsie's cluttered tying tables, a couple of glass showcases, glass-faced wall cabinets for displaying special, fancy "necks" of hackles, dozens of custom-made fly rods up for resale, displays of fly reels, wading sandals, boots, baskets, and heaven knows what oddments of tackle besides. In the room behind there are shelves of fishing books that would tempt me to larceny if I didn't already have so many of them, an incredible number of tin fish boxes, cracker canisters, cartons full of great treasure of feathers, necks, and "materials," and two desks piled high with unanswered correspondence.

Two loud dachshunds and a huge cat striped like a muskellunge get underfoot and, sometimes, under-seat, for it's every critter for himself when we sit down. The telephone rings, Harry ducks out to feed the chickens and Elsie to pick up the eggs, volunteer cooks monopolize the stove and the kitchen sink, and on the table a nonstop meal is in progress from morn to night, for during the season neither Harry nor Elsie can ever start or finish a meal without interruption.

Harry is consultant, counselor, and father confessor to half the amateur tyers who fish in the Catskills; his knowledge is encyclopedic and his experience vast. His particular weakness is the rank novice who, having seen a few flies tied, comes in to acquire a couple of dollars' worth of supplies and some help. I have seen such a beginner, eyes ashine and stammering with eagerness, listen for a couple of hours, lapping up enough concentrated knowledge and instruction to give him intellectual dyspepsia for a week. And beside him may be a hard-bitten veteran grinning sardonically as he relates the mishaps that finally terminated his efforts to raise hackles while Harry chuckles sympathetically and tells *his* troubles.

So there are the Darbees. I've known them intimately for well over a quarter of a century, and I can assure you that you will do well to note carefully, and take at face value, everything they tell you, for it will be not only true and important but unlikely to be found on record elsewhere. *Invaluable* is not too strong a word.

And if, after reading the foregoing, you seem to sense an aroma of admiration and a certain fragrance of affection for these old friends of mine, I will not contradict you.

Mr. Hackle's Fine Hand

There are within sight, praise be, several alleys down which a man can flee toward vacation without pausing to do a day's work first. One is a letter from Mr. Sparse Grey Hackle, that gifted angler and gracious gentleman whose gifts include one most warmly to be treasured: He knows instinctively when a feller needs a friend.

Into such breaches, Mr. Hackle springs agilely, telling tales like this:

"Last Sunday I fished up a certain river most of the day, and through my supernal skill and encyclopedic knowledge of angling was able to take a dozen brook trout. If I had kept them I would have had the makings of a nice can of sardines.

"As I approached the cabin, I was reminded that in it were a bottle of Scotch, ice cubes, soda, and some good cheese and crackers. I reflected that rain was impending, which makes the fish refuse to feed; that it was the worst time of day, 2 P.M.; that from the cabin up, the water is thin and there are no big fish in it, anyway.

Women Are Here to Stay

"Accordingly, I went in and suggested that my wife take over the rest of the river. I gave her an enormous dry fly to keep her from being annoyed by fish. Then I went out on the back porch to enjoy some highballs.

"In an hour my wife came back with something in her net that looked like a Fulton Market halibut. The poor woman didn't know that there never are any fish in the Forks Pool because there is no cover in it for fish, or that big brook trout never take a dry fly, anyway.

"She threw my monstrosity into the wrong place, and a two-pound, stream-bred, native brook trout—speckled trout to you—rolled up and engulfed it. A man who had fished the river for seventy years said it was the biggest brook trout he had ever heard of being taken from it.

"Have I not stumbled on an idea that could be more widely applied? How about sending one's office boy to the ballgame instead of getting deafened and sunburned, mustard-smeared and dyspeptic one's self?

"How about sending the chinless brother-in-law to be trampled on and maybe punched on the nose when he tries to claim his ringside seat in the forty-fifth row at a championship prizefight, instead of undergoing the ordeal one's self?

"And how about delegating any seventeen-year-old boy in the household to take over the chore of getting google-eyed watching sour sports events on television? In fact, how about—look, can Mrs. S. run a typewriter?"

(Red Smith's column, June 30, 1955.)

Momma

Other women find their delight in bridge, sandwiches with the crusts cut off, and the crystallized brainstorms of interior decorators. But Momma prefers to sit around in her woolen-socked feet with the fishermen in some farmhouse kitchen, because she is a fisherman at heart. In fact, it is her proudest title. I referred to her once as a "lady fly fisher" and she retorted heatedly, "I am not a lady fly fisher; I am a fly fisherman." And she is.

It is in fishing that she best expresses herself, and I treasure the memory of her first fishing expedition as a complete revelation of her personality. On that trip, the first time she had ever held a rod or waded a stream, she a) sat down in the stream with tooth-rattling violence, picked herself up, and said nothing about it, ever (she had thought herself unobserved); b) caught the largest trout I had ever seen taken from that brook; and c) found a fledgling wren in the grass and spent the rest of the afternoon trying to get it back into its nest.

As a fisherman she is in a class by herself. I can outcast her both for distance and for beautiful convolutions of the line. I can outwade her, for she is a foot shorter than I am and has an abiding aversion to heavy water. My fishing experience compares with hers as fifty compares with one.

Yet there never has been a time, from the very first day, that she has not outfished me. If we get nothing but rises, she will get more than I. If I get a fish, she will turn up with two. And if I equal her in numbers, hers will be larger fish. A few years ago I had a day on which I solved the riddle of the stream and took two trout on a fly fished deep in water she could not wade. Whereupon she disappeared for so long that I finally started looking for her. I met her returning through the woods with her net held vain-gloriously before her and containing a fish larger than either of mine. "Dry fly," she said loftily.

In fairness, I must add that such small and infrequent taunting is only for me and only in fun. I have never known her to fish competitively, to brag in victory, or to whine in defeat.

Nor to kill a legal limit. And she can and often does return fish, a thing most woman anglers find difficult. I remember one season, late in the year when the fish were getting thinned out in Hewitt's Neversink and the few big ones left were needed to maintain sport, seeing Momma take and return the fish under the big peeled log at the head of York's Ford—I don't know just how big he was but those who caught him from time to time will recall. And she did not mention it that evening until I taxed her with it. Then she merely said: "I had him out last week, too."

All this means simply that Momma is a real fisherman. She packs her own bags, puts out her own wading gear to dry, sets up her own tackle, and asks favors of no one. She even tied her own flies until we both became convinced that the Darbee's superb hackles and fine tying far surpassed the best materials and skill we could muster.

In late years Momma has broadened her scope to include a little wet-fly fishing, but she lives and dies by the dry fly, and it is remarkable how she is able to find fish with it.

Or maybe it's not so remarkable considering the angling elite who have contributed to her education: Jack Knight, Ed Hewitt, Jack Atherton, and, particularly, Ray Bergman.

In the days when Ray did what he called tutoring, I arranged with him for a full course of instruction, coaching, and demonstration of fly fishing for Momma. To this day, she fishes just about the same way he did, and it is a most effective way.

"Don't bother so much with trying to throw curves and loops," he used to tell me. "No matter where a fish is lying there is one spot where you can stand in the same current he is in and thus can cast a straight line to him without drag. Make it your business to locate that spot and go there, even if it means wading a hundred yards downstream to cross over. Don't cast until you're in that spot." That's just what Momma does, and she gets 'em.

She never has had but two bad fishing habits and those were matters of temperament. Momma is of old Yankee stock—her maiden name was Brewster—which means that she gives up grudgingly if at all. One of the sights of the stream is to see her go back into the bushes and retrieve a fly she has lost by hanging up a backcast; she's the only person I ever met who has the eyesight and the temperament to do it. But this New England parsimony cost her some big fish before she finally overcame it. She simply would not give a fish line. She'd run after him, and yield with the rod tip, but give back line that she'd taken in? Not Momma. That was her line, and nothing was going to get it away from her. It took a succession of broken-off two-pounders—and better—and some very vigorous language on my part to cure her of that tightfistedness.

But her other bad habit still clings to her. She consumes flies and leader points like a bonfire because she insists on casting into every hole and corner where she sees or suspects there is a fish, no matter how desperate the risk of hanging up or how hopeless her chances of getting her fly back if she does. She starts out with little No. 20s and No. 18s and winds up fishing 10s and 12s. Give her a leader and half a dozen little flies in the morning and she'll be out of flies and leaders by noon. As the leader gets shorter, and hence thicker at the outboard end because of her mishaps, she has to go to larger and larger flies that have eyes big enough to accept what's left of her leader.

Like every experienced fisherman, Momma has some superstitions and unwarranted conclusions based on erroneous assumptions. One I recall in particular.

In the verdancy of my angling adolescence I had a vast weakness for conceiving of bright ideas which proved worthless. One such was the Hot-Orange Bivisible.

Before changing regulations prohibited fishing close to the dams in New York City's Croton River watershed, my best angling venue was below a high dam from which issues the Carmel section of the West Branch of the Croton. After emerging tumultuously from its tunnel at the bottom of the dam, the stream flows over a sort of stone doorstep which crosses it from bank to bank. In the foaming water at the foot of this small obstruction the rainbows lay like shoats at a swill trough, gobbling any floating fly that was cast over them.

My trouble was that I couldn't see the rises in time to strike, because I couldn't spot my fly in the foam. The obvious answer to this problem would seem to be the white-fronted Bivisible fly of Edward R. Hewitt. But here it did me no good, for the whole base of the doorstep was covered with foam, and my defective eyesight could not see a white fly on white water.

Here entered my bright idea. Why not a bivisible with a hot-orange front hackle instead of the conventional white one? So I ordered several dozen tied in that pattern, and when they arrived I took them at once to the West Branch Dam to try.

My bright idea worked like a charm. I could spot my fly the instant it lit in the foam, and follow its progress effortlessly. But there was just one thing the matter with the wonder-flies—not a fish in the West Branch or in any of the numerous other streams on which I tested them would so much as notice them. I literally never had a rise to the Hot-Orange Bivisible.

So finally I salvaged the flies by painstakingly barbering them with fine-pointed scissors, clipping off every hot-orange barbel until nothing remained but a turn or two of hot-orange quill around the neck of the fly. The Bivisibles thus became mere Visibles, but not to me. To me they were again Invisibles.

So I turned them over to Momma, who was perpetually hard up for flies, and she caught fish on them. What amused me was that she developed a superstition about the tiny hot-orange heads on those flies, insisting they worked better than the standard Gray Hackles they otherwise were. In fact, when she had used up my reclaimed flies she tied some Gray Hackles of her own, each with a comical little head consisting of two turns of hot-orange woolen yarn.

So deeply was she convinced of the virtues of this pattern that one morning she came back almost half a mile along the Big Beaverkill to give me a couple of those flies and tell me the fish had been hitting them furiously. It was such a kind and sporting thing for her to do that I have always remembered it. But it was twenty years later that I had my first intimation that there might be something more than superstition in the hot-orange twist.

One winter night I was re-reading for the hundredth time G. E. M. Skues's perennially amusing, instructive, and fascinating tome, *Sidelines, Sidelights and Reflections.* Ordinarily I skip over Skues's fly and nymph patterns, because they were all for chalkstream fishing, which doesn't exist in my angling territory. But this time I glanced at an article which dealt with a new tying technique he had evolved, "which has been so far applied only to two or three of the Autumn Duns," he wrote. He noted that he had suspended the natural nymphs in a glass of water to observe them, and added to his description of the natural, "the eyes generally being orange."

I carefully read his technical description of the tie. He used hot-orange tying silk for undercolor, and concluded his exposition by saying, "Finish on the eye of the hook with a whip finish thus showing the orange silk (to represent the eyes) quite distinctly."

So if Skues says some English flies have orange eyes, I'm willing to believe some American flies have them, too, even if that belief implies that my Momma just may have a damn fool for a husband.

Letter to Lewis Hull

July 28, 1955

. . . Wish you had been with me two week-ends ago . . . I was over in Pennsylvania with Bob DeVilbiss in the rattlesnake country, fishing a statewide-famous trout brook, Big Bear Creek. Even when full it is about the size of that Black Joe Brook that runs down beside Hewitt's old road, and when I was there the water had disappeared leaving just a little dampness between the stones. The bushes were as close as a well-fitted coat and one could only cast by using a heavy leader and tearing off leaves and twigs until a space had been opened for the back cast. (Tearing them with abortive casts is what I mean.)

Nevertheless, when I <u>could</u> hit the stream-bed with the fly, the damndest most gorgeously colored big and fat brown trout you never saw would dash out, seize hold and—sometimes—be kept from going back into the maze of deadwood in which they lived. We weren't keeping fish so I dunno how many I caught but it had this hard-luck fisherman in a whirl.

In between I fished Dale Furst's Cedar Run, a limestone stream that you could jump across or nearly, and colored up as if someone had been washing milk cans in it. It was hair-raising to drop a big dry fly in the current and see a brilliant orange-washed-over-with-crimson trout materializing under it in the milky water, turning and taking almost at your feet. Big bolivars, averaging maybe 14 inches, and in one pool I got a boil and a schlooop that made DeVilbiss exclaim that it was the daddy of the stream, just from the sound—he had his back turned. Of course I was changing hands on the rod or filling a pipe or something.

. . . That kind of fishing was all brand-new to me until I realized three days later, that I had done it thirty years ago with Ray Bergman on Cedar Brook (I think that is the Ryngip or Pingip that Gordon referred to in his letters) near Haverstraw. I finally remembered seeing Ray cast from his knees, hook his fly around a bend in the stream to a pool that he could not see, and hook a trout by the sound of its rise.

. . . If I were you I wouldn't be too scared of the Neversink in August. They begin to get cold nights up there in that month and although it may be warm by day, you will likely find it distinctly cool by night. The water may continue to shrink, but it will be August; and in August the fish move upstream, water or no water. It can't get dry enough to stop them, and in fact, a low water level just makes them easier to find. I can't forget the monster in the Camp Pool who took crosswise in his big mouth on August early morning the very long shank of a great big polar bear streamer, and held onto it while I hit him three times hard enough to shred the tinsel and padding off the body. I sure wish I could have seen how big he was. I never moved him. He just hung on and bulldogged until he had to open his mouth to take a breath. . . .

A Fey Day

Even though it shatters the unities to admit that I ever caught a fish, this is an essentially truthful book, and I must acknowledge that even my lack of skill and luck has not been proof against the opulence of a certain Long Island pond.

Let me begin this narrative with the name of George LaBranche. George Michel Lucien LaBranche is a very considerable fellow who in his time has been an outstanding athlete, surf- and tournament-caster, and wing-shot. And of course his fame rests on his two great books, *The Dry Fly and Fast Water* and *The Salmon and the Dry Fly,* and on his prowess as an angler.

It will always be a matter of regret to me that I did not become acquainted with him until he had given up stream fishing and so I shall never see him demonstrate his mastery of fast water, but a few years ago I saw him teaching casting at a military hospital and realized that his classic form and perfect control were forever beyond me. So when he invited me to fish with him at the Long Island Country Club I hesitated, for George had the reputation of not suffering fools gladly, and I was afraid that I fell into that category.

But I went, and so found myself next morning in a boat with him on one of the club's famous ponds—cold, clear as glass, floored and walled with subaqueous water-weed, absolutely reeking with natural food, and hence capable of accommodating an enormous head of fish without starving or overcrowding them. For once the Red Gods were with me, for this turned out to be one of those fey days which every fisherman of experience has encountered once or twice; in twenty-five years of angling I can recall but three. It was a brilliant day with a blasting wind whipping the pond into wavelets—not what one would expect to be a good fishing day, but it seemed as if every fish in the water was insanely determined to have every fly that was offered.

The limit was five, and the rule, none to be returned. In spite of my best efforts to prolong the sport, I qualified in eight minutes. Then on impulse I put on a skater fly two inches in diameter, broke off the point, and cast far downwind. On another impulse I began to strip it back in foot-long jerks like a bucktail.

"What the ——?" protested George. He was interrupted by three trout which splashed frantically and futilely at the skimming fly in quick succession, and a fourth which nailed it and sounded into the weed. It frightened me, that fish; I thought I was going to catch it after all and disgrace myself. But after the better part of a minute it let go; I broke off the whole bend of the hook before I cast again.

What followed was a hilarious, lunatic saturnalia. Keeping the fly away from the wildly striking fish became a game at which I could not always win, and whenever it was taken, I had to give slack and wait as much as fifteen seconds before the trout could be persuaded to let go; obviously, they were swallowing the fly the instant it was taken. I twiddled, I teased, I retrieved in giant three-foot jumps, I dapped as the British blow-line fishermen do. And whatever I did, frantic fish almost broke their backs trying to be caught.

The fish quit as if on signal, all at once; and I did, too, for something told me that they were quitting for a long while and I wanted to stop while I was ahead of the game.

Then George went into action. He knotted on a little gray fly and, casting slantwise across the breeze, somehow put it far in under the overhanging willows, against the weed. I felt privately that it was a hundred to one against even George LaBranche moving a fish then, but fortunately I did not offer the bet, for I would have lost. He was evidently feeling in out-of-the-way corners for fish which might have been exempt from the preceding frenzy, and in under those willows he found one.

His next cast was straight across the wind into a tiny pocket in the weed, with the leader draped lightly over a protruding stalk. He found another. Then, in spite of the unpredictable wind, he placed the fly delicately on an overhanging branch and, after a moment, dropped it onto the water with a faint twitch. A fish met it descending. For his last cast he sent his fly riding downwind behind a hearty gust to land with miraculous lightness almost where it had fallen previously. It floated untouched until he moved his line ever so slightly, jiggling the fly without changing its position. Then another fish took it. It was the most beautifully executed fishing and casting I ever saw, but it was scarcely educational; one doesn't learn that sort of thing just by seeing it done.

The fish didn't come on the feed again the rest of that weekend. They had finished their act that morning, an act which I am convinced the Red Gods put on to cover my faults and save my feelings, doubtless because at some time in the past I had been a good boy.

Night Noises

Dear "Rod and Gun":

No, sir, it is not a wonder that "some people" never get over their fear of woodland night noises. That is a fundamental instinct and it is felt, not by "some people," but by everybody, even those who lack the sense to stay in the house at night. Some hide it better than others, that's all.

A night fisherman of thirty years' experience tells me that the splash of a muskrat or a loose cow shaking the bushes still paralyzes him with fright. Me, too. One night, near Margaretville, a big trout cornered a minnow in the shallow near me and went to work on him. It sounded like two skeletons wrestling on a tin roof, and it scared my new English waders and a pair of pants right off me. I still remember that sickish-sweet taste from the pit of the stomach, the real flavor of fear.

My specialty is getting lost when I start wading back toward the bank. I know where it is—oh, sure. But I walk and walk, and the water seems to get deeper instead of shallower. I begin to wonder if the stream is running the wrong way. Maybe I'm walking right into deep water in midstream! I start wishing I had learned to swim, and thinking of my sins, and when I get ashore I'm practically in tears. Of course, you can't light a flashlight in night fishing; it would scare the fish.

Every night fisherman has his worst moment, but none to beat Bill Mackey's. In a raging rapid he stepped into a discarded bedspring. He says he never expected to get out alive.

Another scary thing at night is hitting bats with your rod or line and knocking them into the water. I'm always afraid they'll swim over to me, climb my leg, and take a few bites for revenge. Both bats and swallows will chase a dry fly while it is being false cast, and occasionally catch it. I have hooked a number of bats and one swallow that way. Unhooking them is a problem, but a big turtle or a snake is a worse one.

A ghost cured one of my friends of night fishing. He wandered away from his companions, out into the meadow. When he reappeared he was flitting along in twelve-foot strides, waders and all, while a huge white ghost thundered after him in the starlight. He fainted by the time he reached the stream, and his companions hid in the bushes. It turned out that he had got himself chased by an old white horse.

No, sir, folks getting scared at night is not a wonder. The wonder is that they ever live through it.

SPARSE GREY HACKLE.

(Donald Stillman's column, January 1939.)

Night Fishing

Heat and fear oppressed the land, for it was one of those stifling, humid August nights when the whole countryside is awake and every living thing is abroad on the business of life and death. The darkness was so thick and close that one tried instinctively to push it aside, and the air was heavy with the menace of predators and the terror of their prey. The river was soundless save for a faint spattering at my feet, a mere whisper which I could not identify until I turned on my little flashlight and discovered in the very margin of the stream, where it feathered off to nothing on a sandy beach, a dark line of what appeared to be stranded twigs and chaff. It was a horde of the tiniest of minnows, which had taken refuge in the ultimate edge of the water and still leaped frantically over each other in their efforts to be farthest from the prowling fish they knew would soon be seeking them.

I waded across the broad river to where a little cold feeder entered it and began to cast a big black wet fly on a heavy leader, for this is the season when the hellgrammites rise from the river bottom and swim ashore to pupate under stones before hatching into huge nocturnal dobsonflies. It was too early yet for big fish to be feeding, but there might be a stray around, and anyway, I wanted to be fishing. So for a couple of hours I inched along silently on felt-shod feet working my fly in the cooler water along the bank, where a fish might be harboring. At midnight it was still hot and breathless. Perspiration dripped off my face, and inside my high waders I was soaked with it. I was weary of swinging the big ten-foot fly rod, too, so I went ashore and sat down for a while before I made my way up to the head of the long pool.

The sky had somehow brightened now, and the darkness, so thick and close before, appeared thin and luminous. It seemed as if I could see farther than I really could, but at least I could make out the stranded log on the far bank shining as white as bone. I replaced my wet fly with a deer-hair bug to imitate some blundering moth and began to work out line along my side of the river. It is difficult to get out in darkness just the length needed to reach one's target, but not impossible if one is familiar with the water and his rod, so when I picked up the cast and pushed it straight across the log I was confident that my bug would drop right in front of it.

I brought my hand down hard and the bug smacked the water. A white flower of foam blossomed in front of the log, and blossomed again when I swept the tip back in a hard strike. I was into a fish! It headed down the current, and I held the rod high overhead and reeled desperately to take up the slack. I seemed to be choking, and it took me a moment to discover that it was because I was holding my breath.

Alas, the fish was strong but not strong enough; fighting but not fighting hard. Suspicion at once changed to conviction, and conviction became certainty when I brought the fish into the circle of strange pale light cast by the little flashlight, which by now I held between my teeth. It was a chub—an alderman, the grandfather of all the chub in the river, a chub as round as a rolling pin, one with pretensions to rise above his class and act like a trout, but still . . . a chub.

I unhooked and returned him—gently, because I was grateful to him for providing a little action—stowed away my flashlight, and felt for my pipe. Only then did I realize that my heart was pounding slowly and heavily, like a burned-out main bearing.

That is night fishing, the essence of angling, the emperor of sports. It is a gorgeous gambling game in which one stakes the certainty of long hours of faceless fumbling, nerve-racking starts, frights, falls, and fishless baskets against the off-chance of hooking into—not landing necessarily or even probably, but hooking into—a fish as long and heavy as a railroad tie and as unmanageable as a runaway submarine. It combines the wary stalking and immobile patience of an Indian hunter with sudden, violent action, the mystery and thrill of the unknown, a stimulating sense of isolation and self-reliance, and an unparalleled opportunity to be close to nature, since most creatures are really nocturnal in habit.

Above all, it provides the stimulation of sudden fright at the startling things which continually occur in the dark, and, in fact, I am inclined to believe that that is the greatest lure of the sport. In all of the night-fishing experiences that I recall, the outstanding thing was always that I was scared half to death. Of these experiences, two are notable.

I used to prowl around in the deep stillwater where a small brook entered an ice pond, fishing for big rainbows that worked up into the stream after dark. The banks were swampy and in the stream the mud was knee-deep, but there was firm bottom under it and I could work along an inch at a time, wading almost to the top of my armpit-high waders, onto the boot feet of which were strapped hobnailed leather sandals.

Saplings grew shallow-rooted on the marshy banks and were continually falling into the stream, so when, this night, I encountered the tip of one that had sunk into the mud, I thought nothing of it and backed away. The trouble was that the point of the sapling had run under the strap of my sandal and, having a knob on it, was stuck and could not be withdrawn. I soon found that I could not break the thing off, either, because it was too flexible, nor drag the whole tree loose, because it was too firmly anchored by its roots. So the situation was that I was tethered by the foot twenty feet from shore in mud so thick that I could scarcely move my feet and water so deep I had to move cautiously to avoid filling my waders. And it was darker than the inside of a coal mine.

It was a simple and rather ridiculous plight, but I could see very little about it that was humorous, particularly when I reflected that I was beyond shouting distance of a house or road. In fact, after I had thoroughly tested the possibilities of getting loose I emitted a little cold perspiration in spite of the warmness of the night.

The only thing I could think of to do—which was to discard my rod, dive down, and use my hands to free myself—was neither promising nor inviting. It would leave me flat in the stream with my waders full of water and my feet stuck deep in the mud, probably confused as to the direction in which the bank lay—and I can't swim. If I were unable to regain my feet and my balance in the darkness, and that seemed very likely indeed, I would be in a very perplexing situation. I had also to consider the possibility that I might not be able to free my foot; in that case I would have even less freedom of movement of my legs to assist me in regaining and keeping a vertical position.

I haven't the remotest idea how long I stayed there—it seemed hours—but all the while I was cogitating, I was also twisting my foot and flexing the twig. Eventually it either broke off or pulled out, and although I was even keener for night fishing then than I am now and still had plenty of time left, I headed upstream to the hauling-out place at my best speed. And as soon as I got ashore I unstrapped the sandals and hurled them into the bushes. I have never since worn anything, when wading at night, under or in which a stick might catch.

My other memorable experience was the result of several varieties of folly. It was early May on the Beaverkill and I had not found fish, so, misled by the warm sun and balmy air, I thought there might be night fishing in my favorite pool, the Wagon Tracks. Normally Cairns's Ford, at the head of the pool, is almost out of water except for a little channel close to the road side of the stream, but now I found it knee-deep all the way across, pants-pocket deep in the channel, and of course running like a milltail. It was a tough crossing in daylight; I did not stop to think what it would be like at night.

I found that what was normally the shallow side of the pool had been scoured by floods, and in the high water I had to wade close to the bank. It was not a good sort of night water in that condition, but I was still bemused, so I put on a big stonefly nymph and started working down, casting straight across and letting the fly swing around, then fishing it back close to the bank, an inch at a time. I worked along on numbing legs for hours, staring blankly into darkness relieved only when a car passed along the road on the other side. The water was quiet—dead, in fact; and then I thought I felt a light touch on the nymph, right below me, just as it would be finishing its swing. Action at last! Surely something had lipped the nymph; that was just the right point in its swing to expect it. Could I make the fish come again?

Reeling up the slack I had already worked in so that my next cast would come to exactly the same length, I chucked the nymph across the current again, and as it began to swing I unconsciously leaned forward with my arms extended in an attitude of hair-trigger alertness. The line straightened and I knew the big nymph swinging behind it was approaching the spot. Now. . . .

Something, a mink perhaps, leaped off the bank and struck the water right under my outstretched arms; as it hit, a good-sized fish leaped out and made its escape.

I stood fixed; I couldn't have moved to save my life. The sweet, sickening taste which is the real flavor of fear filled my mouth, and my heart hammered in my throat. I began to strangle and knew I was holding my breath, but I could not command my lungs to function.

When I had recovered the power of movement I decided that I was through, took down my rod, and got my little flashlight out to go back across the ford. Now the ford ran at a diagonal and my target was a clump of bushes on the other bank. I couldn't see the bushes with my little light, but I could see the stream bottom—the shallow ford and the deeper water on either side of it. So I went along all right for perhaps a quarter of the way, and then my flashlight played out.

I had only a couple of hundred feet to go, more or less, but that is a long distance when the water is too high, the night too dark, and the way too uncertain. I worked ahead feeling for the shallower water, but soon got into the position familiar to every night fisherman, in which one seems to be surrounded by deeper water. All right; I would stand still until a car came along to shine its headlights on my brushy marker. But this was wartime, with gasoline rationing in force, and people were not driving much at night. I think only the fact that it was Saturday night, tradition-al "night out" for countrymen as well as city folk, saved me.

I stood there a while beside that short, ugly rapid roaring down into deep water, remembering that I couldn't swim, even without high waders and heavy hobnailed shoes to handicap me. Then a car flashed by and I found my marker and stepped out boldly until once more I seemed to be hemmed in by deep water. As I recall, I had to wait for four cars in order to reach the edge of the deeper channel, ten feet from the bank.

I stepped down into it cautiously with one foot, found a rolling stone, dislodged it, and got solid footing; I brought the other foot forward, worked it in and out of some sharp-angled pockets, and planted it beside the first. The water was halfway above my knees now, tearing at my legs, growling and foaming. The steep pounding rapid was white in the dark-ness, and what I could see looked as bad as it sounded. I shuffled a foot forward, then brought the other one up beside it: the water was an inch deeper. I felt and withdrew with first one foot, then the other, and then inched half a step downstream to get around something high and slippery. I completed another shuffling step. At last I was just two steps from safe-ty, one into deeper water and the next up onto the bank. I put the rod joints in my mouth to have both hands free and resolved to throw myself forward and grab for bushes if I felt myself going. I took a deep breath and stepped out, and, as so often happens, anticipation was worse than reali-ty. My foot held, and in the next instant I was hauling myself out.

I sat down on the running board of my car, filled my pipe, and looked at my watch. It was 1 A.M. daylight saving time. My feet were numb, my legs ached, and my mouth was dry, and when I took off my waders I dis-covered that my knees were trembling slightly but steadily and uncontrol-lably. Fatigue? Not on your life. I was scared stiff.

Nocturne

It is curious that the most vivid memories of a fisherman are those of sight rather than sound. Let him consider the incidents he remembers best and he will realize that they came to him through the eye rather than the ear. Its very uniqueness, then, is an additional reason for cherishing a memory that came to me entirely through the ear. It is an incident of which I heard all and saw nothing.

I was camped on the Willowemoc beside one of those pools that redeem the stretches of broad shallows characteristic of the Catskill rivers in summer. The midnight stars furnished just enough light to reveal the flying bat and the laboring moth. Baked stones and lifeless brush still yielded their heat, but an edge of coolness was creeping into the breathless air. In the shallows the river trickled silently.

I was at last almost asleep when I heard a faint recurring sound up the river. As I listened it came closer, and soon I could identify the swish of a fishing rod and the crunch and rattle of stones shifting under the feet of someone wading along the stream. Clatter, clatter, clatter. Swish-swish. A pause. Then the same succession of sounds again.

It was a night fisherman. The level beds of these flood-swept Catskill rivers, loosely paved with small stones and gravel, are smooth enough for wading in the dark. A few fishermen make a practice of doing so in the hot weather, fishing a bucktail or a large wet fly for the big trout which at that season feed only during the cool hours.

I looked out of the opening of my tent, but the brush was too thick for me to see the unknown fisherman without rising. So I lay in my blanket listening idly for the sound of a hooked fish and half wishing that I, too, had gone fishing.

The Unknown was a workmanlike angler. The grinding of the stones and the recurrent swish of his rod told me that he was systematically covering the water, taking the regulation three steps between casts. There was no interruption to his steady progress except the brief pause to fish out each cast. Now he was opposite me, skirting the pool. Clatter, clatter, clatter. Swish-swish. A pause while he slowly retrieved the lure. Clatter, clatter, scramble—SPLASH!

A tremendous floundering, a rasping of hobnails, a rending of the waters as he emerged, and the sound of dripping garments came to my ears. And then the night was shattered by a spate of profanity from such springs of bitter passion as are tapped only by such a catastrophe. All the disappointment of a fishless night, all the strain of hours of wading, all the primitive, instinctive fear of the dark joined with the shock of a sudden fall and an involuntary immersion to dash the Unknown's self-restraint.

I listened in admiring silence. I have heard an apoplectic sergeant of six enlistments drilling rookies. I have heard a regular army stable detail unloading a car of bad actors from the remount station. Once I heard a high officer ask the driver what was in a stalled truck that was blocking the ammunition going up and the wounded coming back, and when the driver replied, "Officers' baggage, sir," the high officer stood up in his sidecar and loosed a blast that fairly unloaded the offending bedrolls into the ditch.

Best of all, I once heard a gray-headed chief of section on maneuvers extricating an overturned caisson from a nest of rocks under the quiet, sinister admonitions of Charles Pelot Summerall, then a major, afterward chief of staff, and always a prime maneater. That was swearing! "For the love of the bald-headed, paralytic . . ." began the sergeant in a trembling voice, and then ascended to such heights of oratorical frenzy that we stood spellbound. When he sprang into the saddle with a final ". . . and six men and a corporal with sidearms for pallbearers," we knew we had heard the voice of a master.

But compared to the Unknown, these perorations were as the lisping numbers of little children. Louder and louder, higher and higher rose his eloquence, shocking the darkness and affrighting the landscape, until at last he stood upon the mountain peak and hurled a livid, blinding blast at the embarrassed moon. It was the climax. Gradually he slid down from the heights until at last he subsided into a morass of common hells and damns. Silence crept timidly back.

The Unknown resumed his progress down the river. Clatter, clatter, clatter. Swish-swish. A pause. Clatter, clatter. . . .

With an envious sigh, I turned on my pillow and embraced sleep.

The Remembering Machine

Introduction to *The Pleasures of Fly Fishing*

Fish are, of course, indispensable to the angler. They give him an excuse for fishing and justify the fly rod without which he would be a mere vagrant. But the average fisherman's average catch doesn't even begin to justify, *as fish*, its cost in work, time, and money. The true worth of fishing, as the experienced, sophisticated angler comes to realize, lies in the memorable contacts with people and other living creatures, scenes and places, and living waters great and small which it provides.

Memorable, that is the key word. It is the recollection, the memory of all that the angler has experienced or observed, that changes the catching of a few fish for the frying pan into a yearlong and lifelong recreation. And it is these memories of days astream that lead the angler to find in the literature of the art those records and comments, that philosophizing of other anglers, that he will delight to compare with his own.

In the field of memory the camera is, of course, the supreme tool. That little instrument, scarcely larger than two packs of cigarettes, is a remembering machine more potent and accomplished, for the angler's purposes, than the most highly developed computer with its "memory banks." It doesn't lie, that little machine, and it doesn't forget. For all your future days it brings back, strong and clear, the memories that have faded and become distorted in your mind; it sharpens again the worn and rounded edges of your recollections.

But I must remind you that it does these wonders only if you use it. I cannot recall anyone who was ever sorry that he took a picture, but I have heard, and myself have voiced, an infinite number of lamentations that some picture had not been taken.

The world would not know, ever, what George Edward Mackenzie Skues, the greatest fishing writer of his time and the creator of nymph fishing, looked like had not his friend Dr. E. A. Barton taken a wonderful, informal portrait of him with his injured wrists and his big hands that were so deft, his rod and his long-handled net and old, safety-pinned linen fishing bag, and the kindness and generosity he tried to hide behind a crusty expression.

If my dear friend the late Dick Clark had not handed his camera to a bystander to snap a picture of him and another old friend, Charlie Fox, sitting with me on the famous bench beside the placid Letort, I would not now have a picture to cherish as long as I live.

And if Bob Cunningham, a true artist with the lens, had not taken photographs of dreamlike beauty along the DeBruce Fly Fishing Club water on the upper Willowemoc, his fellow-members would be beginning to forget even now how the Clubhouse Pond, the Junction Pool where George LaBranche cast his first dry fly, the Rhododendron Run, the Campsite Pool, and many another fair prospect looked before the catastrophic flood a couple of years ago.

In the following pages "Pete" Hidy shows, in text and picture, how a good fisherman, a good photographer, and a good student of the literature has collected and stored his memories.

Go thou and do likewise.

The Lotus Eaters

No record remains of the early history of the club which a group of wealthy Brooklyn brewers and trout fishermen incorporated as The Fly Fishers Club of Brooklyn. But the late Chancellor Levison, who was a member, told Dick Hunt that the group fished Brodhead's Creek from the Henryville House in the 1870s, and when the brook-trout fishing played out there in the '90s, moved to the Beaverkill and made their headquarters at Ben Hardenburgh's farm.

Legend says that Ben built a log cabin on his farm for a wealthy man who wanted a love nest; that after Ben had discovered what was going on and had run him off, the Brooklyn fishermen took it over for a dormitory; and that when they had a mass disagreement with Ben some years later, they formed their own club and bought the cabin for their clubhouse. At the same time, the club took its pick of the trout water for a price little more than the traditional red apple.

As now constituted, the club has several acres of rolling ground, on the eminence of which is the same log cabin with a separate mess hall behind it; two-and-a-half miles, both banks, of the sweetest dry-fly water on the entire length of the Little River, more than half of it in fee and the rest on long-term lease; privileges of entry and water supply in connection with the late Ben Hardenburgh's farm; and a sound, well-built dam at the foot of the Home Pool, which goes out with the floodwater each year.

The charter provides for twenty-five members, but unwritten law limits membership to twenty, the present number; after a lapse of many years, there actually is now one member from Brooklyn. The shares of stock, one to a member, are valued at one hundred dollars each and the dues are twenty-five dollars a year, besides an assessment whenever the dam goes out. But to stem any rush for the bargain represented by this combination of superb fishing and low cost, it should be noted that a flaming sword bars the entrance to this angler's Eden. It is the membership, the most unique thing about this unique institution.

For these are the lotus eaters. They live in a little world apart, a world which they found perfect upon entering and which, consequently, they strive to keep unchanged. Does there come one with wealth and social position? They do not comprehend the terms. Angling genius and the prestige of authorship? They glance up incuriously and return to their concerns. Sportsmanship, pleasing personality, fellowship of spirit? They regard him with unfocused eyes and murmur that they already have these qualities in the club. Here is one institution by which it is no reproach to be blackballed, for the present members are all agreed that if they themselves were now outsiders coming up for membership, they would be blackballed without exception. This is not a manifestation of caprice, misanthropy, or sadism. It is merely the outward expression of the spirit of the club, that everything is perfect the way it is—let us keep it that way.

This passion for the past carries the members to inordinate lengths, some of which may be described. For instance, the great one-room cabin bears no wall decorations except a thousand nails at which one may pitch his kit and hang it up, a series of penciled outlines of big fish, and a grocery store calendar for the year 1910. Even to stretch a hand toward this ancient, fly-specked relic elicits outraged cries and warnings from all present. The rough board floor is covered with a mud-caked rug of nondescript color; when Malcolm Runyon and the present writer essayed to remove and beat the tattered fabric, Scotty Conover, doyen of the club, leaped upon it in a heroic attitude and exclaimed, "That rug was put down in 1912, the year I joined the club. It has never been off the floor since, and it is not going to be taken up now!" The fireplace below the foot-thick flagstone mantelshelf contains a layer of ashes at least a foot thick. We removed a few inches of this deposit before we were discovered

and restrained, and although we finally escaped expulsion, we never whol-
ly lived down the opprobrium that descended on us.

A new member who naively offered to have the cabin wired for electricity at his own expense shocked the members into literal speechlessness,
and his sacrilege was blamed for a crack that appeared in the fireplace. The
club's shame is the handsome new (twenty-year-old) mess hall, which had
to be built simply because the old one had burned down. But fortunately
it is offset somewhat by the condition of the backhouse, which was torn
from its mooring and knocked askew years ago when the pilot of the
county snowplow was induced to open the lane. Becoming a bit overin-
duced, he turned too short and the plow engaged the corner of the backhouse. It has been allowed to remain just as it dropped when Walt Fassett
reached over and disengaged the clutch, and the members boast of its generous ventilation and erratic geometry.

Aside from the hearth fire, the sole artificial illumination in the cabin
is an old-fashioned kerosene hanging lamp which was salvaged from a
country church. Directly beneath it is a table upon which each member,
as he enters, deposits his bottle. Additionally, there is a pitcher of the icy
springwater that flows perpetually from a pipe in the front yard—water
that is agony to the teeth and a frigid benediction to the palate. No one
can recall clearly how long the lamp and the table have been there, but all
agree that the lamp has leaked kerosene upon the table—and into the
water pitcher—ever since it was filched. You may think that the leak
might be repaired, or that the table might be moved, or at least that the
pitcher might be shifted, but that is because you do not know the
Brooklyn Fly Fishers. Every highball that has been consumed in the club
during all those years has featured a slight but terribly definite flavor of
kerosene.

The same willingness to sanctify a traditional disability prevails in the
dormitory, the single room constituting the upper floor of the cabin. Here
unyielding cots bear mattresses of geologic age, each with its hills and val-
leys disposed in an individual terrain. Each member has learned how to

wind himself between the lumps of his own bed and sleep comfortably in that contorted attitude, and if a newcomer take another member's bed he will hear bitter protestation.

To be at the club for Opening Day is to realize how their devotion to the past inures the members to present hardship. The hardy anglers spend the evening in front of the blast-furnace fireplace, fortifying themselves internally to prevent their entire rear aspects from freezing solid. When the inner stiffness approximates the outer, each picks up a huge load of gray camp blankets and a kerosene lamp and climbs to the loft. How they have failed to burn down the cabin long ago by this procedure is a mystery.

Some take off a few clothes, and there was once an exhibitionist who got into pajamas, but the standard procedure is to take off nothing but the shoes and the hat. Daybreak finds not even an ear or a nose visible, but one cowering figure, more valiant or less enduring than the rest, finally will force himself out of bed to dash downstairs, chunk up the fire, and clench his chattering teeth on the neck of a bottle. When the fire begins to make an impression on the room temperature, the other sleepers come dashing down to seize their bottles and back up to the blaze. The lavatory is the spring-water pipe in the yard. In warm weather they strip down and wash there, shaving with mirrors propped against the porch railing, but on Opening Day they just rinse their hands.

Two things may be noted about that porch in passing. One is that every bottle ever emptied at the club reposes beneath it—it is a broad porch nearly surrounding the cabin, with very little room left under it. The other is that its railing is a favorite spot for the members to cool off in their pelts after a sweaty afternoon in waders—a spectacle that once sent flying two schoolmarms who had driven up the winding lane to inspect the "quaint cabin," thinking it unoccupied.

Two henchmen occupy the club's little world along with the members. One is Joe Hardenburgh, whose farmhouse lies hidden beyond the apple trees; he "keeps an eye on things" in addition to working a hardscrabble farm on which crops are dragged up painfully rather than raised. This laconic descendant of the patroon who received the far-flung Hardenburgh patent is best depicted by his reply to an invitation to attend an auction; "You might find something you want," was the inducement. "I got everything I want now," he said. The other is Bert Cable, the best short-order cook in the world, who looks after the mess hall during the season. He ran the famous White House Restaurant in Roscoe for years and, in fact, starts a restaurant whenever he feels like it, selling out when he gets tired of it. Like Joe, Bert doesn't really work for the club; he just comes up to help out his friends. They are a true part of the atmosphere of this ethereal cosmos.

For so it is. This is the land of the lotus, to enter which is to come under the spell of a dreaming languor, an enchantment of restfulness which makes the world outside hazy and unreal. The energetic visitor ascends the lane in a shower of gravel, hustles in with his equipment, sits down on the porch to catch his breath—and is lost. In this natural bower where nothing can be seen but trees and sky, he idles to watch the line of the hills, to hear the birds at their housekeeping and the river whispering on its stones. He murmurs vague conversation, wanders about the cabin, and dawdles before the fireplace. He smokes the pipe of contemplation over his empty plate. When he goes to his locker for his waders he forgets his purpose; and if he starts for the stream at all he does it late and reluctantly. No one ever strides down to the river at the Brooklyn Fly Fishers. At best, he saunters.

The river itself fits into the spell. This is the Little River, the Beaverkill above its junction with the Willowemoc, the stream to which its alumni return again and again, forsaking the certainties of lordly preserves. The Big River, from the Junction at Roscoe to its junction with the East Branch of the Delaware, is a challenge, whereas the Little River is an invitation. It takes stronger legs and longer chances to wade the Big River, a bigger rod and a better arm to cover its waters. It is here that the ten- and twelve-pound monsters are taken, as well as the five-pound bass that makes the startled angler think he has hooked into a trout twice as big. Here the stalker can watch an hour, a day, or a week until he sees a great trout feeding and then wade armpit-deep and try to keep sixty feet of line off the water as he works out the single cast that will either raise the fish or put him down.

Fishing the Big River is a sport, but fishing the Little River is a recreation. This dozen miles of the loveliest trout water in America, with the Balsam Lake Club at the top and the Brooklyn Fly Fishers at the bottom, is what the old-timers referred to when they wrote about the Beaverkill, the classic water of the Golden Age.

It is still just as it was, at least from the fall of Berry Brook down to the Brooklyn water and the Rockland bridge half a mile below it. A road follows it from Roscoe to the source, but above the Rockland bridge this is a washboarded red-dirt track with an ugly habit of tipping cars into the river, so that visitors to the state campsite above Berry Brook prefer to go in on the paved road from Livingston Manor. All that disturbs the melody of the living countryside along the river road is the bouncing of an occasional farm truck.

And as the river has not changed, neither have the Brooklyn Fly Fishers, for whom the Golden Age still exists. Not for them the state water farther upstream, nor the open water below the Rockland bridge. For years the club leased the beautiful Tempel water in the latter stretch, but they finally gave it up because "nobody ever went down there." No, no one wants to go to any other water. The club leprechaun, Johnny Woodruff, may sneak off to night-fish the Picnic Grounds, and the club juvenile, Ed Myers, may spend his energy on expeditions to the Summer House Pool, but these are the exceptions. Sometimes the members speak knowingly of Foul Rift and the Lone Pine, the Deserted Village, and Painter's Bend, but when you pin them down you discover that they have not fished those pools in the Big River since their boyhood.

Another way remains in which the club stays faithful to the Golden Age. It is the last stand, the loyal Old Guard, the final vanishing remnant of the old-fashioned American dry-fly purists. At first glance it seems strange that this group, more than any other, should exemplify the classic tradition of the dry fly. These are stern and hardy men, unfashionable, contemptuous of innovations, indifferent to foibles; enemies of pretense, averse to strangers, woman-haters; reading no fishing magazines or books—they already know how to fish; immune to British prestige, unknown to Abercrombie's or the Crossroads of Sport, contemptuous of Halford.

But these are the *American* purists. Not for them the long leaders and 4X points, the stream entomology, the tortured science of line calibers and rod action, the elaborate long casting to a rise in stillwater. Here, as nowhere else, there is exemplified the pure gospel of American dry-fly fishing just as its prophet George LaBranche engraved it on the stone tablets of *The Dry Fly and Fast Water;* as Fred White saw it demonstrated by Theodore Gordon; as Chancellor Levison and Dr. Halsey and all the old-timers who grew up in the great tradition practiced it—the gospel that it doesn't matter what fly you use, it's how and where you use it that counts; the gospel of fishing the water rather than the rise, and covering the broken water rather than the smooth. Every inch of the Brooklyn water is broken, or at least ruffled, at normal tides; every inch of it is fished by the members with the dry fly. And with the dry fly only. Scotty Conover assured the present writer that he had not fished a wet fly in more than thirty years, and he is typical.

Here, then, is that echo of the Golden Age, that tiny angling Eden that has survived as the Brooklyn Fly Fishers. Would that it were timeless; but its end is early written. Not too many years hence the adjacent waters will be owned by estates instead of individuals, and when they are sold in settlement, the state, that greedy grabber of dead men's water, will surely get them. With state open water at either end of its unguarded stretch of river, hikers swarming over its acres, and cars churning the dust, the club will see its end inevitable. It will sell out to the state, which will dredge the Home Pool for swimming and put a hot-dog stand in the cabin.

The lotus eaters will die of remembrance.

Author's note: A number of former and present members of the Brooklyn Fly Fishers have expressed approval of the foregoing article, but they point out that a) the 1910 calendar was discarded several years ago; b) the bottles under the porch were sold in a wartime scrap drive; and c) the lamp has been repaired and no longer leaks kerosene into the water pitcher—which, however, still stands on the table beneath it. I record these developments, all of which took place after I wrote the original article, with sadness, for they indicate that change if not progress has at last come to the dreaming land of the lotus.

Letter to Nick Lyons

(undated) . . .

F ine snow is riding the stallion of the wind, which is tapping the window beside me with the tips of the evergreen branches. It's white and cold outside, and dark except for street lights—I just went out to look.

How I'd love to be camping in deep woods tonight, with Nessmuk—or Nick. I'd probably die before morning, but I never go out in dark and storm without planning what I'd do if I were in the woods down at the Big Bend, or the little cup of woods by the Schoolhouse Pool, a little enclave of wilderness beyond sight or sound of Route 17—it's gone now. A heavy pack, no camp made, night and snow falling. . . .

Letter to Nick Lyons

February 17, 1970

. . . This camping trip your friend speaks of was on the East Branch (Delaware) and I think in or close to Union Grove, now under the reservoir. Dan invited me to drive over on the week-end (Saturday) evening and I did, arriving about 9:30 in full darkness. This was a big safari, with wives included; they set up a lot of these umbrella-type "automobile" tents, with folding armchairs and the works. Dan was a pyromaniac and I often wondered how he refrained from burning down his home in Fayetteville many times over; he'd cram in all the wood the fireplace would hold, literally, right up to the top of the arch. This night they had a pile of about a dozen discarded railroad ties and I mean to tell you they had a conflagration that everyone was glad to be 200 feet away from. Each male member of the party had a fifth of Crab Orchard standing in the grass alongside his chair and what with the holocaust and the wild whooping, it sounded like Indians along the border.

I had a spotlight on my car and I turned it on in order to pick my way across the meadow to the campsite. As soon as I did so there was intense silence except for the crackling of the fire, and no one could be seen moving. I finally parked my car, turned off my spotlight, stepped out of the car and here came Dan, nicely mulled, dignified and gracious as an old Roman Senator (which he more or less resembled). That spotlight coming across the meadow had convinced them that a State Trooper was coming to investigate, probably in response to some alarmed complaints from the countryside. All were much relieved when it turned out to be merely Old

88

Sparse. They were a good bunch; but I remember helping several of the more sober ones to rescue the participants in a wrestling match who had wrestled right into the embers but were too distraught to notice it.

The First Camping Trip

A man's first try at anything, from flying an airplane to just going camping, is many things, but above all educational. He learns more—the things that aren't in the books—that first time than a hundred repetitions will teach him.

The first fruits of camping is experience, and experience breeds advice. There is never much demand for this commodity however great its excellence, but sometimes a man of goodwill is tempted to try and help his fellowman by raising the voice of experience. It has long been plain to me that most of the problems, trials, and vexations of camping relate back to mere weight. So once I philosophized about weight, as follows:

The story is that one day long ago an apple fell off a tree upon the skull of Sir Isaac Newton, who forthwith discovered the principle of gravitation. Ever since, outdoorsmen have had to reckon with gravity.

If you're a beginner at camping, take my advice and learn to live with "G," as aviators call this gremlin. It can make you a lot of trouble.

Take water, now. It's handy stuff in small lots for washing dishes, in larger lots for fishing, and in wholesale quantities for boating and swimming. Drops of water combined with "G" are called rain, and because there's so little you can do about it, rain is bad news on a camping trip.

When rain hits, "G" makes it run downhill into the little hollow in which you've pitched your tent. Then you're likely to sleep wet. Camping books say you can prevent this disaster by digging a nice deep ditch all around your tent, sloping the bottom so that the water will drain off instead of flooding in the ditch. But this idea has several important things the matter with it. Sometimes it takes a pretty good civil engineer to get all that sloping and slanting done right.

When I was in East Texas with the Mexican Border Patrol, we got flooded out of our big pyramidal tents every time we had a rainstorm, because our ditches were too small and sloped all ways. We never were able to keep dry until we dug ditches a foot wide and a foot deep, and linked them in an elaborate system of waterways, which we pitched the right way by using the "battery commander's telescope" (an angle-measuring instrument) as a surveyor's level.

You may be able to ditch a tent without engineering instruments so that the water will flow from it instead of under it. It's possible; but just how do you ditch a tent without a shovel? And how can you carry a shovel on a backpacking trip when you have to even take the pits out of the prunes beforehand to save weight?

All right, you have a shovel that doesn't weigh anything! But have you ever tried to dig a ditch, or anything else, in the woods? Well, the forest floor contains more roots than dirt. I won't say you can't dig through it, but I'd rather be watching than helping when you try.

Personally, I don't do much about ditching unless I happen to have a lot of root-grubbing tools handy. Usually I just try to camp on loose, sandy soil and then pray that it won't rain too hard. This defeats "G" most of the time.

However, I'll pitch in a hollow anytime if that's the only way to get on level ground. It rains only part of the time, but "G" never stops. You'll notice this if you try sleeping on a surface that has the least bit of slant. A pitch too slight for your eye to detect will keep you rolling or, worse, trying not to roll all night long. If you *have* to sleep on a slant, have your head, not your feet, highest; and never try to sleep *across* a slant.

There are various outdoor matters on which it's best to try to compromise with "G." The smallest and lightest tent, for instance, is not necessarily the best. I once made myself a one-man tent that fitted me like a nightgown. There was no room for my outfit, or for a little dry wood for the morning fire. In rain it leaked every time I touched it, despite its waterproofing. It got wet inside from my breath and by morning it stank. A tent with a little extra room is worth the little extra weight.

One insidious way in which "G" gets in its work in tents concerns pants. Pants are made to stand up in, and they depend on "G" to make what you put in the pockets stay put. When you lie down, "G" will coax little objects like pipes and jackknives out of your pocket and sneak them under the edge of the tent so you can never find them again. The only sure defense against this is a sewed-in ground cloth.

Such a ground cloth has another important use. Without it, a tent is just a big piece of cloth that you can pull into any shape you please, all of them wrong except one. But if it has a sewed-in ground cloth it will have one definite shape, and once you've pegged down the floor, each pole and stake can go in only one place, the right one. Very nice when you're pitching it in the rain.

Another thing worth the extra weight is an air mattress. People will tell you to smooth off the ground and make a bed of balsam boughs on it. I say, leave the lumps and throw an air mattress over them. Even if you can find evergreens and are allowed to cut them, which is far from certain nowadays, you can spend a whole afternoon making a browse bed that you won't like very well that night. I'll leave food home, if necessary, to make room for an air mattress.

You can save a little "G" trouble by using a sleeping bag instead of blankets, but if you intend to keep a fire going or have any other reason for getting up during the night, you'll be happier with a bag that's easy to get into and out of. Mummy bags that have to be crawled into from the top are not in that class. You might also note that a few people are temperamentally unsuited to sleeping in bags. My most hilarious camping memory is of a partner who dreamed a bull was chasing him and tried to run away inside a crackling canvas sleeping bag. It sounded like two skeletons wrestling on a tin roof.

Still another place where old Sir Isaac's "G" shows up strong is around the cooking fire. Though the books give advice about broiling, roasting, and boiling camp food instead of frying it, you'll quickly find that the frying pan is the camp's basic weapon. But, oh, my aching back, what frying pans they are!

For some reason, women have a bad habit of hammering or warping a big bulge into the bottom of every frying pan they get hold of. So if you're using a utensil that's a fugitive from a kitchen, it will be sure to rock drunkenly and stand every way but level when you put it on the fire. If it's the extra-light type of small pan favored by many campers and the handle proves to be heavier than the pan, you'll be in a terrible fix.

What all this leads to is that when the pan tilts off the exact level, "G" will make the grease flow onto one side and off the other. Then the grease on the bare side will start to burn. Since like all new campers you're using "a thick bed of hot coals," your pan will start to burn immediately and ruin your bacon and eggs.

Build your cooking fire between two parallel logs or piles of stones that are longer than the fire. Put your frying pan across the logs or stone-piles but alongside the fire, not over it. Be positive that the pan bottom is well supported on a true level. Then, with a stout stick, rake coals out of the fire and under your pan. Keep replacing them as they burn to ashes. This gives you heat you can control, protection against scorched knuckles, and no burned grease.

"G" will also remind you that modern man is an upright animal who's uncomfortable crouching by a fire. You'll yearn for a table you can stand up to. I've read that you can make one, or anything else from a pothook to a two-story bungalow, out of forked sticks. But have you ever tried to drive a green forked stick into the ground? It springs instead of penetrating, and when you hit it harder it splits. Maybe you can push it in, but drive it? It splits, friend; it splits most every time.

One place where "G" really comes into its own is in connection with the pack. The most important thing about it is the back and shoulders that carry it. Get in shape and any pack big and sturdy enough to hold your stuff will do your job. How you wear it is another matter. There's a strong tendency among beginners to let out the shoulder straps until the pack rests on what I might call the roof of the wearer's back porch. Sir Isaac Newton says you shouldn't do that. At every step you'll be using good muscle to move that heavy load not forward but upward, and it will soon wear you out. Hitch your pack so high that you won't lift or roll it at every step.

In connection with packing, tumplines—carrying straps that loop across the forehead—offer some unsolved problems. You can't wear a head-strap over a hat without ruining the hat and being uncomfortable besides; if you try it bareheaded the sun's in your eyes, blackflies chew on your scalp, and brush snags your hair. I don't think much of tumplines; but they have a unique virtue. If you are on footing where you are likely to slip and fall, one short motion of your head will throw off the tumpline and, of course, the whole pack. A man hits the ground much faster, and harder, with a pack than without one; be careful about falls.

One way in which campers, particularly new ones, try to mitigate the evils of "G" is to use "combination" equipment to save weight. Combinations are apt to be fairly unsatisfactory for each of the purposes they are meant to serve.

I remember when the army decided to save on shelter-tent poles by issuing pup tents that were high at the shoulders and low at the rump, like a buffalo; a rifle was used for the front pole and a scabbarded bayonet for the rear pole. So what happened when both men in a tent had to go on guard? They took their rifles and bayonets with them, leaving their tent flat in the mud and rain.

Right now I'm trying to keep from inventing a hollow bamboo combination wading staff, rod case, and center pole for a pyramid tent. I'm also fighting the urge to invent a combination Dutch oven and pressure cooker, the two halves of which can also serve as a saucepan and a dishpan, respectively.

I am resisting these temptations by remembering not Sir Isaac Newton but old Nessmuk, who spent a lifetime camping. He was the high priest of the "go light" camping craze and was hipped on saving weight. But it's worth noting that he never used a single combination item in his home-designed and homemade equipment. If he needed a piece of equipment, he made it as light as possible. If he didn't need it—and mostly he didn't—he left it at home.

If you stick to that, you'll be able to pack a tent that's a real tent, a bed that's a real bed, an ax that's ax enough to do your work, and cooking utensils fit to prepare a bellyful of plain, nourishing grub. Carry the rest in your skull. Skill and knowledge weigh nothing, says Sir Isaac Newton.

Letter to Lewis Hull

May 31, 1950

You left a plate of fried something in the ice-box and by the time Momma and I came on the scene (this week-end) there was a very interesting collection of nymphs adorning it!

Also, for your information, frozen orange juice must be kept that way. When not, it ferments. The can that you left in the closet opened from end to end like a grenade and produced a very colorful if not tasteful interior decoration.

In addition, you will find a cord and extra plug attached to the little one-holer electric stove that I brought up and Edgar disdained. It is the cat's nuts for making coffee fast, etc. but if you do any ordinary cooking, remember to keep turning the food if you want to slow down the rate of cooking from a medium fast burn.

If I were you, I would take that goddam toaster and throw it clear across the river where it won't show, and bring up a new one.

. . . You can get frozen hamburger, pork chops, veal chops, minute steak, and steak at Moore's store in Claryville. Very handy. Also ice cream, nice for putting in highballs. Remember those fanny-swatting Navy guys are practically raised on ice-cream; they can't go anywhere, even up in an airplane, without having their goddam little ice cream making machine along. When I was in the military service in France in 1918, we never saw any ice cream when we were in the trenches. Sailors, either.

You can walk down through Christian's woods and hit the Big Bend without trouble (about 20 minutes, maybe 15 without the Navy); that and the pool above are enough for two men for half a day. Carry your waders, etc. This is the way to do it. Put all the stuff, lunch, shoes, etc. in the seat of the waders and tie the top shut with the drawstring or otherwise. Put the wader legs over your shoulders like pack straps and secure the ankles to the belt loops of the waders or whatever with bandannas, cord, etc. Carries perfectly. Adaptation of the old overalls pack; compliments of Sparse Grey Hackle.

A Fishless Day on the Rainbow Run

The phrase "God's country" must have been invented for the Finger Lakes region of New York State because, in all the world, this glorious country fits it best. It is a lovely land of woods and waters interspersed with fat farms, and its climate is perfection. Life there is like something out of a dream. One may live on a magnificent residential boulevard, wider than the Champs Elysées and guarded by four files of immense elms, and still be within half a minute's walk of the principal business street of the town and two minutes' drive of one's cottage on the lakefront, secluded from traffic and trade.

The inhabitants live like kings on the wealth drawn from the soil by field and garden, tree and vine. And yet a more discontented lot of people would be hard to find. Blind to the bounty they enjoy, they look only toward the blazing canyons of New York City. It is their ambition to dwell as often as possible amid the vulgar opulence of a chain hotel and indulge in an orgy of beauty treatments, shopping, theater-going, dining, and drinking, from which they invariably return in an advanced condition of hangover and bankruptcy.

It is probably to punish them that they have been vouchsafed so little fishing for so much water. The Finger Lakes are large—Seneca is forty miles long—but they are deep, with little of the shallow feeding grounds which harbor fish. And they are mostly spring-fed, with relatively few feeders except an occasional small brook foaming over a forty-foot rock wall to blow away in spray before it reaches the lake.

This paucity of spawning grounds crowds the fish into such small waters as Catherine Creek, the southernmost feeder of Seneca Lake. It is an insignificant stream, but in the early season most of the huge rainbow population of Seneca jams into it to spawn. The fish have been established in the lake for thirty or forty years and no one knows how large they grow; five-pounders are standard in Catherine during the run, ten-pounders a commonplace, and fish twice that size far from unknown. Probably the largest never enter the stream.

Taking these fish on the spawning run may be criticized on the grounds of sportsmanship but not on those of conservation, because that is about the only time they are in much danger of being caught. Fishing the lake for them in a hundred feet of water is laborious and not very rewarding since, although there are a lot of rainbows, there is even more water.

The run could provide fine sport earlier, when the fish begin to gather at the mouth of the stream, but then the ice is too thick and the season a month or more away. In fact, in the years when spring comes early, the run may be over before the season opens.

Taking rainbows after they have entered the creek is not really fishing in the ordinary sense but a sort of spree for the participants, a spectacle for the beholders, and an annual windfall of maybe fifty to one hundred thousand dollars for the saloon-keepers and hot dog purveyors of Montour Falls and Watkins Glen, the towns at the head and foot of the creek.

A few years ago, the state conservation department took a group of newspaper fishing writers on a junket to witness the rainbow run in Catherine and a small neighboring brook, Hammondsport Creek. For some reason still unknown to me, I was invited and so was able to witness the fishing of the run on both streams. The conditions did not vary between them.

I quickly found out what kind of party it was to be when, after having breakfasted on the train with several sedate conservationists, I went forward to sit with the newspaper men. As soon as I was seated, an anonymous hand thrust a bottle over my shoulder and a voice behind me brusquely invited, "Here!"

But somehow, I am prejudiced against drinking liquor at nine o'clock in the morning. I will not deny that in my salad days, when we were on the Mexican border, I occasionally sipped rye from a germ-laden bottleneck in the chilly dawn before going down to feed and water the horses. And in the First World War, I was more than once thankful for a morning cup of French Army coffee stiffly laced with *gniol*—a horrible brandy distilled from grape skins, broken glass, and barbed wire—to banish the stiffness and chill of a night of ambulance-driving. I will even admit that one of the pleasantest meals I ever ate was a breakfast of omelette, fried potatoes, and a bottle of champagne, which I had in the little wine shop in Ferrières-en-Gatinais one lively spring morning, with the breeze ruffling the white curtains in the sunny room, after coming off guard. But in later years I have never relished the "army toothbrush," so on this occasion I quickly decided to stay sober and see the fun. It was worth it.

Our camp, near Bath, New York, consisted of a great circus tent nicely equipped with army cots and blankets, and two roaring wood-burning stoves. A chill wind knifed in as the sun went down, so the writers quickly dived into their suitcases for warmer clothing. Now these gentry are just one variety of newspaper man, with the usual predilection for bright lights and strong waters, and disinclination to fresh air. There are some notable exceptions but, by and large, they resemble O. Henry more than Daniel Boone.

I was surprised, therefore, to see the group metamorphosed into something which would have delighted the heart of a Hollywood director of B pictures. Mackinaws, mukluks, parkas, red-top duffel pants, coonskin caps, shoepacs, and *bottes sauvages* made it look like the mob scene from *The Spoilers* or the Klondike gold rush going over Chilkoot Pass. A three-day beard and a bag of gold dust would have enabled any of them to pass as Dangerous Dan McGrew.

This healthy outdoor scenery did not, however, predispose the wearers to a hardy life in the open. Bottles in hand they crowded around the stoves, alternately medicating their tonsils and singing. They suspended operations briefly in order to stoke in some dinner, but in no time at all ribald song and smoking-room story were again penetrating the canvas to assail the sleeping countryside.

The fishing season was to open at midnight, so after a while I broke out my waders and gear and began to grease a line. At this juncture there entered a modest, generous, kindly man who wrought more destruction in less time than an atom bomb. He was a local resident hospitably come down to welcome the strangers in true Finger Lakes style, which is to say with bottles under his arms. His first offering was applejack and, knowing the magnificent quality of the local product, I broke my rule and took a drink with him. We had a moment's conversation about fishing and then he noticed the line I was rubbing down. He picked up the end of it and fingered it curiously.

"You're not going to use this, are you?" he asked. "These fish average five pounds or more. You'll never land them on this."

"This" was the point of a brand-new English Carter tapered line which had cost me thirteen dollars and was, since the Second World War was beginning, irreplaceable. It was the prize of my collection.

"I think it will be all right," I said, suppressing a smile at his assumption that I meant to lift the fish out on the end of the line. No sooner had I spoken than he dexterously took several turns of the line around each palm and, with a sudden jerk, broke it.

"It's stronger than I thought," he said, smiled, and moved on. I just sat there looking at the five-foot piece he had broken off the taper of the line, trying not to weep.

This was only the first installment of his destruction. Applejack by itself is a potent beverage, but its effects can be gauged. Not so when it is taken on top of Scotch or bourbon. Then it forms an unstable explosive compound which is apt to blow the head off the drinker without warning. But worse was to come. Having dispensed his applejack, he returned with several bottles of a sweet, fiery cordial, of which anyone in his senses would have taken no more than a thimbleful. But by this time his customers were not strictly in their senses. They downed hearty swigs of it.

It acted like a detonator to the explosive charge already formed. Men recoiled from the muzzle of the bottle with glazed eyes and sagging knees as from a hard punch to the jaw. The tenor of a quartet faltered on a high note, turned half around, and plunged headlong onto the nearest cot. One little frail fellow, garbed in a ferocious suit of lumberman's gear, sprawled on a cot with his arms and legs trailing off onto the floor and his death-like face turned up to the unshaded electric bulbs.

By midnight, only a handful were able to go out to see the opening of the season, and not all of those were in good shape. One, particularly, chilled my blood by repeatedly running and jumping over a huge bonfire, whooping like a Comanche. Then his voice failed in midwhoop and he hit the ground as limp as a shot rabbit. He had passed out in midair. Four game wardens, one to each arm and leg, lugged him off face downward to the dormitory, and he did not revive until the next afternoon.

It was only a couple of hundred yards from the shouting, flashbulbs, and moving-picture flares to the dim quietness of another pool—quiet-ness but not solitude, for the reflection of the moonlight on snow-covered banks was pinpointed by the orange glow of watch-fires all along the stream. I found a little pool for my own and diligently went to work with a white marabou streamer, ordinarily a killing lure for rainbows that live on shiners or smelt.

The air was crisp but dry and my heavy clothing kept me comfortable as I stood in the shallow water, smoking the pipe which always seems to taste best at such times, and subtly, unhurriedly working my streamer over every inch of the little pool. I had the whole night ahead of me and I proposed to enjoy it. The fishermen mostly stayed where they were, waiting for the fish to come to them, so it was only an occasional wan-derer who interrupted my meditations. I never had a better time on a stream at night. But after several hours of fishing without a response, I decided that there must be some factor in the situation which I did not understand, so I started on a tour of the campfires. In a little while I had my answer.

It is astonishing how little perspective one can gain from secondhand information. I had talked beforehand with several experienced Catherine Creek fishermen but none of them had mentioned the one factor which made all the difference. This was that the fish do not enter the stream until absolutely driven to it by the spawning urge. By the time they do so, they are in the last extremity, ready to drop their eggs at any moment. Obviously, feeding is the farthest thing from their thoughts—and they are abnormal in other ways, also. They have lost most of their wariness, for one thing, and it is strange and somehow repugnant to see a five-pounder which normally would be put to frantic flight by the flick of a hand lying exposed to the sky in shallow water and oblivious to the excited movements of the anglers on the bank above it. They lose much of their fighting power, too, and can be summarily hauled in from the vicinity of brush piles into which, normally, they could not be restrained from dashing at the first bite of the steel.

Once I had comprehended this situation, I was struck with its similarity to that of the shad run in the Connecticut streams. I once fished the big dam pool in the Salmon River for the silvery swimmers, which, unable to surmount the dam and about to drop their eggs, dashed around the water colliding with the legs of the numerous anglers. It was significant of their disinterest in either food or fishermen that, with all the fish and all the fishermen, only about two fish per hour were being taken; and significant also that each seemed to be taken on a different lure, none of which appeared to resemble any natural food. I finally decided that they were not striking at the lures at all, but merely inhaling any which chanced to be near enough. After all, a fish must have its mouth open half of the time in order to breathe, and when it is open there is a stream of water pouring into it.

All the rainbows I saw taken in either Hammondsport or Catherine Creek were caught in one way. The fisherman located a fish and then maneuvered until he could lower his bait or lure directly in front of its nose. As the fish opened its mouth and the hook was sucked in, the fisherman struck quickly and hard. I couldn't help thinking that it would have been more fun to take them as most of them are taken, according to the consensus of local statement—in the darkness of night, with a flashlight and a pitchfork, a bushel basket, or a net improvised out of chicken wire. Catherine is patrolled night and day by wardens during the run, but I was told that the poachers nevertheless got the most and the biggest fish.

When the inwardness of the situation became apparent, I took down my rod, struck the joints under my arm, and devoted the rest of the night to a washerwoman's tour of the stream banks from one watch-fire to the next. I made a rich haul. I inspected fish and admired them; talked shop with wardens and swapped yarns with fishermen; got a complete report on all hunting and fishing activities in the area; gave and received a quantity of free advice; turned down any number of sandwiches and drinks; tried innumerable rods for casting quality and re-set the ferrule on one of them; and in general had a regular festival until dawn's left hand was in the sky.

It was six o'clock and broad daylight by the time I got back to camp. I shaved and shifted into clean clothes amid a deathlike silence; in fact, if the sleepers had been awake, I am confident that many of them would have felt the dark angel was hovering near. I had a lonely breakfast and got myself a ride over to Montour Falls to cover the situation on Catherine Creek so that I could telephone a story to a New York newspaper friend who had asked for it.

It was the night all over again except that the fishermen could now see their prey better and more easily find their way through the brush to the point from which they must lower their lures, which invariably consisted of spawn from a previous victim tied up in a fold of gauze bandage. The use of spawn has since been made illegal but I don't think it has hurt the fishing; a bare hook would probably work at least as well, by the method most popular.

There were fish all along the creek but the throngs of fishermen seemed to take relatively few of them. Everyone complained that it was not a good year, too early, too warm, too dry, and all the other standard lamentations.

The most difficult thing to find that morning was not fish but parking space. I saw clutches of thirty or forty cars wherever there was room enough to put them, and numerous fishermen driving about aimlessly, trying unsuccessfully to find parking within reasonable reach of a decent fishing stretch.

When I came back to the camp at noon for lunch, the first of the celebrants of the night before were just beginning to straggle into the dining tent, and I must say I never saw a less rugged or hearty-looking bunch of pioneers. Their yellow countenances, drooping eyes, fevered lips, and twitching hands proclaimed that, although they might have started out like Kit Carson, they had been unable to finish like him. The demand for coffee was insatiable, but I noticed the cooks did very little business in pancakes.

Even so there were some who could not stand the ordeal. The frail little fellow I had last seen reposing so limply with arms and legs asprawl tottered to the table and buried his head in his hands. He gulped his orange juice and sipped his coffee, but when he was confronted with the staring eyes of two loosely fried eggs, he recoiled in horror and bolted from the tent.

Do you think that these sufferers had, perchance, learned a lesson from their experience; that they might have become converted to a slower pace? That afternoon, the Pleasant Valley Wine Company conducted a tour of its champagne caves. You should have seen us!

A Fisherman's Fauna

Years ago, I was driving along the East Branch of the Delaware on a July morning, looking for a place where I might offer a dollar for the privilege of parking and fishing. The road mounted a small grade, and there below me was displayed a pocket-sized farm which filled the space between road and river. The farmer was mowing a patch and I waited for him to finish, so that when I spoke he would hear me. He was mowing around the outside of the stand of hay, spiraling toward the center, and while he worked he shouted above the clash of the mowing-machine in conversation with a little girl of twelve or thirteen years, clad in gingham and old-fashioned long black stockings. The patch had been reduced to some twenty feet when a half-grown rabbit bucketed out of it in panicky flight across the fallen swathes. Like a shot the little girl took after it and the farmer halted his horse to shout directions and encouragement. It was an amazing performance. With pigtails streaming and thin black legs flying, the child sped over the ground like a greyhound. The rabbit, as is the habit of rabbits, changed its course every few bounds, but the little girl swerved as sharply and almost as quickly and stayed close to its white, cottony tail.

It was over in a surprisingly few minutes. Cut off at each turn from its intended refuge in the standing grass, and finally exhausted of strength or wind, the rabbit stopped, crouched, and made no resistance when the little girl seized it.

"Good! Good!" shouted her father. "You take him in and give him to the cat."

"I don't wanter," she demurred.

"You do it!" he commanded. "Gawddammim, he et up my garden."

A number of considerations naturally presented themselves immediately. Here was game taken in the closed season, doubtless without a hunting license, and held captive without a conservation department permit. But here also was a fine pool, a nice grove to park in, and a dollar as good as spent. I leaned from the car window and spoke in a calm, carrying voice, a voice which combined the persuasive salesmanship of a radio announcer with the authority which my red face and portly figure exemplified.

"I'll give you a dollar for the rabbit," was what I said.

Tableau. The figures in the little stage setting, neither of whom apparently had noticed me before, froze. There was an instant of silence, but I had mentioned a word which is magic in Delaware County, and it quickly broke the spell.

"You take it!" the farmer shouted sharply at his daughter and she, scuffing unwilling feet, approached the car with suspicion written large on her face.

"Whut you goin' t'do with the rabbit?" she demanded in a tone to match her expression. I handed her a dollar bill.

"You don't want to give him to the cat, do you?" I asked softly.

"No."

"All right. Make believe to hand me the rabbit and I will drop him and let him go."

She was only a skinny little girl with tight pigtails and a dirty face but she comprehended this unexpected proposal in its entirety before I had finished voicing it. As quickly as electricity passes through a circuit she had decided to disobey and deceive her loving father and conspire against him with a total stranger for the sake of a dollar and a rabbit's life. She said not a word, but the guile of the whole world's women flared in her slaty eyes. I wish that I had learned her name, for I am sure that I see it, from time to time, in newspaper headlines.

She extended the rabbit. I let it slip through my hands. It landed running and disappeared. The little girl disappeared, too. I drove down into the farmyard and spoke to the farmer, who was, of course, by now an old business acquaintance, so to speak.

"You don't mind if I park here a while and fish, do you?" I asked, and he readily assented.

Considering the known propensities of rabbits and the length of time that has elapsed since that incident, I figure that by now I have a half-interest in all the rabbits in Delaware County.

That was but one of the animals which have enlivened this fisherman's days astream. The others were various, but most of them have been dogs, and of these the two I best remember were Barnhart's dogs. We used to park in his yard for a quarter and walk down through his fields to the Rainbow Pool on the Beaverkill, but this time when I drove up I was met by two dogs I had not seen before, two half-grown yellow curs who took me in charge with authority, not to say officiousness, and saw to it that I went directly to the house without making any felonious attempts against the barns, cows, or other property.

I found that Barnhart had passed on and that his son was running the place. We talked a few minutes about milk prices and the shortage of farm labor, and then I remarked on the dogs.

"I paid six dollars for the pair and I don't think I got stuck," said Barnhart seriously. "They are already pretty good cow dogs. We lost our old one, and of course we can't get along without a dog to get the cows when they cross the river to the pastures up on the hill."

I started down to the river escorted by two canine flank patrols—high-stepping patrols with tails curled up over their backs, alert to see that I kept to the path and let the growing crops alone. But they left me as I passed through the screen of trees along the river and went down to the bank to look for rising fish.

Then the two dogs reappeared like actors coming out on a stage and presented one of the most remarkable performances I have ever seen, a masterpiece of ham acting entitled "How We Go for the Cows." I am not one of those who impute human qualities to animals or exaggerate their instinctive actions into an intellectual pattern. But this was beyond dispute an organized, concerted piece of showing-off that reminded me again how much like people dogs are: in their emotions if not in their reasoning ability.

Brisk and businesslike, the two dogs came out of the underbrush abreast. They gazed up the river; they gazed down the river; they gazed across the river. One could fairly hear them exclaim in melodramatic tones, "Aha! They have crossed the river!" They ran to the edge of the water, posed only long enough to emphasize the frightful chance they were about to take, and, as one dog, plunged in.

Their imitation of a brave swimmer battling for life in a raging torrent was worthy of an old-time stock-theater company. Johnny Weissmuller swimming across Niagara Falls would not have been in it for drama.

They made it! Panting and gasping, they emerged and shook themselves ostentatiously, mounted to the railroad track that follows the river on the far bank, and gazed in all directions. Again I seemed to hear them exclaim, "Aha! They have gone over the hill!" and then they galloped up the cow-path with all the uproar and spurious fury of an opera-house army.

I could hear them returning before I could see them. They were obviously driving cows, for they barked the short, sharp yips of a cow dog at work. Then they came over the crest of the hill marshaling a herd of dangerous, refractory, wild-eyed—and nonexistent—cows. They dashed back and forth to head off strays, barked warning at those that tried to straggle up or down the track, and nipped at hypothetical heels. At last they herded the cows into the river. Climax!

Then like the hams they were they came down to the edge of the bank and mounted a high rock apiece in order to bask in the limelight and receive their curtain calls. The vanity and self-satisfaction displayed on their countenances as they mugged for my approval were so obvious and appealing that no one could have resisted them, and I smote my palms vigorously together and cried, "Bravo! Bravo!" They were not disconcerted; quite the contrary. I really expected them to bow.

Alas, like many other young performers, they did not know when to stop. Flushed with success, they essayed to improvise an act entitled "Helping the Fisherman; or, What Is Going On?" I was casting a big White Wulff on the shadowed water close to their bank, and as it whipped back and forth in false casts the dogs followed it with quick turnings of their heads. When it alighted they immediately ran along the bank until they were opposite, and nearly overhanging, the floating fly, and concentrated their gaze on it as if they were ready to spring in and seize any fish that might offer. That sort of assistance does not conduce to successful fly fishing, so I began leisurely to change to a wet fly, turning my back so that the dogs would go away and allow me to fish down the pool in the last brightness of the sky.

The show was over; the audience had gone home—I was no longer paying attention to them. Abruptly dropping their corny, histrionic mannerisms, the two dogs trotted down to what was evidently their usual crossing place, slipped into the water without the slightest ado, swam nonchalantly across, shook themselves briefly, and disappeared toward home, leaving the farm and all its appurtenances defenseless before me.

Bees

Sparse Grey Hackle's contributions to "Rod and Gun" always are welcomed by its readers . . . "S. G. H." rises to defend the bee as a game animal, game fish, or game something. . . . He learnedly discusses the home life and habits of bees with a nonchalance and surety which prove he is convinced I won't know what he is talking about and so therefore can't bawl him out if he is putting something over on me.

"In your series on local wildlife do not overlook the bee," he pleads. "I have changed my mind about him. I used to regard him as a bum sport, addicted to such vices as hard work, thrift, and sitting down on innocent strangers. To me there was nothing more repulsive than a bee, who works hard all day instead of going fishing and seeing the country; who puts his hard-earned honey into the bank instead of buying handmade rods and English lines; and then lives on it all winter instead of going on relief like us grasshoppers.

"Bees, I have maintained, are too stimulating. Just last summer I met some on a languid day, and in no time at all I had hurled my rod farther than they throw javelins in Stockholm, and was swiftly picking up a pair of hobnailed brogans and setting them down at least twelve feet apart.

"But I went bass fishing in Pennsylvania last week and got some new light. A beekeeper at Wysox told me that each hive has guards at the door to turn away any bees who don't live there. But if a strange bee shows up with a big load of honey the guards let him in, pile on him, take away his honey, and chuck him out on his neck!

"This revelation of clip-joint ethics makes the bee look like a regular fellow and puts him in a class with the trout family, the Wall Street boys, and the gang I was raised with."

(Donald Stillman's column, October 31, 1935.)

Wildlife "Moochers"

"Dear 'Rod and Gun':

"What can I do about a bunch of wildlife 'moochers,' panhandlers who are used to living off the country and are now bumming handouts because food is scarce, instead of getting a job? There's a woodpecker who ought to be riveting at Sikorsky, but he just hangs out around the woods equivalent of a poolroom, playing hot jive on trees and giving out with flams and paradiddles like a trap drummer. Just a bum. There's a frowsy bunch of robins who haven't had their clothes cleaned and pressed since they rode the rods up from the South in them. They show up every morning with hangovers, drink all the water in sight, and lounge around scratching their cooties.

"Tough rabbits shoot craps in my driveway and won't let me in. Two corner-loafing crows make fresh remarks to my wife when she goes out to work the garden and holler disparaging comments on my fishing ability when I pick up worms to catch a meal for the family. Their finger man is a flash bird in a gray hat and topcoat and a blue zoot suit. I think he is casing the joint for those two hoods. The cock pheasant, having been under fire, claims he is a veteran and the country owes him a living.

"But the worst is the squirrel who has an estate next to mine. Last fall he was the irate landowner. If I so much as walked down there it was 'Posted property! Get off! Get off!' and a handful of nutshells on my head. But now he comes around like those strolling entertainers who used to perform in backyards for pennies when I was a boy and puts on an act on the front porch. What a ham! He keeps watching the windows for applause, and for a few nuts he'll put on seven turns a day. The point is that he has savings bank deposits all over the woods. Why doesn't he dig them up instead of bumming handouts?

"My bills for kafir corn, suet, and nuts are something terrible and I wish you would tip off the mendicancy squad. SPARSE GREY HACKLE."

(Don Stillman's column, May 8, 1943.)

Rain on the Brodhead

B rodhead's Creek is called, by those who love this beautiful stream with constancy unalterable, "the biggest little river," meaning that it provides fine fishing out of all proportion to its size. But one who goes on it after being used to the shallow Catskill streams will quickly add another meaning, because he will discover that for its size it contains a surprising amount of water.

The typical Catskill river has its depth in the middle, with thin edges and a stony foreshore which is kept clear by the roaring floods that afflict those streams. Only where there is an occasional short stretch of steep, rocky bank can a tree overhang the water or offer its roots to the trout for a refuge. Not so the Brodhead. It, too, is a lively, tumbling river, but its high, square-cut banks are thick with trees and brush, the roots of which are almost continuous along the streamside. Here the greatest depth is frequently right next to the banks, which are usually undercut, providing the trout with a kind of cover of which the Catskill streams are almost devoid.

As Dick Hunt's guest I have fished both the Parkside Angling Association and the Brodhead Fly Fishers' Club water a number of times, but one in particular remains in my memory as a fishless day. Now, Dick cannot be called an expert, because he claims that there are none, but only "knowledgeable" fishermen; but it is surprising how many "knowledgeable" salmon anglers say he is the best low-water salmon fisherman in America, and how many "knowledgeable" trout anglers say that no one can fish a long flat as he can. This being so, and on such splendid water as the Brodhead, you might imagine that Dick and I had good insurance against a fishless day, but that would be only because you do not know me.

For not only can I exorcise fish like a witch doctor and create deluges like an Indian rainmaker, but I shed such an aura of ill luck that it envelops my companions as well as me.

When we arrived at the boardinghouse that morning, Dick unpacked certain articles with which this account deals. One was a brand-new nylon fishing raincoat so fine and thin it could be carried in any pocket, and another was a brand-new fishing vest, the outstanding feature of which was a back pocket with a vertical, zipper-closed entrance on either side, behind the wearer's elbows. Dick, who is apt to be as casual in his fishing appointments as was his friend Skues, displayed these articles with boyish pride and hearty admiration for his own foresight. The third article was a flat traveling case, familiar to all his fishing friends, holding two metal half-gallon containers, one full of whiskey and the other of martinis.

I must digress here to say that there are two things remarkable about Dick's martinis. The first is their excellence. Ostensibly the dry martini is the simplest thing in the world to make, but in fact it is of a mysterious and esoteric nature. Dick's are made of eight parts of the right gin and one part of the right vermouth; and nothing else. When I try this formula, all I get is an explosive mixture. But by some alchemy, Dick produces a drink with the spicy fragrance of an old-fashioned garden and the tinkling grace of a minuet played on the harpsichord, the most gorgeous firewater that ever charmed the palate and seduced the senses. The other remarkable thing about them is that they have to be earned. We have never set out for the stream without his reminding me that we must earn our drinks by diligent angling and the demonstration of our knowledgeability before we can have them on our return.

This day we set out for the best pool with the most incongruous name of any on the Brodhead. It is famous as Mary's Flat, and I have never ceased to protest that the name brings to mind nothing but an old musical comedy, *Up in Mabel's Flat*. No city boy of my generation can think of a "flat" as anything but an apartment.

The trouble with the river was that there had been a rainy week and the Flat, which normally is pants-pocket deep, was belt-buckle deep, and more, next to the bank. Furthermore, the season was between the two big Brodhead hatches and the fish were cruising, and rising only sporadically. Finally, they were cruising either along my bank, to which I could not cast because of the overhanging verdure, or along the opposite bank—and the river was too deep to wade within casting range.

Besides all that, it was wartime, and new waders were not to be had. I had to trust to my ancient Cordings, and my first step into Mary's Flat told me that my confidence had been misplaced. As I clung to the bushes with one hand and roll-cast a stonefly nymph across the current with the other, I could feel icy water descending from a leak in my seat to meet icy water rising through a leak in my left heel.

Dick was fishing dry in rather shallower water above me, and as I fished down the current I kept turning to see if he was getting any action. He changed flies three or four times and then hit the right one—a No. 16 Red Fox. All I could see was the easy, pushing motion of the rod as he fished a long and beautiful cast in under the branches on the far bank. Then suddenly I saw a dramatic picture that sometimes returns to me in dreams. A thin white streak flashed across the water as he whipped his line off the surface, and in the same instant, white foam surged under the far bank as he struck his fish.

He held his bowed rod high overhead as he reeled in his slack, and then settled to playing the fish—it was a dandy—in the considerate manner which 4X gut demands. He finally grasped it, killed it, and I saw him reach around and slide it into the back pocket of his new vest. The next time I looked, he was pocketing another fish, and pretty soon his rod arched again to the third victim, which followed its predecessors into his back pocket.

It was while I was watching him take off and kill his fourth fish (he wanted to take some home to a friend) that I got what could only be called a bite on my trailing nymph—a savage strike that straightened out my arm and then broke the leader. I was as far downstream as I could wade, so I turned to watch Dick while I soaked another leader point. Imagine my astonishment at seeing the usually staid and sober Hunt striding downstream as fast as three feet of water would permit and at every second step plunging his arm in up to the armpit. He was a sorry sight when he finally desisted and waded to the bank, one sleeve and his shirtfront sopping, and water in the front pocket of his waders and the fly box that reposed therein.

The explanation was simple. Immediately after pocketing his fourth fish, he had been astonished to see it floating away. Only then did he discover that the other entrance to his back pocket was unzipped, and as fast as he had inserted fish at one side they had been sliding out at the other. His race downstream had been a futile pursuit of his fourth fish.

He hoisted himself ashore with many disparaging comments on the new vest, and as he did so the heavens split apart and released a torrent of rain like the descent of Niagara Falls. I whipped out the short raincoat and waterproof hat cover which I always carry and exhorted Dick to do the same.

"Your new raincoat is starting to pay dividends already," I said.

Dick stood still with a very curious expression on his face.

"I left it in the car," he said softly. There ensued what could only be called a pregnant silence, for the car was half a mile away.

"Ah well," he said at last, "here is a good thick tree," and led the way to a bushy hemlock beneath which we sheltered, he soaked down to the waist and I up to the same line of demarcation. We squatted on our heels and I remarked that it was "cowboy style."

"I *was* a cowboy for three or four years. Didn't I ever tell you?" he replied, and then began one of the most absorbing recitals that I can call to mind. As I remember it, he had had no shooting scrapes or fantastic adventures, although there was one pretty thrilling near-stampede and another tense moment when he almost had been left afoot on the prairie after dismounting. But he brought the color and flavor of a cowboy's life so close that I could smell the bitter smoke of sagebrush and taste the dust

that envelops the drag riders. We forgot all about the rain and our discomfort, and in those unlikely circumstances I, at least, enjoyed half an
hour of fascinating discourse.

About noon the rain finally let up and we went back to the house. Wet
waders and sodden clothes were never peeled off quicker, and by the time
I came back downstairs, Dick was opening the traveling case.

"I think," he said judicially, "that we have earned a *good* drink."

We had a hearty lunch and then retired to the living room to plan for
the afternoon. The decision was not difficult to make, for rain slashed at
the windows and charged level along the ground as the gusts swept by. So
we took a fishing book apiece and bade defiance to the weather in the very
best kind of fishing for such a day—reading about it. But not for long; the
ineffable sense of well-being that comes from being warm, dry, and replete
overcame us, and we dozed the afternoon away.

That was long ago, of course, but the memory of this fishless day is not
only clear but doubly precious to me, for Dick is no longer with us, and
two great storms have obliterated Mary's Flat and made the Brodhead,
although still a fine fishing stream, strange water to me.

Observations

My good friend Sparse Grey Hackle contributed the following concerning his late-season ramblings along the edges of the lakes and reservoirs of the Croton watershed. He writes:

"The receding waters of the reservoirs have left broad shores, upon the blank pages of which is written a record of Westchester's wildlife. I wish I could decipher the fascinating stories inscribed there.

"There is a bird which leaves six-inch tracks; another, half that size; and any number more which leave intricate, lacelike impressions of their wanderings. There are animals with little, round feet and one big something with feet like a large dog and claws, but short legs—he gallops in eighteen-inch strides after something which is apparently the size and weight of a rabbit, but which runs instead of bounding. It can turn much shorter than he can; he hasn't caught one yet.

"The bass hang out in six or eight feet of water, preferably over weed until sunset. Then they rise to natural flies and nymphs, working into shallower water as the light fails. The sunfish know it; the big ones stay in four feet of water until the sun goes down, but soon afterward their range is confined to a foot of water, or less.

Bucktail Works Better

"The fish tend to prefer water around the inlets. They are frightened by big, noisy plugs, flashy spinners, and active pork-rinds. A discreet bucktail works better, and worms or minnows would be best if you wanted to bother with them. The crawfish have vanished and frogs are mighty scarce, so the fish don't hang so close to the shoreline at dusk. They seem to prefer shallow water over weed; looking for minnows, I suppose.

"Boats are left stranded by the receding water and dry out. Launched again, they leak in fountains. The six-foot sea oar is still standard equipment and so is the clanking, worn-out oarlock, set so low the oars hit your knees. Some day I'm going to have my own light seven-foot oars, with ring oarlocks that can be clamped to the boat.

"Last week we took our five-year-old Patty fishing. With both of us caddying, she exchanged fifty worms for nine sunfish in three hours. Once when I walked away to try a few casts she reproved me; I explained that I had to go and look for fish.

"'I don't,' she remarked calmly, watching her float disappear. 'Fish follow me around.'

"Hoping you are the same."

(Don Stillman's column, September 26, 1941.)

Letter to Lewis Hull

August 14, 1951

. . . The realization that a chorophyll-green novice took seriously the admonitions of old Sparse, who is notorious for never catching a fish, amuses and still appalls me. I have the awful feeling that comes to a man who voices an offhand and superficial opinion on a stock and next day hears that his listener has bought a hundred shares on ten-point margin.

What tickles me most about your lady's comprehensive report is the naked predation displayed in her statement that "I kept 4. I kept all I landed." That is straight thinking and no nonsense about conservation, higher sportsmanship or the blasé demonstration of self-control engendered by habitual success. A dinner for the family! (A male novice would also have kept his fish, of course; but he would have rationalized his action into an ethical and sporting one.) It ought to remind us that it is never safe to fool around with women; you are liable to get a few fingers bitten off.

How I envy her that first breath-taking glimpse into the strange and wonderful new world of fishing—the enchantment and fascination of discovering (as I recall I did) that rods were not merely tapered but had patterns and hence various actions—that flies hatched from nymphs, and all the lore of the stream-bed; the intoxicating realization, suddenly one day, that you can put the line away out to there, and make it do what you want. If I ever get so that I can catch fish, so that each becomes just another fish, I shall sell or give away my tackle and fish thereafter only in my books. Tell your lady not to learn too quickly, lest she come too soon to the end of her enjoyment.

Letter to Mrs. Lewis Hull

A ugust 14, 1951

Dear Venator,

Your Tab fish must be shockingly ill-bred to ignore a wet because a good big, bright, wet, energetically dragged hither and yon, is their staple diet; they're raised on such. I see that I should have considered the recent return of the fish from the sea where there are no flies. I probably should have recommended bucktails or other fishlike creations.

But then, why do the critters take a <u>dry</u> fly, which represents an insect and isn't even moving? See! Already you are face to face with the first of innumerable mysteries which will always characterize your study of fishing.

I still think they should, and therefore could, have taken a wet fly; probably the reason you could not do it is that you lacked confidence in your lure. Not consciously, of course; but subconsciously you envisioned Failure, a negative quantity. One, by the way, with which you will become increasingly familiar as time goes on.

Look, if you can take a strange rod (<u>any</u> rod would be a strange one, at your stage) and raise 14 fish, what in the world need have you for further counsel—from me or anyone else? If, furthermore, you hooked 4 of the 14, presumably without leaving flies in any of the others (at least you do not mention it), I would say that you had best just keep right on doing what you have been doing.

I am particularly pleased that in your first casting you (a) used an excellent rod, for I am convinced that a good rod will teach casting better than any admonitions, and (b) caught fish on a 25-foot cast. Please do not ever become so obsessed with throwing out long and beautiful casts that you overlook the basic, fundamental soundness of the 25-foot cast. It is obviously silly to throw beyond fish that are near you; and I can tell you it is bad judgment to throw far to fish when you could approach closer and throw near to them. The quality of a cast—that mysterious rightness which presents the fly in a properly deceptive manner—decreases with the length; in fact, I think sometimes it decreases as the square of the length.

There are thousands of fly fishermen, and among them are some who bring in fish when others fail, who never fish more than 30 feet away. But they take the utmost pains to maintain a high quality in their presentation. With a short cast you can do a number of very important things which are impossible with a long cast. For instance, you can fish a wet fly upstream, just as if it were a dry fly, and let it come drifting toward you; and when a fish turns under water after having taken the fly, you may be able to see the flash and tighten up—something which cannot be done on a long line. It will be a long time before you ever learn to fish effectively with that most sophisticated and subtle method of all angling. But if you stick to short casts you may learn it, and then you will indeed be The Master of the Stream, able to designate any fish that you want and say I will catch that one, and do it. Your success will generate an inner serenity built on confidence and a consciousness of superior knowledge and skill, and you will become a ripe and kindly philosopher whose pronouncements on life no less than on fishing will be eagerly sought and respectfully received. All from fishing a short line.

By the way, inasmuch as inconsequential details are so important in judging the exterior of an angler, be reminded that the brown "wolf" is in fact a Wulff, having been designed by and named for one Lee Wulff, a fisherman of parts. On the other hand, it is a mark of virtuosity to refer to a fishing rod occasionally as a fishpole, the point being that only book-learned, provincial and stuffy fisherman are so conventional as never to call a rod anything but—a rod. . . . Always refer to flies (natural) as "fly" in the plural, e.g., "There were a good many fly on the water." Never catch, snag or otherwise uncouthly acquire trout; "take" them. One kills salmon, but one only kills such trout as are kept. Better to say I took four and kept none, or whatever the figures may be . . .

For your solace, words spoken within thirty seconds of raising and either hooking or missing, and then either holding or losing a fish, are not recorded. I have seen Momma lose a 2-pound brown (through her own fault—holding him too hard) and literally jump up and down in the water repeating "God damn it! God damn it!"

I fear that I was smiling a little when I wrote that counsel of perfection about not screeching and whooping. Few can entirely control themselves when the fish is big or the first in a long time. I sat at lunch today by an angler of sixty years' experience and very much skill, who before witnesses raised, hooked, played and lost a huge fish in the Ausable and then waded ashore, lay down on the beach and vomited copiously.

I must also plead guilty to a lapse in my instructions. But it was intentional. If I had put in everything, it would have been a book and not a pamphlet. What I did not say was that all this nonsense about keeping a tight line on a hooked fish is—nonsense. A fish fights according to the resistance he encounters, and if you take all the pressure off him he will slow down and move but a short distance, sometimes not at all. Of course if you are alongside a snag or other imminent danger, the only thing to do is to bundle him the hell out of there and the sooner you start the better; one of the tricks of playing big fish is to skulldrag them with a plain steady haul, all the leader will stand, out of danger before they get started, which takes a moment to happen.

If I am being fancy, I grasp the line with the forefinger of my rod hand so that I can check it or release it under whatever pressure I wish to impose. I drop all the loose line held in the other hand and use that hand to wind up the reel, meanwhile holding the vertical rod as high above the water as possible to keep as much line as possible off the water, hence away from my feet, hence out of such trouble as being stepped on or through. (It is entertaining but confusing to have a good fish on and find that the line runs from the hand guide, between your legs up your back, over your shoulder and onto the reel. It gives more mirth to the bystanders than to the subject.)

However, I don't usually believe in being fancy. Reeling against a tight line sends vibrations down same which galvanizes a fish no little. So I just drop the whole damn slack, hold the rod high and reel energetically. When I take up and put the spring of the rod against the fish, he begins to fight again.

Of course there are always exceptions and I hit one two weeks ago. Threw a long line across a big flat pool to the high bank, got a rise from what I thought was a little brook trout and could not restrain myself from a slow lift which set the hook. As soon as the fish started I knew he was solid—I don't know how big, but he was no 12-incher. I dropped my slack, reeled it up, felt of the fish, and by the great horn spoon, he had hung me up. It was a ledge, and I had been looking at it and knew there was no sunken wood, downed trees, etc. in it and hence thought there was no obstacle. But he was hung up—I could feel the obstacle and also dimly feel the fish tugging at the other end. I used all my craft, roll-casting a loop across the pool, throwing slack to try and float the line off the downstream end of the obstruction, etc. But it was no soap and he chafed through the 4x leader in a moment. I think he ran in a hole.

I am pleased (and want to say that you have done well) to hear that you did not break off in your fish and that you did let them run and not try to snub them down like handlining codfish. It seems to me that you have a natural instinct for fishing (as a great many women do, contrary to popular opinion) and will show up you husband even as Momma shows up hers.

I suppose that as long as there is a guide on hand he will always insist on the netting, but it goes against my grain to see it done and every once in a while it loses a nice fish, even when both parties know their business. Netting is intrinsically a one-man job. If you never bring a fish to the net until he is turning on his side and never scoop fast at him, you will never lose a fish in the netting, which is the toughest way to lose a fish except having him slip through a hole in your fishing coat pocket after he is stowed away.

So you will not humanely dispatch your fish with the pliers. Very well. If you prefer to let the poor creature agonize to a slow and lingering death by strangulation, sobbing and gasping as the oxygen fails in its bloodstream, it is all right with me. But each convulsive flop in your creel is a reproach to you, whether you believe it or not.

Apparently you learned in one easy lesson to sit on the knee of the Red Gods and chuck them under the chin. It is very apparent that they like you. If you serve them well they will make you an inheritor, and ultimately your golden sceptre will become a magic wand with which to unlock the mysteries and treasures of the stream.

Hearth and Field

"**A** s a man who knows the ropes of both fatherhood and field sports, I think you ought to speak a word of warning to the many fathers who think it would be a fine thing to take a small boy on a hunting trip. They mean well but they ought to be warned that they may unwittingly cause a great deal of suffering.

And the Hunter Home from the Hill

"Take, for instance, my son-in-law Ted, who is a very nice man and devoted to his family. He is a knobby-legged ex-football player who, as an infantry captain, galloped up and down every contour in Italy. He is built like a two-story brick smokehouse.

"Last week he and one Don, a friend who is just as big as Ted and has hunted big game up and down the Rockies, took my grandson Tad hunting on one of those game farms. Tad is sturdy and game as a rooster, but he is only seven years old, and when I note that he took along a broomstick as his 'gun' you will realize that he is just a *little* boy.

"Those two big bruisers quartered all over the game farm all afternoon, up hill and down dale, sometimes traveling so fast that Taddie had to trot to keep up. They must have covered four or five miles. It was a thoughtless thing to do.

"The consequence was that, just about dark, Taddie burst into the house carrying the two shotguns in addition to his broomstick, and demanded urgently to know what was for dinner and when. And where were Ted and Don? Outside, said Tad.

"My daughter opened the front door and recoiled, thinking for an instant that the two men had been involved in a shooting accident. They were trying feebly to crawl up the front steps on hands and knees. Their dry tongues were hanging out and they croaked hoarsely, 'Martini! Martini!'

"She said afterward that they had even gasped 'Water! Water!' but I don't believe it; they couldn't have been *that* far gone.

The Lethal Broomstick

"It is a terrible thing for a little boy to learn so soon in life that he can show up his own father in a trial of endurance. It makes him feel insecure, and may lead to juvenile delinquency. You should warn fathers of the peril they face in taking a boy hunting.

"Oh yes, there is one curious thing about this incident. They had managed to gather in one pheasant, but when it was plucked it did not show any wound or so much as a single pellet of shot in its interior. My son-in-law intimated that he had shot so close to the bird that he had scared it to death, but this unlikely explanation does not convince me. I keep wondering about the broomstick of Taddie's."

(Red Smith's column, November 7, 1962.)

Down the Great River

Dawn was breaking on the Great River and our craft floated far out on the vast expanse of hurrying waters, gliding past wooded bluffs and tangled, swampy shores. A mist overhung the river; only the lapping of the wavelets against our boat relieved the silence.

It was especially designed for the Great River, our boat; seven feet long and five wide, square-ended, it had a freeboard of two feet. It had a low bow and high stern, over which was now draped a fabric that served us as a sail by day and a tent at night. Under it my partner, Bill, sprawled in sleep.

In the sweet coolness of early morning I jointed up a rod and cast out. A two-pound rainbow smashed at the fly.

"Fish for breakfast, Bill," I called gaily as the rod arched, and Bill emerged sleepily to seize the net and boat the fish. Together we laved faces and hands in the Great River.

But it was not to be fish that morning. Over the waters came a light craft propelled by a native woman who evidently wanted to barter with us. The natives of this section are still very friendly to explorers, so we beckoned her nearer and soon had acquired a variety of the native foods which she bore—tropical fruits, "siryal," and the eggs of birds.

Breakfast over, I plunged in for a swim, forgetting the perils of the Great River; and so I experienced an adventure which might well have ended fatally. I was stroking along when a giant alligator broke water and made a dash for me. I struck out frantically for the boat, calling to Bill for aid, and to his quick response I owe my life. Snatching up a rifle, he sped a bullet into the saurian's brain, and we looped a rope over its jaws as it threshed in the water. It measured over twenty feet, a real man-eater.

Then the fishing began. The variety and size of our catch were almost unbelievable, for few flies have ever been cast in this stream. We took salmon, trout, and bass in profusion, fish to make an angler ecstatic. Occasionally we were surprised to land saltwater fish, sharks and tarpon and tuna, which endure the river waters without discomfort. I doubt if anywhere in the world is there to be found such fishing as the Great River afforded us.

At intervals flights of ducks and geese appeared. Then we would muffle ourselves in our tent until their calls sounded overhead. *"Now!"* I would cry, and we would fling off the tent and fire into the massed birds with such deadly effect that they rained into the river around us.

We were hailing the shore to discover a native with whom we might trade for the noon meal when a tiger appeared on the bank. Usually these beasts slip quietly away, but this one swam out and attempted to board us. Again Bill saved the day, hitting it between the eyes with two slugs from a double-barreled shotgun, a deadly weapon at short ranges. As the beast slipped from the gunwale over which it had hooked its paws I seized it, and together we got it aboard and whipped off the pelt. It was an enormous old male with worn and broken teeth, obviously a man-eater.

A lion which appeared immediately afterward met a better fate, for when he approached the boat we threw the tent over him, effectually muffling his teeth and claws, and hauled him aboard. Bill put a strap around his neck and soon tamed him so that he became our companion, sharing our rations and spending most of his time in the boat.

Thus the day wore on, with a magnificent wild panorama of wooded banks continually unfolding. Rod and gun at hand, we reclined at ease while munching native "kukis" and "arnjes." When a breeze came up we rigged the tent as a sail and crested the waves at speed, Bill steering with a paddle. Rapid after rapid we shot without mishap, and once we even went over a falls, fortunately without shipping water.

As the sun declined, we ate a hot meal brought from a native village nearby, smoked our pipes, and prepared our staunch craft for the night.

Dusk veiled the sky, and our sail came down to become a tent again. Side by side my partner and I sat by our little fire and discussed hunting, fishing, and other topics appropriate for explorers.

It had been a hard day. Exhausted by the ardors of combat and the chase, replete with nourishing fare, and lulled by the easy motion of the boat, my partner, Bill, slipped away from me into slumber.

Safe in his tent, a convalescent little boy with gold in his hair and cookie on his face smiled in his sleep as the shadowed banks of the Great River of Life swept unheeded past his bed, and a stout man with sparse grey hackles crept sheepishly down the stairs.

A Boy Fishing

Apparently Sparse Grey Hackle has been taking trout-fishing lessons from his boy, for he writes that the best cure for boredom is to take a boy fishing on a well-stocked trout stream. He says that not even a wooden Indian could watch unmoved the spectacle of a boy with protruding eyes and rattling tongue whirling his line over his head and trying to cast to rising seven-inch fish front, rear, right, and left at one and the same time.

"His technique of fishing seems to be 1) strike with a rock-shaking whoop; 2) draw a formidable landing net; 3) reel in slack; 4) describe the battle with the speed, excitement, and vocabulary of Graham McNamee; 5) lead the fish between his legs, behind his back, under rocks, over snags, and into fast water; 6) scoop the fish up on the fifth try in a tangled net not over six inches deep," writes Sparse.

"Once dispatched, the 'fine proportions' of the fish must be pointed out and his length overestimated by fifty percent. Thereafter he must be withdrawn from the creel at ten-minute intervals for further admiration, his length increasing miraculously each time.

"Between fish the boy will wade with an impetuous skating stroke, alternated with pirouettes and a water-skimming effect. It is a combination of adagio dancing and calisthenics. In spite of this novel method of locomotion in slippery boots, immersions are imminent rather than actual. One feels that if the boy should fall, he would merely bounce off the water.

"When a boy fishes he requires plenty of food, which will be demanded at one-hour intervals. Doubtless this is the source of his energy, which carries him through the day at a gallop while his adult companion droops and puts him in the car still gabbling vigorously and incignantly resentful of any suggestions that he sleep. Thirty minutes later, however, he will collapse like a shot rabbit and sleep over the worst roads while coiled on the seat.

"Just for the record, I must admit that I maintained my record of never catching a fish, while my companion ended the day in a blaze of glory by hooking a fourteen-inch rainbow and bringing him to net like a veteran. Apparently my equal is in the infant class."

(Don Stillman's column, July 10, 1936.)

Letter to Dana Lamb

F ebruary 26, 1965

. . . My son, whom I see about every two years when IBM sends him
East from San Jose, Calif., on business, spent the week-end with us. His
news is depressing. It appears that certain operations in some of their
newly developed data-processing devices (etc.) have to perform certain
functions within a period of four "anaseconds" [nanoseconds—Ed.] as
nearly as I can spell what he said—one "anasecond" (or whatever it is) is
a billionth of a second. During the said "anasecond," electricity can only
travel a distance of 12 inches—a single foot—since its speed is only
186,000 miles per second. The result of this is that it is impossible to have
the control unit separated from the operating unit by a cable more than
20 feet long; no one can have a 25-foot cable because it would take the
electricity too long to go out and back, there being only four "anaseconds"
available for this journey.

So we face an existence confined and limited to 20-foot cables as
respects certain electronic (etc.) operations, a drab existence devoid of 25-
foot cables or even 30-foot cables. Of course, if someone can invent fast
electricity——. But I hate this uncertainty, and am inclined to be pes-
simistic about the prospects for moving electric impulses faster than
186,000 miles per second. . . .

To hell with everything, including us. Particularly us.

The Little Maid

One warm, lazy afternoon I took the little maid to the meadow stretch through which Windbeam Brook meanders from the mountain to the lake, she being nine and wishful of learning to fish with a fly. We halted under an old apple tree grown brushy from the nibbling of cows and I set up the six-foot rod. The wily brown trout is not for little maids the first time out, but rather the enthusiastic and undiscriminating rainbow, so I looped a wet Campbell's Fancy to the leader. Then the little maid drew on the new boots and pulled them up under the pretty blue dress.

I showed her the way of casting and she took the rod and duplicated it with a child's unconscious perfection of coordination. So I led her into the stream. Alas, the pretty blue dress. It hung below the tops of the pulled-up boots and draggled in the water so that the glorious crispness of its lower part disappeared and it became limp and clinging. But the little maid paid no heed. With a loop of slack held daintily between thumb and forefinger of her left hand, she plied the rod with her right, casting straight across the little brook and letting the fly sweep down and around below her.

I had just turned my back when I heard a gasp and turned to see her standing transfixed, her eyes protruding like teacups. Something—a raiding predacious Something, with swaggering mien and evil leer—had snatched two feet of slack line from her light grasp and then had fled basely, without waiting to be hooked. Thereafter the little maid fished with three solid turns wound grimly around her fist.

But he came no more, and we went from pool to pool through the meadow, shooing away the cows as we walked along the bank, without finding another trout. We came to the big boulder at the head of the Birch Tree Pool and I swung her up to a seat on it, leaving her to drift a fly down the pool while I went up to the run above. Casting a wet Quill Gordon so that it came down at the current's pace, I was at once fast in a nice brown. "You've caught a fishie!" approved the little maid at the top of her voice, and I glanced up a moment to see her great sparkling eyes and smiling rosy face, and the sun on the pretty blue dress.

I netted my fish and went back to casting, and then—"Daddy!" No need to ask why. The little boots were planted on the boulder now as the little maid stood erect and held the rod high overhead. In two strides I was ashore, driving a wave ahead of me. I pitched my rod recklessly into the brambles and desperately stretched my legs.

"Is he still on?" I panted. She nodded, then under my tutelage drew in yards and yards of line until finally we came to a little silver arrow, a four-inch rainbow. Here was a case for diplomacy, for to the uncritical mind of a child a fish is a fish, and one of four inches is as good as one of twelve. I discoursed eloquently on sportsmanship and conservation, but when I announced that the trout must go back she was first incredulous, next indignant, and finally downcast. Then inspiration came and I pointed out that it was just a baby fishie. She brightened up at that and agreed that it ought to be released, for she adores babies. So we admired the lovely medallion blotchings on its sides, gently unhooked it, and let it dart away.

We went on down the brook. The little boots twinkled along the bank and flew through the air in graceful curves as the little maid leaped from stone to stone with a confidence that made me apprehensive. Gaily she ignored my warnings and then, oh then, the slimy rock reared its treacherous head. "Look out! Don't——" But alas for the poor little maid and alas for the pretty blue dress. Up flew the little boots and down went the little girl.

The waves parted and she emerged salting the stream with tears of fright and chagrin, but only for a moment, for the little maid was both blithe and game. She giggled when I held up her heels to empty the boots and laughed when I wrung her out. When I had finished, the pretty blue dress was nothing but a twisted wad of wet cloth, and she was arrayed ludicrously in some of my spare duds.

We stopped in the village for cocoa and sandwiches and while we were waiting discovered one of those marble-shooting game boards which are commonly called pinball machines. The little maid's New England thrift was dismayed at the sacrifice of nickels to a machine which did not return gum, candy, or even music, but she stood up to it and played earnestly until the victuals came. And so home.

"Jeannie! You fell in!" Mother exclaimed from the doorway as the strangely-clad figure stepped from the car. The little maid shrugged indifferently, then summarized the events of the day out of her New England conscience and the recollection of a careless word which I had spoken in warning as we went through the meadow.

"We wasted fifteen cents and found lots and lots of cow flops," she reported tersely.

Letter to Young Jennifer Lyons

April 15, 1972

Thank you so much for a perfect gift. It is the best-looking boat I ever saw, and I just wish I had one exactly like it, about 12 feet long; it would be unbeatable for river fishing, for one man.

It accommodates, exactly, two pipes; and I always smoke two although not at the same time. . . .

This is a remarkable hull and I wonder who designed it; or did you just dream it up? It is as nearly untippable as any boat I ever used, and I have used many. This one can be rolled down until it is virtually flat on its gunwale, and still it will right itself.

It has a slight drag toward the stern and is correspondingly a little finer forward. This is just exactly right for a one-man rowing boat in running water, and one of the hardest things to find. . . . I just wish I could take this one down a good strong current.

The one thing it won't do is work well in strong wind because it has no keel, but that makes it all the better for maneuvering in rapids and rough streams where short, fast turns are necessary.

The finish on this model is the equal of anything I have ever seen on a piece of fine woodwork. It feels like satin; I think it was done with No. 500 sanding paper, or very, very fine steel wool. In any event, there was a lot of hard work done on that finish and it's a credit to you indeed.

And finally, I think it's a piece of Philippine mahogany, one of the very best boat woods and so, appropriate. So thank you again for a fine gift which will carry many a cargo of briarwood to a safe port.

The Young Conservationist

W hen John Miller came to Wethersfield, Connecticut, from Sussex,
England, he was a farmer, and farmers his descendants remained
right through nine generations into the early manhood of my father and
his brother. True, my grampa took his young family to the Pennsylvania
oil fields to make his fortune barging oil in barrels on Oil Creek; my father
was born in a leased shack on the Tarr Farm, site of the world's first gush-
er. But the pipeline came and Grampa went broke; thereafter he was,
variously, a drill-rig engineer, a coastwise trader in vegetables, a horsecar
conductor, a Sing Sing prison guard, a customhouse clerk, a door-to-door
salesman of patent oil lamps, and, later, of life insurance, and a store-
keeper in Tarrytown, New York.

But first, last, and in between he was a farmer, and managed or operated dairy farms from Lewes, Delaware, to Ballston Spa, New York, including two on Staten Island, even then a part of the city of New York. When
he died at the age of eighty-three on a tiny subsistence farm in Orangeburg,
New York, he still had a plow horse, a Jersey cow, and one milk customer.

In my boyhood we spent our summers on Grampa's farm and in his late
years it was my job to service that one customer. So each day, after an early
supper, as soon as Grampa came in from milking, I'd set off with my two-
quart pail, trudging up the Sparkill road in the afterglow of a summer sunset.

There are no roads like that one anymore. It was a dim dirt lane that
meandered through old meadows growing up to brush and trees, almost a
tunnel under the great overhanging branches where the air was sweet with
fresh-cut hay, spicy with weeds, and perfumed by the sun-warmed fruit of
abandoned orchards. Each clump of woods provided a zone of cool air fra-

grant of cedar, and each marshy spot yielded the dank earthy smell of mosses. It was so quiet, so still; nothing moved in that breathless evening hour and even my footsteps were silent in the dust of the road, fine and soft as talcum, a grateful cushion for a little boy's bare feet.

Once emptied, the pail had to be rinsed in a tiny spring brook that ran beside the road a way. It flowed less than a kitchen faucet would, and it must have been fresh out of the ground, for it was so cold my bare feet could not stand it. But it had the mystery of all running water, it provided crisp peppery watercress which no little boy could resist, and, best of all, it was populous with frogs.

Boys and frogs have gone together ever since there were boys and frogs, and I entered joyfully into my heritage. Instinct taught me that a frog could be trapped in a hurled lump of mud and made to spring into an open hand or even a milk pail by touching his opposite end, or just by pouncing on him. So each evening I put a little water in my milk pail and then added half a pail of frogs. For I had a mission.

Across the road from our farmhouse was a marshy meadow and beyond it curved a little brook, a feeder of Sparkill Creek. It was a gentle, purling, cool, clear brook that was my favorite playground; I caught my first speckled trout in it. But there was one thing about it that puzzled me. There weren't any frogs in it; at least, none that I ever saw or heard. It seemed to me that when we sat out on the porch evening under the magnolias, we were entitled to have the night noises of birds, katydids, and crickets accented and dramatized by the juggurums of a goodly frog population. Obviously, this was an oversight of Nature, and Alfred Miller was just the boy to show Nature how things should be done. So for some weeks I paused at one end of my milk run to load frogs and at the other end to liberate them. Then one evening I forgot to liberate them.

Here is where Gramma came into the story. Gramma was six feet tall, a Hempstead of Saxon bone and bulk, and she lived for battle; if no battle was handy it was her delight to start one. She had a short-fused temper and a rampaging sense of humor, as well as a great mop of blonde hair turned sort of white and a pretty good soprano voice—and lots of it. She was the ramrod, the driver that had really got the family through the terrible starving times of the 1870s and '80s. She was thirteen years younger than Grampa and, as I remember it, she was always bossing him around and giving him a hard time. But six months after he died, she just sat down in her big old rocking chair and died of "heart trouble." But it wasn't heart failure; it was heartbreak.

In summertime we used an old board shack beside the well for a summer kitchen, because it was handier to the water supply, and cooler. It had a dirt floor, an old table and chairs, a kerosene cooking stove, and a wooden sink with a pail of well water and a tin dipper beside it. This night Gramma was sitting on a high stool washing the supper dishes and belting out "The Son of Man Goes Forth to War" like a captain leading a charge. Without missing a note she took the lid off the milk pail and abstractedly poured a cascade of indignant batrachians into the dishpan.

Gramma weighed three hundred pounds and she was lame besides, but she unloaded off that stool and sashayed out the door like a schoolgirl while hitting the highest, loudest note I ever heard her emit. She came back instantly, mad enough to chew nails. Any little boy who did that to his loving Gramma deserved, she opined, A Good Whipping; and she strongly implied that she was ready, willing, and able to do the job right then. As Gramma had raised four kids with a short-handled buggy whip, the situation looked a bit critical. But my mother, who was wiping the dishes, came to my rescue. My mother was meek and mild, but she was tougher than boiled rawhide; and she and Gramma didn't like each other very well anyway. She allowed softly that nobody—*nobody*—was going to whip her little Alfred. This confrontation provided the diversion I needed to retrieve my livestock and head for the marsh. I didn't return until Gramma had departed the shack.

The curious part of this adventure is that despite my exertions and the risking of my backside in the cause of conservation, I never afterward heard so much as a single croak from our stretch of the brook. The ungrateful little beggars must have taken off for other parts as soon as they were freed.

Letter to Nick Lyons

December 28, 1970

. . . I sent the extra <u>Fisherman's Bounty</u> to my second grandson in the Maryland branch, mostly because I've never sent him anything previously but kid stuff. He doesn't even fish so far as I know; it's not fishing country.

So he avows that "Murder" is simply the best story ever written, insists (until stopped by acclamation) on reading it aloud at the breakfast table, and has selected for his term theme the title, "My Grandfather as an Author." He is fourteen.

Nick, how shall we ever learn to fathom the human heart? I'm deeply touched, and some day you will be too when you suddenly encounter the very last approbation (or rather, the approbation from the very last source) you ever expected to receive. . . .

Who shall fathom the human heart in its mutations?

Murder

" If fishing interferes with your business, give up your business," any angler will tell you, citing instances of men who lost health and even life through failure to take a little recreation, and reminding you that "the trout do not rise in Green Wood Cemetery," so you had better do your fishing while you are still able. But you will search far to find a fisherman to admit that a taste for fishing, like a taste for liquor, must be governed lest it come to possess its possessor; that an excess of fishing can cause as many tragedies of lost purpose, earning power, and position as an excess of liquor. This is the story of a man who finally decided between his business and his fishing, and of how his decision was brought about by the murder of a trout.

Fishing was not a pastime with my friend John but an obsession—a common condition, for typically your successful fisherman is not really enjoying a recreation, but rather taking refuge from the realities of life in an absorbing fantasy in which he grimly if subconsciously reenacts in miniature the unceasing struggle of primitive man for existence. Indeed, it is that which makes him successful, for it gives him the last measure of fierce concentration, that final moment of unyielding patience that in angling so often makes the difference between fish and no fish.

John was that kind of fisherman, more so than any other I ever knew. Waking or sleeping, his mind ran constantly on the trout and its taking, and back in the Depression years I often wondered whether he could keep on indefinitely doing business with the surface of his mind and fishing with the rest of his mental processes—wondered, and feared that he could not. So when he called me one spring day and said, "I'm tired of sitting here and watching a corporation die; let's go fishing," I knew that he was not discouraged with his business as much as he was impatient with its restraint. But I went with him, for maybe I'm a bit obsessed myself.

That day together on the river was like a thousand other pages from the book of any angler's memories. There was the clasp and pull of cold, hurrying water on our legs, the hours of rhythmic casting, and the steady somnambulistic shuffling that characterizes steelworkers aloft and fly fishermen in fast water. Occasionally our heads were bent together over a fly box; at intervals our pipes wreathed smoke; and from time to time a brief remark broke the silence. We were fishing "pool and pool" together, each as he finished walking around the other to a new spot above him.

Later afternoon found me in the second pool below the dam, throwing a long line up the still water. There was a fish rising to some insect so small that I could not detect it, so I was using a tiny gray fly on a long leader with a 5X point. John came by and went up to the Dam Pool, and I lost interest in my refractory fish and walked up to watch, for there was always a chance of a good fish there. I stopped at a safe distance and sat down on a rock with my leader trailing to keep it wet, while John systematically covered the tail of the pool until he was satisfied that there were no fish there to dart ahead and give the alarm, and then stepped into it.

As he did so his body became tense, his posture that of a man who stalks his enemy. With aching slowness and infinite craft he began to inch up the pool, and as he went his knees bent more and more until he was crouching. Finally, with his rod low to the water and one hand supporting himself on the bottom of the stream, he crept to a casting position and knelt in midcurrent with water lapping under his elbows, his left sleeve dripping unheeded as he allowed the current to straighten his line behind him. I saw that he was using the same leader as mine but with a large No. 12 fly.

"John, using 5X?" I breathed. Without turning his head he nodded almost imperceptibly.

"Better break off and reknot," I counseled softly, but he ignored the suggestion. I spoke from experience. Drawn 5X silkworm gut is almost as fine as a human hair, and we both knew that it chafes easily where it is tied to a fly as heavy as a No. 12, so that it is necessary to make the fastening in a different spot at frequent intervals in order to avoid breaking it. I kept silence and watched John. His rod almost parallel to the water, he picked up his fly from behind him with a light twitch and then false cast to dry it. He was a good caster; it neither touched the surface nor rose far above it as he whipped it back and forth.

Now he began lengthening his line until finally, at the end of each forward cast, his fly hovered for an instant above a miniature eddy between the main current and a hand's breadth of still water that clung to the bank. And then I noticed what he had seen when he entered the pool—the sudden slight dimple denoting the feeding of a big fish on the surface.

The line came back with a subtle change from the side-sweeping false cast, straightened with decision, and swept forward in a tight roll. It straightened again in front of the caster, whispered through the guides, and then checked suddenly. The fly swept around as a little elbow formed in the leader, and settled on the rim of the eddy with a loop of slack upstream of it. It started to circle, then disappeared in a sudden dimple, and I could hear a faint sucking sound.

It seemed as if John would never strike although his pause must have been but momentary. Then his long line tightened—he had out fifty feet—as he drew it back with his left hand and gently raised the rod tip with his right. There was a slight pause and then the line began to run out slowly.

Rigid as a statue, with the water piling a little wave against the brown waders at his waist, he continued to kneel there while the yellow line slid almost unchecked through his left hand. His lips moved.

"A big one," he murmured. "The leader will never hold him if he gets started. I should have changed it."

The tip of the upright rod remained slightly bent as the fish moved into the circling currents created by the spillway at the right side of the dam. John took line gently and the rod maintained its bend. Now the fish was under the spillway and must have dived down with the descending stream, for I saw a couple of feet of line slide suddenly through John's hand. The circling water got its impetus here, and this was naturally the fastest part of the eddy.

The fish came rapidly toward us, riding with the quickened water, and John retrieved line. Would the fish follow the current around again or would it leave and run down past us? The resilient tip straightened as the pressure was ended. The big trout passed along the downstream edge of the eddy and swung over to the bank to follow it round again, repeated its performance at the spillway, and again refused to leave the eddy. It was troubled and perplexed by the strange hampering of its progress, but it was not alarmed, for it was not aware of our presence or even of the fact that it was hooked, and the restraint on it had not been enough to arouse its full resistance.

Every experienced angler will understand that last statement. The pull of a game fish, up to the full limit of its strength, seems to be in proportion to the resistance which it encounters. As I watched the leader slowly cutting the water, I recalled that often I had hooked a trout and immediately given slack, whereupon invariably it had moved quietly and aimlessly about, soon coming to rest as if it had no realization that it was hooked.

I realized now that John intended to get the "fight" out of his fish at a rate slow enough not to endanger his leader. His task was to keep from arousing the fish to a resistance greater than the presumably weakened 5X gut would withstand. It seemed as if it were hopeless, for the big trout continued to circle the eddy, swimming deep and strongly against the rod's light tension, which relaxed only when the fish passed the gateway of the stream below. Around and around it went, and then at last it left the eddy. Yet it did not dart into the outflowing current but headed into deep water close to the far bank. I held my breath, for over there was a tangle of roots and I could imagine what a labyrinth they must make under the surface. Ah, it was moving toward the roots! Now what would John do—hold the fish hard and break it off; check it and arouse its fury; or perhaps splash a stone in front of it to turn it back?

He did none of these but instead slackened off until his line sagged in a catenary curve. The fish kept on, and I could see the leader draw on the surface as it swam into the mass of roots. Now John dropped his rod flat to the water and delicately drew on the line until the tip barely flexed, moving it almost imperceptibly several times to feel whether his leader had fouled on a root. Then he lapsed into immobility.

I glanced at my wristwatch, slowly bent my head until I could light my cold pipe without raising my hand, and then relaxed on my rock. The smoke drifted lazily upstream, the separate puffs merging into a thin haze that dissipated itself imperceptibly. A bird moved on the bank. But the only really living thing was the stream, which rippled a bit as it divided around John's body and continually moved a loop of his yellow line in the disturbed current below him.

When the trout finally swam quietly back out of the roots, my watch showed that it had been in there almost an hour. John slackened line and released a breath which he seemed to have been holding all that while, and the fish reentered the eddy to resume its interminable circling. The sun which had been in my face dropped behind a tree, and I noted how the shadows had lengthened. Then the big fish showed itself for the first time, its huge dorsal fin appearing as it rose toward the surface, and the lobe of its great tail as it turned down again; it seemed to be two feet long.

Again its tail swirled under the surface, puddling the water as it swam slowly and deliberately, and then I thought we would lose the fish, for as it came around to the downstream side of the eddy it wallowed an instant and then headed toward us. Instantly John relaxed the rod until the line hung limp, and from the side of his mouth he hissed, "Steady!"

Down the stream, passing John so close he could have hit it with his tip, drifted a long dark bulk, oaring along deliberately with its powerful tail in the smooth current. I could see the gray fly in the corner of its mouth and the leader hanging in a curve under its belly, then the yellow line floating behind. In a moment John felt the fish again, determined that it was no longer moving, and resumed his light pressure, causing it to swim around aimlessly in the still water below us. The sun was half below the horizon now, and the shadows slanting down over the river covered us. In the cool, diffused light the lines on John's face from nostril to mouth were deeply cut, and the crafty folds at the outer corners of his lids hooded his eyes. His rod hand shook with a fine tremor.

The fish broke, wallowing, but John instantly dropped his rod flat to the water and slipped a little line. The fish wallowed again, then swam more slowly in a large circle. It was moving just under the surface now, its mouth open and its back breaking the water every few feet, and it seemed to be half turned on its side. Still John did not move except for the small gestures of taking or giving line, raising or lowering his tip.

It was in the ruddy afterglow that the fish finally came to the top, beating its tail in a subdued rhythm. Bent double, I crept ashore and then ran through the brush to the edge of the still water downstream of the fish, which now was broad on its side. Stretching myself prone on the bank, I extended my net at arm's length and held it flat on the bottom in a foot of water.

John began to slip out line slowly, the now-beaten trout moving feebly as the slow current carried it down. Now it was opposite me and I nodded a signal to John. He moved his tip toward the bank and cautiously checked the line. The current swung the trout toward me and it passed over my net.

I raised the rim quietly and slowly, and the next instant the trout was doubled up in my deep-bellied net and I was holding the top of it shut with both hands while the fish, galvanized into a furious flurry, splashed water in my face as I strove to get my feet under me. John picked his way slowly down the still water, reeling up as he came, stumbling and slipping on the stones like an utterly weary man. I killed the trout with my pliers and laid it on the grass as he came up beside me; and he stood watching it with bent head and sagging shoulders for a long time.

"To die like that!" he said as if thinking aloud. "Murdered—nagged to death; he never knew he was fighting for his life until he was in the net. He had strength and courage enough to beat the pair of us, but we robbed him a little at a time until we got him where we wanted him. And then knocked him on the head. I wish you had let him go."

The twilight fishing, our favorite time, was upon us, but he started for the car and I did not demur. We began to take off our wet shoes and waders.

"That's just what this Depression is doing to me!" John burst out suddenly as he struggled with a shoelace. "Niggling me to death! And I'm up here fishing, taking two days off in the middle of the week, instead of doing something about it. Come on; hurry up. I'm going to catch the midnight to Pittsburgh; I know where I can get a contract."

And sure enough, he did.

Letter to Harry Darbee

M arch 26, 1962

. . . I am figuring on getting up for the opening, and the principal reason for doing so is to see Elsie Belle and you, and to wet my feet in the Sacred River one more time even if there's no fishing left in it. The dear and beloved Beaverkill will always be first in my heart.

. . . Yesterday (Sunday) I washed my fishing vest for the first time in four or five years and discovered that the green dye is what we used to call "fugitive" in the cotton-goods business in my youth. Also am putting in a new grass bag; the mice who lived in my creel damn near destroyed it. Also put a new net into my Geo LaBranche flopover net, and shortened the handle. Also tested a pair of wading stockings and for heaven's sake they were tight. Also oiled a pair of hobnailed wading shoes. Also assembled a skillion little flat spools of nylon so I can design my own leaders. I finally had to give up when Farlow just plain never filled my last order. I know why; I gave them hell about having points measuring .005, .006 and .007 instead of .008 and .009 which they sent me last time. They wrote quite a plaintive letter in acknowledging the order (sent a year ago) but they never filled it or wrote. . . . Now I will have a good excuse for not catching any fish.

Sam Day and I are inventing leader tapers. We are going to make the fly touch the water before the line and leader.

I still have to get the flies out of all the little boxes and put them into all the big boxes; repack the fishing vest (a night's work by itself); put the LLBean superweight pants and other heavy woolens out on the line to get rid of the paradichlorobenzene; pack the boot-foot waders, the boot-foot stockings, the stocking-foot waders, the stocking-foot stockings, the felt-soled wading shoes, the hobnailed wading shoes, the four pairs of wading socks, the boot hanger and bootjack, the extra laces, the hang-around-the-neck plastic glow-light for changing flies at night, the falling in clothes, the dock workers' long underdrawers, the flannel shirts, the alarm watch, the extra flashlight, the shoe trees, the dressing gown, the flasks and the black dinner coat and trousers.

I also have to pack the wading staff, the flopover net, the Harrimac Folding Landing Net, the 6'9" rod, the 7'6" rod, the Garrison 8' rod, the Payne 8' rod, the Garrison 8'9" bass big rod, the Garrison 10' dry-fly salmon rod, the no-name 12' two-handed fly rod, and the 5' bait-casting rod. Also the Zwarg 4/0 salmon reel, the Medalist 4" bass and dry-fly salmon reels, the Hewitt custom-made trout reel, the four Medalist 3" trout reels, the four-foot gaff, the three-tined spear and the double-barrel shotgun.

I will probably start fishing around 11 AM (have to wait for the sun to warm up the water) and quit about 2 PM (have to warm myself up internally). But it won't make much difference because I will have discovered that I left my belt worm-box, my wet fly book, all my dry-fly boxes, my streamer book and my bass plugs home. . . .

Only Yesterday

(Introduction to *Great Fishing Tackle Catalogs of the Golden Age*)

What fisherman cannot recall his boyhood excitement at the arrival of a new tackle catalog—the ecstasy of looking into a new Eden and the despair of beholding the angel barring the way with the flaming sword of penury?

What little boy of "only yesterday" did not beguile his rainy afternoons with pad, pencil, and the Sears "Roebook," compiling lists of "what I would buy if I had $50," then $25, then $10, and finally a mere $1, all fantasy because his allowance of pocket money, like mine, was 5¢ a week?

Frustrating? No, for the icy blast of economic reality was tempered by a divine providence to the scanty fleece of the forlorn lamb. After a catalog had been studied long enough, the hellfire flare of the fell figures faded into a rosy celestial glow as the opium of the copywriter bemused the senses of the little boy, lulling him into a blissful dream of owning all those magnificent gadgets and thereby becoming king of the water, the emperor of the fish.

From the days of the earliest settlements in America men fished and hunted. But even on the frontiers, fishing and hunting provided no important sustenance for many or for long. No natural population of fish and game ever could support permanently any sizable human population, which likely is why the first explorers of North America found no more than a scattered, scanty population of aborigines. Notwithstanding the incredibly rich resources of this vast area, only those Indians who had been able to develop agriculture—the tribes on the Muskingum in Ohio, the Five Nations in the Finger Lakes area of New York, the pueblo-dwelling tribes of the Southwest—were able to create a population numerous enough to establish permanent communities.

The Puritan coming home from the woods in high-peaked hat and buckled shoes with a wild turkey slung on his flintlock is a myth. It took only a year or so for even a tiny settlement to kill or drive off game until it cost too much, in ammunition and time, to feed a family by hunting.

After that, hunting and fishing were mere diversions, and therefore considered to be not respectable. In 1847 the Reverend George Washington Bethune signed his fine, scholarly "biographical preface" to the first American edition of Walton and Cotton's *Compleat Angler* simply as The American Editor. He feared the wrath of his elite congregation if they were to learn that he countenanced and even engaged in the idle, trivial, frivolous, disreputable sport of angling. And "only yesterday," President Calvin Coolidge manifested honest surprise at being invited to go fishing. "A pastime for boys and loafers," this canny, hard-case politician called it, until his advisers pointed out the size of the "fishing vote."

"Only yesterday" the United States ceased to be predominantly agricultural and rural, when the last census disclosed that there are more people in cities now than on the land. Only now has fishing become a major sport, for actually, angling has always been primarily a sport of sophisticated city dwellers. For many years the sporting goods industry dwelt on the number of millions of fishermen there were, including a horde of saltwater fishermen, and liberal estimates of the number of fishing landowners, none of whom required a license. But I can easily recall when the trade's own estimate of its annual sales volume was only about $3 million.

Legend to the contrary, fishing was never the big thing for the country boy that hunting was. To be sure, he cut his pole, dug his worms, and went "trouting" in April, but the onset of spring quickly drove him back to the plow and the harrow, the cultivator, the hoe, and the mowing machine. By the time the bass season came in, the livelier, more gregarious pastime of baseball was in full swing. Only after the harvest could the country boy fire a couple of shells through his Montgomery Ward shotgun to clear the rust out of the barrels, and go hunting for rabbits, squirrels, quail, or grouse.

So there were no fishing tackle stores in the country; the hardware dealer and the general store sold tackle as a sideline. Only in cities of substantial size were there stores devoted exclusively to the sale of "sporting
goods." It is the catalogs of such houses that are sampled in this look
backward to yesteryear, before the glass rod and the fixed-spool spinning
reel, the new leisure and the new affluence, doubled and redoubled and
doubled again the ranks of well-read, sophisticated young recruits to the
sport of angling.

   As a boy who earned the 50¢ to buy his first rod by eating health-
giving prunes at 5¢ for each eight prunes, and lived to refuse a $300 offer
for a treasured wisp of bamboo less than 7 feet long, I have run the whole
course. So walk with me through the catalogs that my colleagues have
assembled and permit me to add a few comments and explanations.

Letter to Harry Darbee

January 15/16, 1948

. . . I never recall catching a fish on one, which undoubtedly means that I don't know how to fish a nymph—something I have long suspected. Even when my eyes were better, I never was able to see a fish flash under water and take a wet fly on a loose line. I suppose it is easy to make excuses, but I am sure that a part of my lack of fish-catching ability is due to my inability to see. A long while ago I became convinced that all really good fish-catchers have two things in common—fathers who were fishermen and remarkable eyesight. The fishing father simply means that the guy has a lot of experience, particularly when he was a kid and had time to waste watching the water, etc., which is one of the best ways to learn. Check over your own list and see if I am not right. . . .

Did I ever tell you about my famous bead-chain nymph? After reading Needham's <u>Better Trout Streams</u> I was much taken with his picture of the Rhyacophila caddis nymph. It does not make a case but crawls around the bottom. It is segmented very perceptibly, according to the photo he showed. . . . I decided to make a Rhyacophila that would crawl around the bottom, be segmented and bright green. I took four beads of an electric light pull chain (after reduced it to three because it was too awful damn heavy) and tied on one side a very light wire small (No. 14 or 15) hook, so that it would ride on top and not on the bottom; then painted it green—I mean <u>green</u>—with Duco (cement).

Forgot about it until one day in I think July when nothing worked. I knew I needed a heavy, deep run and found it in front of the Swiss

American, where there used to be some good fish. I cast as far as I could upstream with a big 9-foot rod (it was a terribly bitching thing to cast, that nymph), let it come down on a loose line and straighten out below me. I got a strike that nearly straightened out my arm, and brought in the biggest chub I ever saw in the Beaverkill. I kept getting these big chubs and then I got a hell of a strike that took off the nymph. That week-end and the one following I lost all of these nymphs that I had . . . the same way. . . . It was such a lousy thing to cast that I finally lost interest. . . .

Letter to Harry Darbee

August 17, 1950

Dear Harry:

Those are just lovely flies. You never did nicer—or was it Elsie? If you two can't tell your own work apart, how do you expect me to? I think myself Elsie probably does them a little better, just because she is so much better than you are in every other way.

It certainly was a treat to open those boxes; in fact, I had a hell of a time keeping myself from rising to them. I am always careful when I handle your flies—one time I had a Hendrickson of yours on the table and the wind moved it suddenly, and I nearly broke my neck striking at it. . . .

Dammit, Harry, the longer I fish the more I am convinced that the quality of the hackle is the one thing that determines the efficiency of the fly above everything else. If the pattern is far enough wrong, a fine hackle may not raise a fish; but no matter how good the pattern is, bum hackles raise far fewer fish—frequently none at all—than the user has a right to expect. Next to the quality of the hackle I will put the amount of it, which is a factor sometimes, I think. A very lightly hackled fly probably sits lower on the water and hence seems to be more attractive when the fish are taking spent flies. But overly hackled flies <u>never</u> work well for me unless they are all hackle, bivisible. Sometimes I think the attractiveness of bivisibles is principally the commotion they make when they land. They must really "explode" a light pattern when they come down. . . .

The Indomitable

All was quiet along the river as I cast my fly up into the pool, but before it floated back battle had been joined in the next valley. The forces of heaven were attacking over there, for I could hear the war drums of the thunder. Reeling up hastily, for these mountain storms come fast, I waded ashore and took shelter under a hemlock.

It was a brief engagement. The forces advanced rapidly, and in a few minutes rain topped the high crest and charged with flashing bayonets down upon the valley. It stamped the river flat and passed over the thick woods with the sound of a marching multitude. With it came the lightning running a brilliant scale like bugles sounding the charge, and thunder for the accompanying drums. Clouds scudded by like massed battle flags.

The storm passed over, the thunder sounding the long roll beyond the crests until it died in the distance, but the rain continued to march steadily past like the train of an army. Behind me the river frothed under it; it slashed the dirt in muddy streams from the gravel of the narrow path before me and dripped steadily through the branches onto the thirsty moss. A wet, earthy odor arose.

Suddenly the close unstirring air was pierced by a military summons whistled with martial vigor; far up the path sounded the notes which a leaping memory identified as "First Call for Guard Mount." The whistler was evidently no recruit; he knew army routine, for it was succeeded by "Assembly" and then by the plunging cadences of "Adjutant's Call." A sharp command followed, then a series of stirring bugle marches. He was mounting the guard. "You're in the Army Now," "Payday," "There She

Goes"—an old soldier this, one who had walked many a post, for these were all favorites of the Old Army.

Now he was in sight, a big man, square and well set up. His lined ruddy face was wet with rain. Rain plastered his flannel shirt to his shoulders, his breast was black with it, and his back was streaming. Above his boots his trousers were sopping, and my ear detected the squelching of wet feet in cadence with the thud of his heels. Behind his hip a creel rode so lightly as to suggest that it was empty, and in his right hand he bore the joints of a fishing rod, upon the butt of which an automatic reel was still mounted. With this rod he thrust rhythmically before him in the arm-swing of a marching soldier.

The man was as wet as if he had been in the river, but he did not know it. His face was composed, even pleasant, and his eyes held a faraway look. With wings on his ankles and drums in his heart he was striding across some sun-baked parade ground. He never saw me.

"Route order—*march!*" he commanded and then loudly, unmelodiously, but with unquenchable spirit, broke into song. The years fell away, and I saw again a brown line of packed and helmeted figures streaming along a white road, for the song he sang was "Mademoiselle from Armentières." The charging rain beat against that song, broke, and turned back. The trees took it in their arms and meshed it in their leaves. The river bubbled in time with it.

He was past, now, the grinding of the gravel under his heels growing fainter. The bawdy words and rollicking tune sounded farther off. Now he came to the turn of the path.

> *An officer came across the Rhine, parley-voo,*
> *An officer came across the Rhine, parley-voo. . . .*

The well-remembered words trailed into indistinguishable sound, and the sound into silence. I heard again the marching of the rain and the dripping of the branches.

I took the pipe from my mouth and saluted. It was a sentimental indulgence, but I had just seen a brave man. I have said that he was swinging his right arm, but I failed to add that he was not swinging the left. That sleeve was empty.

The foregoing fantasy was written many years ago as a tribute to the indomitable crippled veterans of my World War who were making new successes of their lives despite seemingly insuperable obstacles. I would like to add now the account of an incident which I witnessed in Halloran General Hospital after the Second World War as my tribute to the crippled veterans of the succeeding generation.

Here came two kids jockeying their wheelchairs down the corridor with the expertness, spirit, and almost the speed of dirt-track racers. They were bound for the telephone booth beside which I stood, and it quickly developed that, with one nickel and one telephone number between them, they purposed to call up some girl and kid her five cents' worth. Along came a nurse, young and, easy to see, a favorite of the troops.

"What," she demanded amiably, "are you guys up to?"

The younger of the two—they were both heartbreakingly young—broadened a grin already wide and flipped a hand in an airy gesture.

"Just roving around," he said jauntily, "looking for adventure."

Adventure! A game leg and a wheelchair apiece, one telephone number and one nickel between them. Adventure? Yes, for they had, besides, the high indomitable hearts in which and only in which the true spirit of adventure dwells.

I did not salute, because it would have embarrassed them.

Chance Meetings

During nearly half a century of fly fishing I have of course encountered a veritable host of fishermen. Some were great figures of angling, some were as able with pen as with rod, most were anonymous, conventional types—good-hearted, friendly, helpful, kindly "regular fellows." But a few had something unique or at least unusual about them that has made them linger in my memory. Most were encountered by chance and my contact with them was fleeting or no more than brief. Others became warm acquaintances; a few, friends.

They were a diverse lot; if they had anything approaching a common characteristic, it was the way they had come into fishing. The most unlikely types, city born and city bred without even the remotest previous contact with fishing, suddenly conceived a passion to go fishing, assembled equipment, and forthwith went, all without seeking counsel or even taking a preliminary dip into the literature of the sport. Their utter inability to explain how they got interested in fishing and their great valor of ignorance are the only things they had in common. Let us look at a few of them.

The Novice. I was coming out of the tail of Cairns' Pool one time on my way to an early dinner when I spotted a fish rising close against the bank. It took the Gray Variant I offered and immediately proved itself to be a lowly eight-inch stocker, which was quickly netted and released.

"Congratulations! You played him very nicely," said a pleasant voice above and behind me, the voice of a young man who had been watching me from the edge of the road. Since neither the fish nor the handling had merited congratulations, I deduced that this was a novice but also a man of goodwill and sportsmanlike instincts.

He proved me right. It was his first day astream, with an outfit he had bought complete in a discount store, on impulse and without knowing why. Luck had been with him; he had had a wonderful day. His outfit had proved adequate if not fancy; he hadn't been able to cast with his new fly rod, of course, but he had let his big wet flies run down in the current; and, wonder of wonders, he had caught three fish. And now he was on his way back to the hotel, at peace with the world, but had stopped to watch when he saw me hang my little fish.

"Would you like to see my trout?" he asked, hauling a canvas creel from his car and drawing forth three small fish. Right then I faced a decision which I still wonder whether I made correctly. But as I still see it, I had either to well-nigh break his heart then or let someone else do it later; I could just imagine him displaying his catch to the fishermen in the Antrim Lodge bar.

"Look," I said gently. "There is one mark by which you can always identify a trout. Every trout has it and no other fish have," and I explained about the adipose fin.

"What are those, then?" he asked.

"Chub," I told him, and explained about chub.

"Then I suppose I might as well throw these away," he said miserably, his happy day ruined.

I did the best I could. "Why did you come all the way up here just to go fishing?" I demanded. "It was to have fun, wasn't it?"

"Yes, of course."

"Well, didn't you have fun when you caught those fish?"

"I certainly did!" he said firmly and even smiled for an instant at the recollection.

"Then you got what you came for; you had fun. And you learned something very important. You learned that it's not fish that make the sport but just catching them—or even just trying to catch them."

He seemed to look a little less disconsolate as he drove away, but maybe that was just my wishful thinking. I still wonder whether I made the right decision.

The Paratrooper. My wife once belonged to a women's fishing club that leased a clubhouse and some water on a Catskill stream, and we were fishing there with our daughter Patty.

We were surprised to receive, on our first evening, a call from a most personable young man, a paratrooper just out of the service, who was our neighbor by virtue of living two miles up the road. He knew two other members of the club who were also staying at the house and his call was ostensibly on them.

But within five minutes he had executed a turning movement and realigned his advance with us as his objective. Then he put down the best-directed and most skillfully laid barrage I ever saw, so well organized that we did not recognize it as a holding action. He was awaiting an anticipated tactical development, but when it did not materialize he finally had to make a frontal attack.

"Where is your daughter Miss Pat?" he asked with a most charming smile. "I hear she is very pretty." He glowed like a neon sign.

"She's in bed," said Lady Beaverkill.

"In bed!" exclaimed Airborne in shocked surprise. "But it's only nine o'clock."

"Well, she's only nine years old," said my wife mildly.

He never dimmed his smile or flicked an eyelid, but behind him the two ladies developed severe cases of internal mirth. I didn't learn until afterward that, chancing to meet Airborne that morning, they had told him we were coming up with our pretty daughter but either by accident or, more likely, by design they had omitted the very vital statistic.

Airborne had had it but, like all paratroopers, he was a master of minor tactics. In five minutes he had cleared his flanks, disengaged his forward elements, and was falling back under heavy covering fire to a previously prepared position. But the last volley to ring in his ears as he started his half-hour walk home in the darkness was the pealing laughter of his unsympathetic acquaintances.

Fly Tyers in Left Field. Back in the days when Charlie Kerlee was one of the very best commercial photographers in New York, I stopped by to say hello to him. He had a girl on the model stand, and you will believe that she was a toothsome dish when I say that she was the highest-priced fashion model at that time and, I believe, the first to receive one hundred dollars an hour for her work. She was wearing a gorgeous fur coat, which was being brushed meticulously by the furrier who owned it so as to get the right play of light on it.

Then entered a mutual friend who was a dedicated amateur fly tyer. At the sight of this fur-clad lovely he stopped short and pointed like a bird dog, then bounded forward with a glad cry.

"Wow!" he exclaimed. "What a gorgeous body. . . ." The model jerked her head around to slay another fresh guy with a dagger look, but the newcomer ignored her to fondle a corner of the coat while he finished his exclamation. "What a gorgeous body that would spin into!"

Just in case these lines are read by someone who is not familiar with the fly tyer's method of constructing an artificial fishing fly, I will explain that the tyer sometimes "spins"—twists—clipped fur around a sticky silk thread and then winds the furry thread in close turns around the shank of a fish-hook to make a body for his imitation of an insect.

"What is it?" continued the fly tyer as he gazed at the glorious, creamy, cinnamon-tinged fur.

"Fisher," said Charlie. "*Only* twelve thousand dollars."

"Yeah?" said the unimpressed fly tyer. "Gosh, I wish I could get just a little piece of it."

"I could give you a few trimmings," said the amused furrier.

"You can? Oh boy! Thanks!" chortled the fly tyer, almost beside himself, and hastily hauled out his business card.

As we walked out together I remarked, "That girl is really a cupcake, isn't she?"

"What girl?" demanded the fly tyer vaguely. "Gee, I hope that guy remembers to send me those clippings. What a body!"

I have known, and know of, fly tyers who were farther out in left field than that. For instance: For some years during and after World War II a chap named Harlan Maynard, an accomplished amateur tyer, worked as a volunteer teaching fly tying to disabled veterans at Halloran General Hospital on Staten Island, New York. This hard-fisted, hard-faced, hard-talking, and soft-hearted Maine man had a magnetic personality, and his classes tied with a fanatical fervor that persisted after they had been discharged and sent home. He once showed me letters from two of his grateful graduates, the following extracts from which illustrate my point.

Wrote one: "I am back to tying. I want to get a dozen of each size of twenty patterns in time for the opening of the trout season. My wife gave birth to a boy yesterday, nine pounds. I have picked up a very promising pointer pup and am training him, but most of the time I tie flies. . . ."

Wrote the other: "I sure miss the class and wish I were back tying with you. I am getting tools and materials to start again. My wife went out for the evening three days ago and hasn't come back yet. Wait till she gets home. How are all the fellows in the class? I have found a place with some good blue necks and the price is right too. . . ."

But I think the most in fly tyers was the chap who came into the smoking compartment of a Pullman sleeper one night when the late Walter Sill of The Anglers' Club of New York was using a portable fly-tying kit to tie salmon flies to while away the time.

"Thunder and Lightning!" said the young man, which was not an exclamation but the name of the fly Walter was tying. He sat down to talk, and in half an hour the porter came in.

"Your wife sent me to see where you were, suh," he said.

"Tell her I'll be right back," said the young man. Half an hour later, while they were taking turns at the tying vise, the porter returned. He addressed the young man again.

"Your wife says to come back, suh," he said.

"Right away," said the young man, waxing another piece of thread and never looking up.

Half an hour and two salmon flies later the porter returned for the third time.

"Your wife says to come right away, suh," he said.

"I guess I'll have to leave you," the young man said with an apologetic smile, "or my wife will be sore at me. You see, we were married just this afternoon."

He was a *real* fly tyer.

The Singers. It was a time of gloom and sorrow, for the disaster at Pearl Harbor and the hopeless plight of our troops on Bataan cast down our spirits. The military had refused me firmly and there was little I could do to help, so I went fishing, as I could after I discovered that a 1940 Ford would run on unrationed kerosene.

Thus it was that early one Saturday morning in August my wife and I, on our way to the Beaverkill, encountered on the forward deck of the Newburgh ferryboat a group of men enjoying the rising sun and cool breeze on their way to work in the war plants across the Hudson.

Clad in scrubbed, faded blue bib overalls and blue denim shirts, they were middle-aged men with gray hair and comfortable waistlines but with wide shoulders, too, and strong, callused hands. One of them reminded me of my Uncle Frank, who had the front of a buffalo and a handlebar moustache all across his broad Saxon face; who could lift anything he could get a good hold of and, besides, made the most marvelous wooden guns for my cousin and me to hunt deer and bears all along the fencerows of the old farm.

They did not mind being up early or going to work on a Saturday, those men, but joked and laughed together, and I think they must have been members of some sort of singing society or chorus, for several times during the long trip they broke into snatches of harmony of which they sang but a few bars each time before lapsing into mirth and banter.

The ferryboat came into the slip and made fast. The gates went up. The group started off the boat. Then suddenly one of them raised a strong baritone voice.

"Onward, Christian soldiers . . ." he sang, and the others came in with a heart-stopping crash:

"MARCHING AS TO WAR!"

On the instant they were all in step, pounding their heels on the planking and swinging their tin dinner pails in unison to the cadence of the greatest marching song ever written.

Through the cavernous, echoing ferry shed and out onto the cobbles of the old river town they went, still singing, in an irregular formation that somehow reminded me of skirmishers going forward under fire. As I eased the car past them, the one who looked like Uncle Frank stopped singing a moment and smiled as he saw the aluminum rod cases stacked in the back of the car.

"Good luck," he said, and I seemed to hear Uncle Frank add, "Olfurd," as he always used to pronounce my name in the old-fashioned country way.

My heart was uplifted, and suddenly all was made clear to me.

"They'll never beat us; *never!*" I exclaimed. "Men like that made America great; men like that will keep her great."

And so they did.

Letter to Frank Woolner

September 22, 1975

. . . There is no substitute for the facts; no substitute for knowing what you're writing on, and the more you know the better. When I've done my research and my reporting assignments, I'm a lion; as long as I can stand on my own ground I defy the world. But when it comes to throwing a bluff, or covering holes in my background with a rose-colored mist, I'm a rabbit, an antelope or whatever frightens easily and departs fast.

If it's straight reporting, such as writing for the ticker under a deadline, I want the essential news in the first page, the first paragraph thereof, the first sentence of that paragraph, and the first words of that sentence. Be accurate above all, of course; be complete enough to give the outlines of the picture; sneak in a line of background if it is pertinent and you have one to use; and STOP.

In writing I also take advantage of a highly unreliable and often non-functioning long-range total recall. . . .

My most remarkable recollection however had to do with what I always called my best ambulance drive. I took a French captain with a broken back halfway across Paris (from the Gare de La Chappelle to the Ritz Hotel on the Champs Elysées) on a midsummer day of boiling traffic, over cobblestones and "pavé." It was 40 years later that I lay awake one night chuckling to myself about the swear-words, French and English, that I had exchanged with volatile French cab drivers . . . (I drove two miles an hour, up the front and down the back of each cobble). And suddenly I saw myself receiving back from the attendant at the receiving room entrance

one of my stretchers, on which the captain had been carried inside. . . .
And then I heard as plain as I can hear anything, the attendant saying,
"The captain said thank you for a good ride." . . . Well, I'm only human
and I must admit that the captain was a gentleman and an ornament to
the French Army, and I get out his thanks once in a while and look at
them. But I also grin at the recollection of a skinny American driver
shrieking frantically, "Species of green camel shit——" As they passed me
slowly I'd lean over quietly and say, "Grand blessé; dos cassée." And they'd
say "Oh, oh," because they were almost all reformés—healed up and discharged casualties.

My Old Girls

I had never so much as ridden in an automobile when we entered the
First World War in 1917; I was a "milishy" horse-gunner and we de-
rided them. But my old outfit and over a dozen others turned me down
for defective vision, and I didn't find a doctor who knew less about eye
examinations than I did until The United States Army Ambulance Service
with the French Army (its official title) was organized to take over the
American volunteer services in France.

War was still a horse-and-mule affair in 1917, and the iron-pants West
Pointers who ran the army didn't take this gasoline stuff seriously, so I
enlisted as an expert driver and was never called on it. We were carefully trained as stretcher-bearers and first-aid men—work that we never
did—but I went to France with exactly 125 miles of automotive driving
experience, almost all of which I had obtained for myself in extracurric-
ular ways.

My section was stationed at American Hospital No. 1 in Neuilly, on the
outskirts of Paris, and there I was assigned to Mlle Tillie, a French 1910-
model Panhard with dual rear wheels and a big wooden 12-seater ambulance body. This was a fine car. Her delicate cast-iron pistons had skirts as
thin as a postcard and were Swiss-cheesed to lighten them still further. She
had such refinements as a miniature air-pump to boost the gravity gasoline feed at high speeds, and an automatic accelerator on the oil pump—
when you go twice as fast, you need more than twice as much oil. And the
four-speed gate-type gearshift sticking out on the right side was as smooth
and fast as any synchronized stick shift made today. On it I learned to
really shift gears.

Mlle was practically a virgin because no one could get any work out of her; she had no power. But I found she was timed very late, so I set the spark as far ahead as it would go and depended on my gears for the low speeds. When we took the cars over in the Bois one Sunday morning for drag races, Mlle Tillie turned out to be the top banana.

But there were several things wrong with Mlle. The high-tension magneto was useless in rain or even fog (and Paris has better peasoupers than London) until I made an oilskin hood for it; and it leaked electricity all over the engine. The 1910 updraft carburetor, besides having a foot-long intake manifold and no choke, had a low float, so that it flooded slowly but incessantly except when I turned off the gas (which I had to do at every stop) or when the engine was burning it faster than it could leak.

This combination of loose electricity and loose gasoline made Mlle Tillie, like any other Frenchwoman, apt to catch fire whenever she became overheated. The first time it happened I was so excited that, when I found the Pyrene extinguisher rusted fast in its bracket, I removed the Pyrene, the bracket, and no less than eight wood-screws with one flick of the wrist. But when the weather got warm, Mlle caught fire whenever she was slowed down in traffic, and I became nonchalantly expert at putting her out.

Those Panhards had another exasperating failing. There was a spring button on the dash, which one pressed momentarily to short-circuit the magneto and stop the engine. But the button would stick occasionally, and then no amount of hand-cranking would start the engine. One wise guy got rich on us, starting engines at a franc a throw; he merely pulled out the button when no one was looking. It was months before he got drunk enough to blab his secret and release us from financial bondage.

Our work was with the wounded who came, with the trench mud still damp on their uniforms, in trainloads to La Chapelle freight station. We distributed them to some 150 hospitals ranging from big municipal institutions like Kariboisière and Pitié to little converted dwellings hidden in back streets and alleys. We all provided ourselves with French-English dictionaries, maps of Paris *"par arrondissement,"* and some means of defense against holdups at knifepoint by "apaches." Mine was *le coup-poing Americain* ("the American punch"); I think I was the only soldier in the A.E.F. armed with brass knuckles.

My first duty call was when the hand-grenade factory blew up in La Courneuve, the other side of Paris—a fearful catastrophe which never got much publicity. In my first two blocks I beefed a mudguard on the hospital gate, came within a whisker of being caught between two converging tramcars, and banged into a truck that stopped suddenly ahead of me.

That was dramatic. The radiator leaned back, the fan bit into it with a hair-raising screech, and a large hump appeared in the hood, all simultaneously. So I leaped onto the hood and jumped up and down on it until the hump flattened and the radiator moved away from the fan. This caused bystanding French to regard me thoughtfully and then depart talking to themselves and making circles at their temples with a forefinger. But I got to the doings, worked all afternoon, saw all the sights, and made friends with a beautiful French nurse who spoke no English. I tried to make a date with her but she kept saying something about 18 o'clock and I thought she was kidding; I had never heard of the European 24-hour clock.

My introduction to night driving was by being booted out of La Chapelle with 12 sitting cases—gassed—in a car that I couldn't drive very well, an address in a city that I didn't know and whose language I couldn't speak, and a map that I couldn't read because the street lights were blacked out. I delivered them, too—finally.

But I soon came to know the streets and how to drive them at night. There is always a little luminosity in a city, and on clear nights I could guide myself by watching the strip of sky showing between the treetops or roofs on either side of the street. In fact, it would have been easy except for the damnable French habit of creating *"rond-points"*—traffic circles—at intersections and putting monuments on them. I was barreling happily along on the Rue Something-or-Other one night during an air raid, taking a French doctor to his post, when he seized my arm and shrieked, *"À gauche!"* I whipped the wheel hard left without parley, and a good thing I did; I stopped with my right running-board almost touching a durable granite monument that was too low to show against the sky.

Another night, while cutting across the Étoile during an air raid, I encountered a group doing some last-minute sandbagging around the Arc de Triomphe. A man walked across ahead of me so I passed behind him, leaving plenty of room for him but not for the 16-foot plank that I couldn't see on his shoulder. Mlle Tillie had a roof over the driver supported by two sturdy irons (and no windshield, of course), and next morning I found that they had hit the plank right at the level of my eyes, a night-driving hazard which, like low monuments, I included in my calculations thereafter.

If night driving was fascinating, day driving was exhilarating. There never was anything like the Paris wartime traffic—no lights, no cops, no regulations, and the streets jammed with everything from bicycles to tanks. I soon saw that it was every man for himself and drove accordingly. I will admit that I always got clear off the road and up in the weeds when the French 155 mm GPF howitzers, towed on rubber-tired mounts by huge automotive "prime movers," dashed at 50 miles an hour from Paris to the outer forts during bomber alerts. Those blacked-out juggernauts turned out for nobody. But I defended my right-of-way against everyone else, so that I had considerable social intercourse and no little shredded tinware thrust upon me.

Between contestants in an impromptu race, etiquette required the loser to shrug off his dents nonchalantly; but when an innocent, i.e. woolgathering, third party was involved, there was trial by combat (verbal, usually) and the verdict was with the crowd. For of course there was always a crowd. My theory is that in Paris crowds do not gather; they are always present, in suspension in the air, and the slightest *crrrump* of a fender precipitates or crystallizes them.

The French love a good show, and I always took pains to give them one—drama, emotion, pantomime. I had two good assets. English is the only language for real swearing, and I was just off the Mexican border, where for seven months I had honed my vocabulary on a horse-drawn caisson section composed of 14 mouth-breathers and reform-school alumni, and a single-mount which could, and often did, kick me in the calf when I had my feet in the stirrups. Besides that I developed a magnificent Gallic shrug which outdid the French themselves.

I also, at first, used wit—the barbed and trenchant word. But I gave it up; it worked too well. That was the time I gave an argument to a French officer who was trying to pull rank on me, and he finally drew himself up and said coldly: "*I* am a French officer." I drew myself up, too, and replied: "*I* am an American private. Same thing." I figured that would get him, and it did. He summoned a file of tough Senegalese and chucked me into the clink.

So mostly I leaped from my car waving both arms and roaring in bilingual and profane rage, endeavoring to get maddest first. But sometimes I just shrugged, like the time a cyclist raced down a long hill behind me, passed me on the right, and then suddenly tried to cross my bows.

He landed on the seat of his pants, slid some little distance on the sharp new concrete road, and came back breathing fire and demanding identification. Wordlessly I handed him a leaf of my notebook and a pencil, and pointed to the mass of stenciled initials and numerals which covered one whole side of the ambulance. A single look told him that he was licked, and small signs of amusement on the faces of the crowd told me that I was about to win.

But then he hauled the slack of his britches around and said: "You must pay me for my *pantalons;* they are *dechirée.*"

They were, too; dechirée all to hell. There was a dramatic pause and I could feel the sentiment of the crowd change, for money is a sacred thing to a Frenchman. After all, the rich Americain, why should not he pay the honest, poor Français, no matter whose fault it was?

This was negative thinking and had to be changed. I stood stock-still until everyone was silent. Wordlessly I reached into my pocket, every eye following my hand. Deliberately I withdrew 15 centimes—about a nickel—and displayed them. Then I raised my eyebrows, drew down the corners of my mouth, spread my palms, and slowly, magnificently elevated my shoulders clear above my ears. There was an instant of spellbound silence and then the crowd breathed, "Ah!"

It was the verdict. The shoulders of the cyclist dropped despondently. He essayed a feeble imitation of my shrug. Then, placing his dechirée backside tenderly on his bicycle, he pedaled gloomily away. I was 10 kilometers beyond the *octroi* gate before I realized that I hadn't said a word during the whole performance.

Mlle Tillie had a wonderful life with me but it was kind of hard on her. Besides the normal attrition of social intercourse, there were times when someone just plain hit me. And then there was a game that I invented when I discovered that I could put the gearshift into reverse while the car was still moving forward. I'd turn into the Panhard Yard as fast as I could, with my clutch out, and shift into reverse while still moving ahead at 30 miles an hour. Simultaneously I'd floor the gun and drop in the clutch. Mlle would stop dead with a jolt and instantly shoot backward, I spinning the wheel to guide her into her stall. Then if I stood on the brake soon enough, she'd stop an inch from a brick wall. We laughing boys all played that game and I got so I could do it nearly every time.

After six months in Paris we were ordered to the front, and as we left I saw Mlle Tillie being towed away to the boneyard.

I'll never go back. Paris was a lovely town, a city of gay behinds and bucks on leave; brakeless truck drivers gleefully shouting *"Houp-la! Attention!"* as they charged indomitable bicyclists reading newspapers while pedaling through a puree of traffic; neighborhood *buvettes* which thought Scotch was a kind of vermouth and poured, and charged, accordingly; gentlemen politely tipping their hats to lady friends over the sheet-iron screen around sidewalk *pissoirs;* horse meat for dinner (we always shouted *"Eu! Eu!"*—French for gidyap); vines growing down the Seine embankment and children playing in the golden dusk while their concierge parents gossiped under the chestnuts on the Cité; stoic wounded and sweet-faced nuns—I saw it all, at dawn and noon and midnight, in fog and rain, moonlight and sunshine. But I'll never go back. Paris is not what they say, a state of mind. It is a time in a young man's life, and that time comes but once.

For the front we got the most amazing vehicle ever made, the comical little roller-skate that the French first barred from the combat area for fear it would break down and ultimately extolled as the one automobile that wouldn't; the vulgar vehicle, butt of a million jokes, that nevertheless led the whole world into new industrial, economic, and social areas. That was the Model T Ford.

She was The American Girl of her time—the farmer's wife who could cook, wash, iron, sew, feed the chickens, slop the pigs, milk the cows, hoe the garden, and breed a baby a year. She never wore her shoes, her corsets, or her teeth, and so she always looked like hell; but she was the backbone of the nation.

Model T's probably had more things wrong with them than any other mechanical contrivance ever made in quantity, but they were made wrong on purpose, so that there would be one thing right. In an age when no automobile was even faintly dependable, one could rely on Tillie T because *she always ran*. (In English, that is; in French she walked— *marché*.) She'd run with pistons so slack you could drop a nickel past them, valve clearances set by eye, ignition timed by sighting alongside a bolt-head, and spark-plugs drenched with oil; and she'd do it on anything from powdered coal to Campbell's Soup. You could run her a mile without water and then fill her up without cracking the block, coax her along all day on three cylinders, and bring her in on a fence-rail skid if a wheel collapsed. When the gas got too low to feed on a steep grade you could go up backward, and if the brake burned out you could come down on the reverse pedal. And in an era when every other kind of electrical automotive equipment was a curse and a blight on mankind, the low-tension magneto built into the Ford flywheel ran safe and unfailingly, submerged in the engine oil.

Admittedly, Tillie T had minor failings. She had no true "neutral," and cold weather stiffened the oil between her 16 clutch plates. Then she was rough to crank unless one could get oneself a good shot of *gniol*—a frightful brandy which the French distilled from barbed wire and broken glass for their troops. Rain would wet the coils on the dashboard that stepped up the low-tension current, so that one had to steal an extra set to use while drying the wet ones by body heat. And if she hit anything hard enough to bend the "wishbone"—the radius rod, a V-shaped front-axle brace—the axle would turn over and the car dart irresistibly in either a full left or a full right turn.

Our little three-stretcher ambulances were admirable for the work— light, strong, and practical—but they had one defect. Although the body was so short that holes had to be cut front and back for the stretcher handles to stick out, it still greatly overhung the back axle. When it came down from a high bounce, it pulled upward on the front spring and often broke it. So we wound German barbless entanglement wire over the frame and under the front axle, leaving only enough room for normal spring movement. It delighted the French troops to see our cars going down the road like kangaroos, lifting their front wheels off the ground at every bump.

Incidentally, they had fun with my car especially, for on the side of it I tacked a printed placard that I had salvaged from a shell-wrecked dwelling, one of the signs that were seen by the thousand all over France, and America, too, for that matter. CHAMBRE MEUBLÉE À LOUER ("Furnished Room to Let"), it said. War is, among other things, unspeakably monotonous, and even a feeble jest is a priceless thing to the infantry. Sometimes, when I'd overtake a marching column, a wave of laughter and wisecracks would follow me its whole length, with those ahead craning round to see what the joke was. The French were grand troops.

Our work was carrying the wounded from a rescue post, usually in the rear line of trench, to the advanced dressing station, and from there to the field or evacuation hospital. Most of it was done at night and all of it in the chalky, soupy mud of France. I had to clean Tillie's spark plugs at the foot of every steep hill, but then that grand old girl would hoist her skirts and just march up that hill, her cylinders ticking off as deliberately and evenly as footsteps.

I really learned night driving up there. The only lights on the road were the glowing cigarettes which rear-rank infantrymen cupped in their hands and waved vigorously when they heard an engine approaching. The chalky roads gleamed on clear nights and I could sky-drive, besides; but when it rained, and that was mostly, both road and sky turned as black as the woods and fields. Typically the roads were three-lane, with infantry and horse-drawn guns, fourgons, etc., streaming up one side and down the other, while automotive vehicles went both ways in the middle lane, ducking in and out as they had to and could. The one thing that everyone yielded to was the French truck convoys, long lines of indestructible White trucks driven by wild Annamites with black teeth. There wasn't a radiator cap or gas-tank cap in the lot, half of them were always towing the other half, and the last car was always a big *remorqueur* ("tow truck") with a winch on it. They boiled and clanked and rattled, but they kept going.

To this day, I don't know how I did it; every night, when I got to the main stem and waited for a hole in the traffic, I'd think: "This is it. This is the night I can't do it, and have to go back and admit it." But in half an hour my vision would accommodate and I'd go ahead and "do it," although afterward my eyes would burn so that I couldn't get to sleep. Strangely enough, I never hit anything on those roads at night.

I had a lot of fun with Tillie, but a few incidents are more vividly remembered than the others. For instance, there is the roughest ride she ever gave me. I got a little flu and was ordered into (U.S.) Evacuation Hospital No. 6 on a stretcher. Emmons, who used to ride with me sometimes, made the run. This was a chubby lad, critical of the driving of his betters and overfond of slumber even on the seat of a Ford, so that I used to amuse myself by making tight left turns, trying to shoot him off the slippery cushion into the bushes. He evened the score this time by rattling my noggin on the floor like dice in a box.

After some days I got homesick for Tillie and decided to resign from the hospital. So I neglected to march onto a hospital train with the other walking cases and hid out. The next morning I walked the full length of the main drag in Souilly, then Pershing's headquarters town, clad in a short French Colonial brown overcoat and purple-striped pajamas—just marched up the stem as if I owned the whole joint, and no one said a word. I even talked a Marine M.P. at the edge of town into stopping a truck to give me a ride back to the billets. There (after a fruitless search for Emmons) I shaved off 10 days' whiskers, ate a dozen pancakes, and, that night, went dancing with Tillie in the Bois de Consenvoye. I guess I was tougher in those days.

Another time I had just loaded a bunch of gas cases, in that same Consenvoye Woods, above Verdun, when the *boche* started shelling with a big piece, about a 9.2-inch naval gun. I watched the bursts moving toward us in a line and decided to capitalize on my expert knowledge of artillery by getting out of there before they got to me.

I was about 100 yards off on the flank when one of those shells inexplicably landed about 6 inches from my car. Maybe 4 inches. There was a formidable explosion; the man beside me leaped convulsively across my arms and the steering wheel; dirt and stones rained down on the roof; and about a company of lollygagging infantry lay down in the road. For the next few seconds I ran a complicated obstacle course between prone and cursing troops, and as soon as I got my passenger back onto his own seat I resigned from the artillery.

One night I had just gone on duty at that same advanced dressing station when a runner came up with word that a soldier had been wounded on the road. I was dispatched and soon found him standing on the shoulder with his medic, bandaged and ready to go; shrapnel in the thigh. I wanted to put him on a stretcher but he bucked so hard the medic finally said okay, and so I put him on the bench inside, lit the lantern, and fastened the back blackout curtain.

The hospital was in Glorieux, a suburb of the walled city of Verdun, and to reach it I had to follow a road outside the walls and over a maze of narrow-gauge railroad tracks. I kept worrying about what those tracks would do to my wounded passenger—*un blessé.*

That whole Verdun terrain—Mort Homme, Hill 301, Côte de Poivre, and all those terrible names—had been leveled, plowed, and harrowed, over and over, by storms of shell fire inconceivably violent and intense during the great attacks in 1916, so that not merely was there no brick atop another but, literally, no brick or even half-brick. The M.P.'s had had to put up signs—VILLAGE OF SO-AND-SO—so that guides and drivers could locate themselves on their maps. The ancient city of Verdun itself had suffered pitifully, for scarcely a house but was demolished or badly damaged, and there were no inhabitants now except a small French garrison in the citadel.

An M.P. hailed me as I passed the gate and, when he learned my destination, assured me that I could cut right through the town to Glorieux: "Just go down that street and. . . ."

I thought about my poor *blessé* and fell for this foolish idea—foolish because the M.P. didn't know what he was talking about. By the third turn I was hopelessly lost, and then my *blessé* became delirious, moving around, kicking the side of the car, and talking to himself in an unintelligible mumble that would rise at intervals to a loud urgent tone and then dwindle again to a murmur.

Verdun commands a natural invasion route into France, and for centuries it has been no stranger to war. It was an eerie feeling to be alone at night in a ruined and desolate city in which so many people had died violently. Their spirits seemed to press around me, weeping with terror, mute with despair, searching hopelessly among the ruins. The air was tainted with ancient agony and old woe.

I drove very slowly, looking for signs of life, for with so many troops around it was likely that someone would be in there, orders or no. And at last I saw faint candlelight in an upper window. *Aha,* I thought, *some French who have sneaked in there for a quiet place to play cards and dodge details.*

But when I got out to look for the entrance, I saw that the light upstairs was merely the sky showing through where the roof had been. The building was a ruined shell, and the windows blank eyeholes in a skull. Except for the faint ticking of my engine and the mumble of my *blessé,* it was silent—grave silent. Not a breath, not an echo, not a footfall, not a buzz of plane, muted chatter of machine-gun, or muffled slam of distant shell. Only the occasional trickling fall of a fragment of stone or crumb of mortar. I went away from there.

The moon was rising, brightening one side of the street, casting the other into dense shadow as I drove into a medieval square from which there seemed no way out. It was a little square, maybe 50 yards on a side, steeply tilted, walled, and with a barred iron gate at one side. Moonlight shone through the gate but the shadows under the wall were black and opaque, and the square only faintly illuminated. I stopped to consider what to do. The ceaseless murmuring of my *blessé* underlined the silence.

And then, as I sat there, the hair rose on my neck and suddenly I had the utter conviction that in the next instant I should see the gate open and a man in wide-topped boots, long coat, broad plumed hat, and rapier walk into the square followed by a knot of men-at-arms dragging a sweating, quivering wretch to torture. Suddenly those old walls seemed saturated with screams and groaning, soaked with tears and blood. I went quickly, blindly out, taking every turn I came to, and then I was hailed; I was back at the gate from which I had started. This time I took the road I knew, and in 20 minutes my poor *blessé* was in safe hands.

My last adventure with Tillie was in the Vosges Mountains on our way to the Rhine with the French Army of Occupation. About dark one day I delivered a measles case in another town and, as I had no headlights and didn't have to be back that night anyway, I decided to return in the morning. But later the lieutenant came along in his touring car and offered to lead me home. He had lights.

The touring car was faster than Tillie and the looey too green a driver to understand that when he went around a turn he left me in the dark. So he kept right on while I had to feel my way, and when I topped a hill I saw him three bends ahead and going away. I just had to get back on his tail so I pulled down the spark and gas handles and started sky-driving. I soon came to where the road dropped down and turned left into a notch between two big mountains; I couldn't see it but it had to be there. The tough part was that I'd have to estimate where it turned.

I watched the edge of that left-hand mountain, sharp against the sky, come back and back until it was opposite my left elbow. "Now!" I told myself firmly, and turned left. It was the greatest, and the most difficult, act of faith in myself that I have ever performed.

I almost made it; I missed it by only a foot. My left wheels scalped the base of the mountain for 30 feet before I could wrench the car out of the ditch and back onto the road. But the drop had bent the wishbone; next morning the wheel marks showed that Tillie had shot straight across the road into the opposite ditch. I stayed with her and wrestled her back onto the road a second time, but that heavy tail swinging in a half-circle was too much for her—I was doing about 40 miles an hour.

She started to roll on her radiator cap and the front wall of the body, flipping her tail high in the air. Down she went on her side with a crash of loose tools, up onto the roof while the floorboards dropped down on my legs, and over onto her other side. The canvas hood above the driver's seat collapsed over my head and I shot out of the tangle like a flushed grouse as soon as the car stopped rolling.

Even in this extremity Tillie had done her best for me. She was clear of the road, with her radiator on the edge, and her tail across the ditch so that I could crawl underneath and get stuff out of the running-board toolboxes. I was eating beans by lantern light when the looey came back looking for me.

The infantry was on the road at dawn, and my liveliest recollection of the whole incident (aside from those floorboards) is of the kidding that I received.

"What are you doing, *bouleversée comme ça?*" they'd sing out jovially, one after another, and each time I'd reply that I'd been flying too low and had brushed the treetops. They'd nod approval of this correctly jaunty attitude and march on laughing. What grand troops they were!

The head-high front wall of the body was what saved my bacon, and it is easy to understand why nowadays I like a steel roof and plenty of good, strong, <u>vertical</u> body pillars, and view dimly the current engineering practice of figuring in the window glass as part of the supporting structure of the car. I keep remembering those floor-boards.

I left the section soon afterward but some months later I saw Tillie when she passed through the Base Camp on her way to the motor pool at Romorantin. She had had a wonderful nine months with me, but she looked haggard and I knew she was not long for this world.

The Last Race

Ere the drivers start for the front-line posts,
For their duty tour at a first-aid "shop"
They chat of their work with the battling hosts
As they crank their cars at the *relais* stop.

They tell of new pockets of mustard gas,
Of a crossroads shelled and a byway stopped,
Of a road where a *voiture* still may pass
With only the risk of a chance shell dropped.

Then a driver calls to his parting mates,
As they climb in their cars and the motors roar,
"There's a straight, smooth stretch by the city gates
And we'll race at dawn. Are you on? *Au 'voir.*"

Then they roll away in the murky night
To lonely adventure in death's wide courts,
And they meet at the dawn's first graying light
To burn up the road to the city port.

When Peter, the night before Judgment Day,
Drafts the Final Evacuation plan,
He will call all those drivers up and say,
"To the graveyards! And bring me every man!"

They they'll talk, as of yore, of unknown roads,
Of a hollow deep and a high hilltop,
And they'll wonder who will be in their loads,
As they crank their cars at the *relais* stop.

Then one will call out to his parting mates
As they climb in their cars and the motors roar,
"There's a straight, smooth stretch by the Pearly Gates
And we'll race at dawn. Are you on? *Au 'voir.*"

Then they'll roll away in the murky night
To lonely adventure in death's wide courts
And they'll meet in the Last Dawn's graying light
And burn up the road to the Golden Ports.
                            —Verdun, October 31 (ca. 1919)

The Smartest Critter

A n agreeable surprise is the discovery that Mr. Sparse Grey Hackle, an occasional correspondent who is an authority on hellgrammites, Royal Coachman bivisibles, and railroad trains, also is a deep student of mules.

Mr. Hackle read a tale published here recently about Dave Camerer's homesick horse, Timber—part Cleveland Bay, part Irish, part Borden's, and part homing pigeon—which broke out of winter quarters and bucked Sunday traffic for 7 miles up the Merritt Parkway on a foggy night to return to the Camerer homestead in North Stamford, Connecticut.

Sparse put down the paper and took up his typewriter. He deposes:

"That horse you mention may have been part Borden's but his intelligence tells me he is also part mule. This is the most intelligent of the animals, including man.

"Mules do not bet on basketball games, pay $50 for 'ringside' seats, drink flavored alcohol under the name of whiskey, kid themselves that a fishhook with feathers on it looks like a live insect, sit all day in a leaky boat trolling, or write letters to sports columnists."

The Earliest Guided Missile

"Mules remember people they don't like and wait until they get a chance to get even; mules don't like everybody. They do not have to peek through a telescope or line up a set of sights to hit the target; they just listen until they locate it and then shoot by estimate. The lowest target score ever made by a mule in this way is 100 percent.

"Mules do not require a Dedeaux system or the National Labor Board to figure out for them what is a full day's work. They know it to the ounce-inch, and when they have done it they refuse overtime, with or without time and a half. You can build a fire under a mule who has done his day's work and he will only move far enough to get the wagon over the fire.

"Although many people don't know it, horses can faint, worry, get hysterical, and become neurotic. Mules make the other guy faint, worry, etc.

"Unlike men and horses, mules have sense enough to keep away from women. You can see women handling horses but never mules. It takes men to handle mules. Mules understand and appreciate masculine language and prefer names which do not sound good in mixed company. It would break a mule's heart to be named Timber.

They Get You in the End

"I doubt that horse story you related. Horses haven't enough sense of direction to find the open door of the barn they live in. Down on the border, when our horses got loose they would permit themselves to be caught up when they became thirsty; they couldn't find the water tank, 300 yards away, at which they had been watered three times a day for six months. But mules can find any food or water within walking distance and go to it in a straight line.

"If a horse bumps his head on a low overhang, he will toss his head higher and harder until he kills himself. One bump educates a mule for a lifetime; he will never hit that spot again.

"If you always pay attention to what you are doing and always do things right, you can be around horses a lifetime without getting hurt. But no man can be around mules without eventually getting it.

"That is why mules are disappearing. They are just too smart for men to cope with."

(Red Smith's column, January 31, 1950.)

Panther's Scream

Those New England "panthers" have set Sparse Grey Hackle reminiscing. He writes:

"Back in 1916, the First Battalion, Second New York Field Artillery, was camped at the target range at Monte Cristo Ranch, Texas. I was corporal of the guard. During the day, one of my sentries, named Mason, had hidden his blankets in a boxcar on the adjacent siding so he could sneak in at night and sleep in some loose straw. But he had been seen.

"A panther had been active in that wild section, and we were having a fine Mexican mountain lion scare. So three of our jokers spent the evening plying Mason with lion stories and then hid in the boxcar before he got there. As he came into the pitch-black interior they rustled the straw and emitted a few meows. 'Who's there?' quavered Mason. Then they let loose with the Brooklyn conception of a mountain lion's scream.

"It worked. The petrified Mason was the worst-scared man in Texas. He pulled his Colt and distributed seven .45 slugs in a panic-stricken circle. After that he was only the fourth worst-scared man in Texas. Yelling twice as loudly, the three 'mountain lions' charged Mason, who was blocking the doorway, and they all poured out of the car.

"For an instant, as I viewed the pile-up, I sure thought I had some dead men to explain to Colonel Wingate. Then the pile exploded because Mason, who was on the bottom, still thought he was attacked by mountain lions and was defending himself with fists, teeth, brogans, and an empty pistol. You never saw so many black eyes, bloody noses, tin ears, and lumps in your life.

"The moral of this story is that it is just as dangerous to be panther as to meet one.

"Sparse Grey Hackle, who in those days was known as 'Jockey Miller.'" (Donald Stillman's column, January 9, 1946.)

To Arms!

Three o'clock in the morning. Moonlight, bright enough to read by, flooded the camp and the deathlike hush of a Texas night pervaded it. I stood behind a clump of cactus, outside the military lines, and furtively watched the sentry walking his beat.

Suddenly, off to my right, an automatic shotgun yammered out five shots, and a burst of pistol fire answered. The sentry ran that way, dragging out his weapon. There were more pistol shots. Then footsteps sounded behind me and Private Handshakin' James O'Malley appeared, shotgun in hand.

"Come on!" he whispered, stooping to help me lift a gunnysack containing twenty dead ducks. He ran for the horse lines, dived into the shadow of a pile of baled hay, and tossed gun and bag under the protecting tarpaulin. I looked over the forage pile and saw the trumpeter run into the company street. He hesitated an instant, then raised his bugle, and the high, hysterical beat of the "Call to Arms" rang over the camp. "To arms! To arms! They're coming! They're coming!"—Men clad in long white "issue" underwear boiled out of the tents.

We certainly had started something, I reflected morosely, another crack-up to the credit of flitter-headed Handshakin' O'Malley, the corner-loafing son of a New York politician. He, the crackbrained harp, had started this episode and brought it to a catastrophic conclusion.

I thought of the fine day he had broached his idea and reflected bitterly that we had not known when we were well off. It had been a brilliant East Texas morning in the fall, with the trade wind booming, as always, through the camp. Chewing our after-breakfast tobacco, we had been idling in the picket lines, draped comfortably over shovel handles, between the protecting horses which hid us from the top sergeant.

We were National Guardsmen who had gone from New York to Texas to fight "the Mexican War" and had remained to chambermaid the horse lines for months after the war scare had vanished. We felt imposed on and were doing as little work as possible until the War Department should release us from our bad bargain.

O'Malley spat copiously and I did, too, for we had but recently learned to chew in order to be tough artillerymen, and we were not yet too friendly with eating tobacco. I regarded him with distaste. His round vacant face, with its scattering of freckles, reminded me of a half-baked cup of custard. *Half-baked* was a term that just fitted O'Malley. Now his china blue eyes roamed the heavens and an expression of interest disarranged his freckles.

"Lookit the birds," he invited.

High in the sky was a sight to stir the blood of a sportsman. Four flights of ducks, each moving in a lopsided V, points forward, were sweeping across the heavens in parallel flight, headed due south. I knew that this was the vanguard of the great fall duck migration from their breeding grounds under the Arctic Circle to their winter quarters in Mexico and Central America, and as I watched the regular, rapid beat of those powerful wings boring the streamlined bodies through the air, a prickle of restlessness ran up my back and into my hair.

"Ducks. Swell shooting. I used to go duck hunting with my father in Great South Bay," I offered reflectively.

O'Malley's cup-custard face assumed the expression of a child regarding a new toy as his protruding eyes swiveled in my direction. "Tell us about it," he invited amiably, and rearranged his carcass around the shovel handle. I began, nothing loath, for a new topic of conversation was something to cherish in those days of boredom, and had conducted the hunt in great detail as far as the placing of the decoys when a harsh, loud voice assaulted my ears.

"What are you guys doin'—posin' for animal crackers?" it demanded. Automatically we stopped talking and started shoveling.

"Nah, nah, none of that! Attention!" barked the voice. We faced the top sergeant and came to attention.

First Sergeant Brandenburg was undoubtedly the prototype of the famous A.E.F. character, The Hard-Boiled Top. Although he had Old Soldier written all over him and possessed an easy assumption of authority that argued a former status as a non-commissioned officer, he always denied having had any service prior to the time he had left his job at the Fulton Fish Market to come to Texas with us. I have always thought privately that he had been a non-com in the regular army under some other name, had deserted at the promptings of his noble thirst, and was back with the horses and guns because he couldn't keep away. But he was a soldier, every inch, and a dandy top kick.

"A fine pair of goldbricks! Always duckin' the detail! You'll do an extra tour of guard for this—both of ya. Report to Sergeant Brady at first call for guard mount. And now bear down on these banjos, you crackerbacks, and get that picket line cleaned," he barked, and strode away.

O'Malley spouted tobacco juice—he had nearly drowned—and went languidly back to shoveling.

"Big hunk of cheese," he grumbled, using an expression which was then the last word in slang. "Guard, guard, guard! I gotta snootful of it. I was on a week ago and now I have to stay up all night again."

It was true. Ours was a large camp requiring a numerous guard detail. What with the other details required in an artillery outfit, we were always short of men for the guard, and this unpleasant assignment came all too frequently to those on the duty roster. So Brandenburg was always on the lookout for guards, and his favorite punishment was to move the offender up out of his rightful place to the top of the roster.

"To hell with him," grumbled O'Malley. "I'll soon be out of this. I wrote my old man a month ago to get me out and he said he would.

Believe me," he added with a gleam of pride, "when he goes after any-thing, it's as good as his. He can go right to the governor."

Alas, potent as Old Man O'Malley might be with the governor, his hypothetical intervention did us no good with Sergeant Brandenburg. At six o'clock O'Malley and I, clean and shining, were marched off after the ceremony of guard mount and assigned to adjoining posts along the edge of camp, on the McAllen Road.

A little guard goes a long way with me, and as soon as I had seen the officers safely off to the mess hall, I ceased to "walk my post in a military manner" and sauntered toward O'Malley. I found him in conversation with a stranger whose battered and muddy automobile was parked by the roadside.

It was a friend of O'Malley's, Doc Hutchinson, a typical elderly Texan, sunbaked and windburned, who just by chance was one of the best duck hunters in this part of the state. Well, you can guess what happened. Doc came by and picked us up the next evening around seven o'clock, passes in pocket, and we drove out, seemingly forever, over the flats of East Texas until we came to Doc's favorite duck pond just before daybreak.

As we approached, the whole surface of the pond seemed to heave into the air as a great flock of ducks took off at once. We improvised a mesquite, sagebrush, and reed blind and soon were dealing with the incoming flights. It seems unbelievable, but I assure you that all day long, at intervals of a few minutes to half an hour, ducks came into the pond, one to four or five flights at a time. Mallards, black ducks, redheads, blue and green teal, butterballs. Without decoys, and with only the sketchiest kind of blind, we killed ducks until we tired of it. With Doc's deadly shooting, my hit-one-miss-one, and O'Malley's ineptness, we nevertheless ended up with 114 ducks!

We piled into Doc's car, soggy and bushed, and headed back to camp, not realizing that we were in for a much longer ride back than we planned. First the old-fashioned magneto went dead, then we punctured a tire, then the clutch started to slip. We managed to get going again after each breakdown, but when we got to McAllen it was not the anticipated 11 P.M., but 3 A.M. We were over pass, and due for the guardhouse.

"I got an idea!" said O'Malley, although he didn't look it. "Drive down the back trail and leave us off behind the camp. We can run the guard if we pull all the sentries over to the other side of camp. Leave us take the auto gun, will you, Doc? I'll get it to you tomorrow."

So Doc left us in the brush behind camp, with the shotgun and a gunny bag full of twenty ducks. We waited until the clank of Doc's car died in the distance, then threaded through the brush until we could see the sentry walking No. 12 post on the edge of camp.

And then O'Malley had pulled his idea, which was nothing less than to empty the shotgun in the air at a point sufficiently removed so that, when the sentries naturally ran there to see what was going on, we could cross the unguarded line and get into camp before they came back. The pungent and unconsidered result had been that he had nearly been killed by the return fire of the sentries and that we had precipitated a call to arms to which the whole camp, in momentary expectation of a Mexican bandit attack, was boiling out like bees from an overturned hive.

As we hid in the shadow of the forage pile, men came running through the gun park toward us in the brilliant moonlight, fastening pistol belts as they came. Shoes, underwear, and pistols they all seemed to have, but only a few wore breeches, the laces flying. O'Malley and I slipped into the picket line, untied our teams, and started to back them out.

Shouting, the firstcomers dashed into the line of dozing horses, which exploded into the air like a covey of grouse. In an instant they were rearing wildly, snorting, kicking, squealing. I saw one with his forelegs over the picket line, another down and lashing out frantically. White-clad men flew out of the line, squeezed or kicked out by frenzied horses.

O'Malley and I were clear just in time. We led our pairs to the gun and started harnessing. In a moment the other pairs were coming up on the trot and all around I could hear the clash of steel collars latching, the clap of saddles, and the jingle of trace chains. The "milishy" was turning out!

The white-clad drivers of the First Section—one gun and one caisson—swung up into the saddle and the cannoneers scrambled onto their seats. A great shout of "Gangway! Gangway!" went up, and galloping hooves battered the baked ground while gun-shields and pintle-hooks clanked. Lieutenant McSweeney thundered after it on his big roan, quirting on both sides and volleying short blasts on his whistle for gangway. Bright in the moonlight, the drivers bent in their saddles, whipping wildly, while the cannoneers on the bouncing ammunition chests clung to the hold-on straps and shouted "Let's go! Let's go! Yay-y-y-y!" The caisson slewed around the corner and a white figure shot it off in a low arc, over the far wheel and into the cactus. A huge cloud of dust rose behind the flying carriages. The flying gun was going to its post with the cavalry screen, a mile from camp.

The rest of the battery was ready to roll. Drivers stood to their pairs, holding the horses by their heads and hopping on one foot to pull up trailing shoelaces. Cannoneers stood by the carriages. Noncoms checked the harnessing. The captain came by.

"Nice work, boys," he said in his quiet way, and went off to a conference with the officer of the guard. In a moment the bugle sounded "Recall" and we went to unhitch and unharness.

Knots of half-clad men stood around the gun park and horse lines, too excited to go back to bed. Rumors that someone had "run the guard" began to spread. I retrieved the shotgun and hid it in my bed, but it was impossible to carry a sack of ducks through the wakeful camp without discovery. We had to leave them under the tarp and trust to luck.

"The Top wants to see you," our non-com informed O'Malley and me as we were preparing to turn out for drill call. We went to his tent in silent trepidation.

"Jockey," said the Top incisively, "you and Handshakin' were the first men out on the call to arms and you were the only men fully dressed. How about it?"

"Why, Sergeant, what do you mean?" I protested virtuously.

"Just a couple of good soldiers," smirked Handshakin'.

"Well, never mind," said the Top. "We don't want a scandal, so you won't get a court. But you'll both do guard duty, every other night, until further notice! While I'm about it, take a month apiece in the kitchen, too.

"Go over there now, they've got a job for you, picking the feathers off twenty ducks. The non-coms are going to have a duck dinner," he concluded, and walked away.

O'Malley and I glared after him. He was laughing, silently but heartily.

Christmas in Bed

For several years now Mr. Sparse Grey Hackle, angler, has passed Christmas Day in bed for one reason or another, though he gets up between holidays and becomes a man of action in a trout stream. It wasn't altogether a surprise, therefore, to get a Christmas letter from Lenox Hill Hospital. It hasn't much to do with sports, but it's about Christmas, more or less:

"This big hearty nurse grabbed the sheets and gave a heave. The bedclothes came flying. So did my watch, which was under the pillow; it exploded against the wall like a grenade. I sent it to a repair man with a hurry-call for a 'lender,' because even in a hospital a man is not a man unless he has a railroad watch and a straight razor.

"I got a peach of a 'lender.' Next morning this big, hearty girl grabbed the sheets and gave a heave . . . yep.

"I am back in my favorite Christmas resort having my tonsils out. I have been waiting eagerly for Dr. Oberrender to show up and check me out, but now I dunno. It has been snowing all day and if I go home I'll have to clear the driveway.

Snow and Cactus

"There is a resident doctor here to whom the Christmas snow looks entirely different. He is Dr. Alberto Amaya of Bogotá, Colombia. Until this morning he had never seen snow. He galloped wildly from window to window and finally accumulated, and proudly displayed, a real snowball—a trickling, walnut-sized lump of city-colored snow. It reminded me of something and at last I remembered what.

"Back in 1916 when we were on a huge troop train bound for the Mexican border, our train came to one more of its innumerable halts. I gazed wearily at the landscape and then bounced high with excitement. I hustled out, sprinted fifty yards to seize my treasure, then legged it back as the train started up.

"The skipper, coming down the aisle to reprove me for leaving the train, stopped spellbound when he saw what I was carrying. I marched proudly with it through the cars, attracting great interest, until a captain cornered me and said: 'Throw that away! I understand the Mexicans make liquor out of it. I'm having enough trouble with this so-and-so battery already.'

"What I had found was a single lobe of prickly pear, the commonest variety of cactus in that part of the world.

Christmas on the Border

"Within two weeks we had amassed a pile of prickly pear sixteen feet high and a half a mile long in the course of clearing our campsite. I personally (with the aid of two mules) transported tons of it. And nobody ever found out how the Mexicans made liquor out of it.

"What I mean is, Dr. Amaya may soon find a lot more snow than he needs. 'I want to go skiing—Zwee!' he exclaimed at one point in our interview. Too much snow and too little experience with skis add up to the Fracture Ward, Doctor.

"I am just remembering that we were not home for that 1916 Christmas, either. We had been expecting orders every day for seven months and we felt pretty low. So we decided we would make our own Christmas, and we started with a tree.

"There wasn't a tree of any description within three hundred miles of the border, so we took a sixteen-foot tent pole and nailed on tent stakes for branches. Big two-notchers and little single-notchers and a few tiny shelter-half pegs to finish off.

"Of course, this was a horse-artillery outfit, so you can understand that some of the gifts had a humorous angle which we cannot go into here. There was a Bull Durham bag for the top sergeant.

O Tempora! O Mores!

"The homemade Christmas tree invented by C Battery, Second New York Field Artillery, became a legend. When the regiment's successor, the 205th Field Artillery, went to camp in Spartansburg, North Carolina, in World War II, the boys bowed to tradition and made a tent-pole Christmas tree.

"They were roundly criticized by the local newspaper for their 'sacrilege'!

"If they don't let me out of here pronto, I'm going looking for a sixteen-foot tent pole. Merry Christmas!"

(Red Smith's column, December 25, 1955.)

Lunch with Sparse Grey Hackle

One recalled that there had arrived last winter a letter from Mr.
... Sparse Grey Hackle which had not been published. It had been
written during the run of the Sportsmen's Show here, and it conveyed a
friendly warning against associating with two of the show's performers—
"especially," Sparse wrote, "if they show signs of martinis.

Mr. Big George and Mr. Little George

"Mr. Big George," Sparse explained, "a cop in my town, stands six and a
half feet, is as slim as a greyhound, and eats only one meal a day, starting
a 8 A.M. and ending at 11 P.M.

"Mr. Little George, a Nova Scotia lumberjack, is built like a fireplug
and for many years has owned and operated a food foundry. Naturally, a
beautiful friendship has developed, but you must know of their hobby to
judge how perfect their confidence in each other is.

"These guys are addicted to shooting at small objects with big black
pistols and large heavy rifles having one barrel to shoot through and the
other to look through. The objects are in their hands or mouths or on
their persons. They stage an act which is a great hit on the fruit-cup-and-
half-broiled-chicken circuit on account of the audience expecting someone to get killed.

"For instance, one stunt is shooting holes through Alka-Seltzer tablets
held between the other guy's fingers. Since the bullet is one-quarter of an
inch thick and the tablet three-quarters of an inch wide, it makes a fairly
tight fit as shooting fits go. The situation is complicated by the fact that

these firearms shoot higher and higher as the barrel gets warmer. They haven't put on thermometers yet, but they have been figuring on it ever since one of the Georges suffered a light finger-scorch from a .22 high-speed bullet. At twenty yards, yet.

The Prudence of Sparse

"The pistol is used for coarse shooting, exploding balloons—small balloons, under-inflated—which Mr. Little George holds between his knees or under his armpits.

"There is also the matter of trimming the ash off a cigarette—not a long, new cigarette, but a short, old butt—held in the lips. Spectators who are invited to hold the cigarette usually decline for fear of getting ashes in their eyes.

"The two Georges are so much in love with this activity that they not only do it for free, but also furnish their own ammunition. The matter of hospital expenses has not arisen yet, but it will. My own idea is that anyone who allows people to shoot things off his head has the kind of head that is not injured by ordinary bullets, but they resent my saying so.

"They keep inviting me to participate passively in their act, but don't you waste any carfare coming out to Darien to see me do it. I stick to safe, humorous pastimes like sneaking up behind Brink guards and saying, 'Hands up!'

Keep Your Hands in Your Pockets

"The two Georges make a big thing of the Sportsmen's Show. Last year they attended on a schedule which started with nine martinis apiece before dinner. Later in the evening Mr. Big George bought a complete spinning outfit, which for a fly fisherman is the equivalent of appearing in Times Square with no pants on, and Mr. Little George attempted to enter the wood-chopping contest with his pocketknife.

"If you should meet these guys, keep away from them, particularly if they show signs of martinis. Above all, do not hold up any small object in your hand while they back away from you."

(Red Smith's column, September 20, 1950.)

Sparse Holiday

Homecoming from Saratoga was cheered by two items in the accumulated mail. Besides the customary chummy little greetings from the Warm-hearted Finance Company, there was a note from Mr. Sparse Grey Hackle, the gentleman angler, reporting a successful completion of a vacation, or survival, anyway.

"It ought to be a relief for you to read about it," he writes, "because it had no fish in it at all. I spent it in an aluminum canoe with a 65-pound pointer named Boy and his owner, Big George the ex-cop."

(Though Mr. Hackle's square name, Miller, suggests that his heritage could include a wee dram of German blood, he has never been one to fret about *Lebensraum.* He drives, by preference, one of those foreign bugs which fits his ample torso like a lady's girdle, and it seems improbable that they held any dances in that canoe. Assuming that Big George is the size of the average ex-cop, the craft had well over 500 pounds aboard not counting fishing tackle, camping gear, and provisions.)

Anyhow: "Boy has a nose like the muzzle of a double-barreled shotgun and he can rest his chin on the table and pull a slice of bread toward him from a foot away, 2 inches at a sniff. And he can strike with the speed of a rattlesnake.

Love and Caviar

"One evening my hostess unwrapped a quarter-pound bar of butter and put it on the table. A moment later she exclaimed fretfully that she was sure she had put out butter—where was it? She unwrapped another bar, turned to the stove, turned back, and the butter was gone.

"She spoke querulously about this at some length, which is understandable at present prices, but she couldn't quite convince herself that the blandly dignified Boy could have ingested half a pound of butter in two winks. I knew better.

"I took Boy outside and put my ear against his stomach and there was a lot more internal activity audible than an unfed dog should contain. I didn't say anything in the house—I wouldn't squeal on a fellow dog; but I gave him a private talking-to and he manifested contrition as well as appreciation of my leniency.

"Then we went out on the porch for cocktails and Boy came up behind me, put his chin on my shoulder, and laid his velvet cheek against mine. He then removed the caviar canapé from my grasp and looked longingly at my martini.

"I didn't reproach him. It was my own fault for forgetting something I learned long ago, that love always has a solid financial foundation. Anyway, how many dogs can appreciate an 8:1 martini made of the best imported ingredients?

Cheval en Casserole

"For lunch one day we took a can of hash apiece for George and me and a can of dog food for Boy. George fed the dog and we started on our hash, but halfway through George glared at the label on his can and spoke anguished words. He had eaten half a can of a well-known kennel ration.

"I tried to cheer him by telling him how much horse meat I had eaten in the French Army, and made funny remarks like 'giddyap, whoa!' but he seemed to have lost his appetite. He refused the rest of my hash. After a while I didn't think so much of it, either, so Boy got the whole business.

"His victory was brief. This dog goes ashore from a canoe while it is still 5 feet from the bank. This time there were 10 feet of lily pads fringing the shore and he decided to walk across these. He took his customary 5-foot leap and, of course, disappeared.

"Have you ever seen a double-barreled shotgun spouting two streams of water like the twin monitors on a fireboat? It is the sort of fishing memory that brightens one's declining years.

"Oh yes; I didn't catch a damn fish."

(Red Smith's column, August 21, 1961.)

Man's (Sportswriter's) Best Friend

Let us give thanks for blessings large and small, namely: the log in the fireplace, the ribbon in the typewriter, the fried bologna on the festive board, and, above all, the United States mail. Without the postman there would be no letters from Mr. Sparse Grey Hackle, gentleman, sportsman, and friend of all sportswriters in need. In need of a holiday, that is. With an unfailing sense of timing, Mr. Hackle writes:

"Our mutual friend Mr. Big George Evans is just back from a week's woodcock shooting in Maine with Boy. Boy is a 65-pound, jet-propelled pointer who doesn't like automobiles. He publicly insults the cars of George's visitors, and when traveling he whizzes around inside George's Pontiac like a misguided missile, treading on George's countenance and jumping on the accelerator.

"So before starting on this long trip, George consulted the vet.

"'Sure,' said the vet, 'give him these tranquilizers when he gets restless.'

Houdini with Liver-Colored Spots

"I cannot get a coherent account of what happened, beyond the statement that, although Boy habitually eats pillows, furniture, briefcases, and parts of the milkman, he does not and will not eat tranquilizers. In the end, George took the tranquilizers himself.

"The first night in Maine, the cabin turned colder than a curb broker's heart"—Mr. Hackle works in Wall Street—"and Boy decided to sleep in the bed. Not with his master, but instead of him. The next night, George put an old sweatshirt on Boy and tied it securely around the dog's waist. It looked a bit improbable, but it kept Boy warm.

206

"In the morning George drove into town and locked Boy, still wearing the sweatshirt, in the car while he went to breakfast. Now, I do not expect you to believe that a pointer measuring 2 feet tall at the shoulder and 10 inches across the chest can unlatch, push open, and climb through the ventilator window of a 1953 Pontiac.

"I will merely bet you 10 bucks that this one can and, as soon as George had crossed the street, did.

Bright College Years

"Certain invalids were tottering down the main street of Cherryfield on their way to the dispensary for their morning dose of health-restoring bitters. They leaped violently upon beholding a liver-colored dog wearing a Notre Dame sweatshirt extruding through the ventilator window of a car. They departed rapidly, looking straight ahead and muttering.

"Boy paid them no heed. He walked directly to a parked automobile and insulted it. George did not notice whether the car had Oklahoma license plates but I think it likely, for that was the day you-know-who defeated you-know-whom at football.

"The sweatshirt and the affronted car are no longer available, but I can produce the dog and the Pontiac anytime you produce the 10 bucks."

(Red Smith's column, November 28, 1957.)

Old-Timer Puts Oar In

Rowing Is Called Best Propulsion
When Fishing for Bass or Pickerel

An oarsman on an ancient galley made himself immortal by his plan to leave the sea when his hitch was up.

"I'll march inland with an oar over my shoulder until someone asks me what it is," he vowed.

Today he would get no farther than the Fifty-Seventh National Boat Show; boatmen have forgotten rowing, and think sculling is throwing at the batter's head.

Gasoline has supplanted muscle for utility and even for pleasure, but for sport, particularly for fishing, a rowing boat is needed. The dinghy, built square to hold a dozen people, and the "rowboat," built wide at the stern so it will not squat under power, are not real rowboats. To see a real rowing boat, one must look at the lovely lines of an old-time whaleboat, a Grand Banks fishing dory, or even a slim river rowboat on the upper Susquehanna or Delaware.

The trout angler doesn't need a boat; he wades the stream to cast his fly. But a sport, no more than a nation, cannot exist with only a population of royalty; a viable social order must also have a peasantry. So besides trout anglers, there must be fishermen for black bass, pickerel, salmon, and walleyes; and most of this fishing is done from boats.

A Machine-Age Holdout

An outboard motor is a handy thing for a long trip to the fishing grounds, but what one needs for propelling a boat noiselessly along the shoreline of a bass lake at one-half to two-thirds of a mile an hour—the proper speed for fly-rod fishing with bass bugs—is not an outboard motor but a well-trained wife. Another fisherman will do, but then you can only fish half of the time; the other half, you'll be rowing for him.

But even a real rowing boat needs some improvements that will be hard to find at the show. Casting from the stern seat requires the fisherman to twist his body ninety degrees, a position no one can hold for long without cramps. Some sort of swivel-top stool, preferably one that can be fastened to the boat, would be a godsend. If the caster stands—and that's the best way to do it—any small jerk with the oars will send him overboard, and some wives are small jerks! To prevent this, every whaleboat was provided with a "clumsy-cleat," a board with a notch in which the harpooner could brace his leg. Captain Ahab, in *Moby Dick,* had a special notch in his boat to accommodate his wooden leg. A clumsy-cleat in a fishing boat would avert many an involuntary bath.

Fifty years ago bow-facing oars, a simple parallelogram of steel rods that allowed the rower to face the way he was going, were a standard article. For years after they went off the market, the guides and fishermen who used the winding waterways of the Great Dismal Swamp repaired their bow-facing oars by welding and brazing as the parts wore out. It is a mystery to me why no one is making these useful devices now.

There is also need, particularly by the lone fisherman, for what I might call an un-anchoring device. He can anchor in a strong current by just chucking the anchor overboard. Un-anchoring is another matter if, as often happens, he needs a little slack to get his anchor loose, because no one can row against a current and simultaneously pull up the anchor.

A Memory on File

I once anchored in the spillway current below the power dam in the Chicoutimi River and, if I hadn't had a sharp knife and an anchor rope instead of a chain, I'd be there yet. I also met a chap once whose anchor *was* on a chain, and the chain bolted to the boat. His anchor was caught in some bridge-builder's scrap in the Farmington River when it was rising rapidly after an all-night rain.

When I encountered him his bow was only two inches above the water and in another hour he'd have had to swim for it in an ugly current. Fortunately, I had a file in my fly book. It was only four inches long, but it was brand new and sharper than a serpent's tooth so it took me less than a minute to clip a link out of the cow chain and earn the fisherman's hearty thanks.

Car-top boats can be a problem, particularly on a windy day. One of my friends has a Volkswagen camper with a boat on top, and in a steady gale he can get across the Tappan Zee Bridge only by carrying two points of weather helm—but if it is gusty he requires all three traffic lanes to make the transit.

There is also the matter of having muscle enough to unload and launch a boat. Some fishermen, especially those who go it alone, have to rely on livery boats. On these a cement block anchor, stubby six-foot sea oars, worn-out open rowlocks, and a tin-can bailer are standard equipment. The user of livery boats can double his enjoyment by providing himself with a pair of seven-foot, wide-bladed spruce oars equipped with leathers and full-ring oarlocks so mounted that they can be clamped to a boat gunwale; a little five-pound mushroom anchor on a strong, light line; a scoop bailer with a rubber edge (scraping with a can scares the fish) and a big sponge; and a low stool with a revolving top.

Better yet, he might just switch over to fly fishing for trout.

Houseboats . . . Bah!

So now the marine tenderfoot has discovered something new: House-boats are big this season. Someone should tell him that for a full century after the Louisiana Purchase in 1803 the Ohio and Mississippi Rivers and their major tributaries provided far better and faster transit, and carried far more traffic between the Great Lakes area and the Gulf of Mexico, than the few miserable, unconnected roads that existed before the coming of the automobile.

Today's houseboats are temples of luxury compared to the shantyboats of yesteryear, but they do not go on voyages; people just tie up in some quiet spot and devote themselves to bathing and drinking cocktails. Today's vacationing houseboater is only a pallid imitation of the lusty shantyboaters who thronged the rivers less than 100 years ago.

For in those days, besides the rafts of commercial barges pushed by steam towboats, there was a great, continual migration along the rivers of craft on which people dwelt and, one way or another, made their living.

When Nathaniel Bishop rowed a Barnegat sneak-box—a duck-hunter's skiff—from Pittsburgh to the Gulf in 1875, he passed more than 200 of these shantyboats and family boats on the 1,000-mile length of the Ohio, he noted in his book, *Four Months in a Sneak-Box*.

At Best a Scow

At its best, the family boat was a scow strongly built of white oak, anywhere from 15 feet wide to 60 or 70 feet long, on which a wooden cabin was built.

The principal sources of this floating population were, I think, the Civil War, which taught the manhood of the nation to live a rough outdoor life and engendered wanderlust, and the economic convulsions that made the latter half of the 19th century an era of hard times during which innumerable industrious, capable artisans and craftsmen were continually out of work through no fault of their own. Many of those took to the rivers.

Tinsmiths, shoemakers, barbers, sewing-machine repairmen, harness makers, carpenters, cobblers, and other craftsmen lived on the river, tying up at a town as long as they could find work there, then dropping down to the next settlement on a never-failing 5-mile current.

Besides these were all sorts of performers, professors, teachers, musicians, lecturers, actors, minstrels, and entertainers who traveled in a variety of small craft and whose efforts, however meretricious, were welcomed in dreary villages so starved for even the simplest entertainment that a new face or a chance to pick up fresh river gossip was a thing to be prized.

About a year ahead of Bishop, an actor named Cloud rowed an ordinary Delaware River skiff from Pittsburgh to within sight of New Orleans, keeping himself in whiskey simply by billing himself as "the Great Oarsman" who was rowing the river to win a $5,000 bet for the relief of his family—a story of which every word was false. He nevertheless succeeded in financing enough whiskey to drink himself to death before the end of his voyage.

The Redoubtable Captain

The most colorful of these strollers was undoubtedly Captain Paul Boyton, the inventor of an inflatable, deflatable, reflatable, floating rubber life-saving suit. The redoubtable captain paddled himself across the English Channel in this suit, and shortly after Bishop had come down the river Boyton paddled himself in his suit 100 miles from Bayou Goula to New Orleans in 24 hours.

To avoid being overset by the vast amount of waterlogged driftwood with which the Mississippi was virtually blocked, he deflated his suit until only his head was above water, and in this trim propelled himself with a double-bladed canoe paddle that he held in his upraised hands. He reported that a man and a woman who had been crossing the river in a skiff were so terrified at this spectacle that "the man pulled for dear life" and "the woman's screams could be heard miles away." Well, why not—who wouldn't scream at such a sight?

Today's houseboater has no prospect of such delights and opportunities. An artisan who tried today to work his way down the river or along the coast by plying his trade would immediately encounter the impassable obstacle of union membership—local union membership.

And the entrepreneur who tried to set up a floating peripatetic grocery store, restaurant, or barbershop would strand at once on the shoals of local licenses or permits to engage in business, federal, state, county, and municipal sales, use, income, and gross business taxes; inspections; and the admonitions of various boards of education to send his kids to school.

Come to think of it, about all a feller *can* do with a houseboat nowadays is tie it up in some quiet place, go bathing, and drink cocktails.

Me and Those Canoes

Canoeing was invented by the Indians for torturing captives. The Eighth Amendment prohibiting cruel and unusual punishments meant canoeing. Irvin Cobb had canoeing in mind when he wrote that sport is hard work for which you don't get paid.

Canoeists are different from ordinary people. In some cases the difference probably is a matter of courage, resolution, endurance, or fortitude, but in my case it was what my old top sergeant said about a rookie who tackled all the dangerous horses. "He ain't brave," snorted The Hard-Boiled Top. "He just don't know no better."

The fact that every time a canoeist embarks he runs a measurable risk of drowning or coronary thrombosis and a greater one of hernia or heat prostration indicates that there are things basically wrong with canoeing; it is, in fact the most inadvisable means ever conceived for the transportation of man by his own efforts.

Take paddling. If you wanted to move a bureau, you'd stand behind it and shove it with the big muscles of your back and legs. If you had a boat instead of a bureau, you'd dig in your oars and do the same thing. But what would you think of a man who moved a bureau by sitting alongside it, a foot away, and twisting around to give it a feeble shove? If he had a canoe instead of a bureau, he'd use a paddle the same way.

Rowing with two oars drives a boat as straight as a bricklayer heading for a saloon, but paddling with a single blade zigzags a canoe like a bricklayer leaving a saloon. The beginning of the stroke turns the prow aside, so to keep from traveling in a circle the paddler must end the stroke by turning his blade and pushing with it sideways away from him. That off-center body twisting and straining is man-killing. An Amateur Athletic Union official has said that the nearest a man can come to the pangs of childbirth is the twisting and wrenching of competition walking, but he's wrong. The agony of paddling against a headwind is like giving birth to cement blocks.

Carrying a canoe over portages hurts less than paddling only because it is done less. Any carrying at all is too much; there is no, repeat no, canoe light enough for portaging. There is one that weighs only 45 pounds, although it is aluminum, and a careless fisherman in an aluminum canoe sounds like two skeletons wrestling on a tin roof; but even that is too heavy, and besides, a canoe is three times too long to be carried through brush without catching and hanging up worse than a militia officer's saber.

The difference between canoeists and other people is emphasized again in the matter of white water. Canoeists ascend, and sometimes descend, rapids by poling. Unlike the paddler, the poler stands up to the job, but he not only reaches over the edge of the boat—he leans over it. The results of throwing one's weight on a pole which then slips are dramatic but not necessarily enjoyable.

Poling downstream can be even more dramatic and even less enjoyable. The standing poler shoves his pole ahead, sets the point, and the snubs the canoe, letting it downstream slower than the current. The exciting part is when the pole sticks fast among the rocks. If the poler lets go, or if he holds on and the pole breaks, the canoe is out of control until he can squat and grab a paddle—usually too late. But if he hangs on and the pole doesn't break, the canoe goes ahead without him and he remains in the middle of a roaring torrent, waving like a flag. He can try to walk ashore or he can take a chance and let the current carry him down through the rapids, but most well-traveled stretches of white water are studded with canoe poles thrumming in the current, still supporting the skeletons of polers who held on until they starved to death.

With the paddle, white water must be run faster than the pace of the current, to maintain steering way. Since this ordinarily amounts to 10

miles an hour or more, a loaded canoe which encounters a granite mountain in the midst of a rapids is likely to absorb so many foot-pounds of
energy that it abandons its unity like a dropped watermelon. For these reasons most canoeists carry around most rapids, blackflies or no blackflies.
Some make a point of never doing so, but they are not numerous; they
keep getting used up.

It is not surprising that a sport which makes such demands on its devotees should boast its full share of characters. Three of them, all identified
with the canoeing craze of the 1880s and '90s, are fair examples. They are
MacGregor, Bishop, and Nessmuk.

John MacGregor, a brawny (168 pounds) Scots barrister, started it all
back in 1865 by designing a wooden kayak that fitted him like a coat (his
words) or a coffin (my words) and made history as the *Rob Roy*. With a
Cambridge hard straw hat on his hard head, a folded raincoat to sit on,
and his Sunday suit—and damned little else—in a folded cloth bag,
MacGregor cruised on the Continent for three months, fascinating children with gifts of rubber bands, petrifying the yokels with the spectacle of
burning magnesium, and handing out evangelical tracts. On his return he
set the sporting world afire by writing *A Thousand Miles in the Rob Roy
Canoe on Rivers and Lakes of Europe* and, subsequently, *The Rob Roy on the
Baltic* and *The Rob Roy on the Jordan, Nile, Red Sea and Gennesareth &c.*
The cheerful, hardy, sincere, and most engaging personality which these
fascinating books reflect was undoubtedly the principal instigation of the
worldwide canoe craze that ensued.

It came to America in 1871, when a group led by William Livingston
Alden and M. Roosevelt Schuyler organized the New York Canoe Club
and built a fleet from drawings of *Nautilus*, a modified *Rob Roy*, which
they obtained from MacGregor's first disciple, Warrington Baden-Powell.
In 1885 the club established the New York Canoe Club International
Challenge Cup for decked sailing canoes, which is still in competition.

In the winter of 1874–75 an early member of the New York CC,
Nathaniel Holmes Bishop, *rowed* a canoe from Troy, New York, to Florida

down the coastal inland waterways, and in the following winter rowed a
Barnegat sneak-box—a light cedar duck boat—from Pittsburgh to Florida
via the Mississippi and the Gulf. The two trips aggregated about 5,000
miles, and since Bishop had earlier walked across South America from
Buenos Aires to Valparaiso, it must be judged that he was obsessed with
distance. He weighed but 135 pounds, and no wonder. Bishop was the
real founder, in 1880, of the American Canoe Association, which today is
still the governing body of organized canoeing. He wrote three uninspired
chronicles of his journeyings, none of them improved by his dissertations
as an amateur geographer but all reflecting his courage and resolution.

Our third character is Nessmuk—George Washington Sears, the foremost outdoor writer of the 1880s. All the early canoeists were fanatical on
the subject of saving weight, but Nessmuk made a religion of lightness,
perhaps because he weighed only 105 pounds. He was the creator and
high priest of the go-light craze in camping out.

Beginning in 1880 he and his builder, Ruston of Canton, New York,
created a series of clinker-built wooden canoes, the first of which weighed
18 pounds and the last, built in 1885, just an ounce under 10 pounds. But
his best-known craft, approaching MacGregor's 80-pound *Rob Roy* in
fame, was the *Sairy Gamp*, 10½ feet long, 26 inches wide, and less than 7
inches deep. Her sides could be sprung like a cardboard box by mere hand
pressure and her planking was less than ¼ inch thick, but Nessmuk cruised
her all through the Adirondacks without mishap. She hangs today in the
Smithsonian Institution, a miracle of cabinet-work and varnish, a cedar
bubble that floats on the water as a soap bubble floats on velvet.

Aside from the barrel-hoop and bed-sheet canoes that all boys build,
my own connection with the fascinating craft began with a $25 no-name
and ended with an Oldtown guide model in which my bride and I hon-
eymooned on Barnegat Bay. I had sport in all of them, but just as there is
no kiss like a first kiss, so there is no canoe like the first one. That cheap
but sturdy craft gave two 17-year-old boys an unforgettable summer during which we furrowed Long Island Sound like a cornfield. In that great

burst of exaltation the true philosophy of canoeing—and of canoeists—
was made clear to me.

On July 4, 1910, my cousin and I started before daylight to cross the
sound to Execution Light, but the wind came up with the sun and stalled
us within pistol-shot of our goal. So we made a grand swooping run back
to the sheltered inlet beside Travers Island, summer home of the New York
Athletic Club, and hung around the rest of the day taking in the
Metropolitan Senior High-Diving Championships more enjoyably than
those who had paid to watch from land.

The wind died as darkness fell. A string orchestra struck up on the
veranda of the clubhouse, and richly garbed ladies and gentlemen began
arriving in their Rolls-Royces from their lordly estates. Rare wines and
costly viands were served, fragrant Havanas ignited.

By contrast, we had ½ pound of smoked beef, a box of soda crackers,
and a jar of water. We still had before us the long paddle home, a 2-mile
carry on our sunburned shoulders, and, for me, three hours on trolley and
subway to farthest Flatbush.

I washed down the last salty, crumby mouthful with a long swig of
warm water and lit my pipe. The music wafted soft and sweet as a baby's
sigh over water which stirred gently as it slept in the arms of the land. The
trees were inky against a spangled, luminous sky. The reek of salt marshes
mingled with the pungence of the tobacco.

My fingers felt thin and hard as I wrapped them around the shaft of the
gleaming spruce paddle, and I was eager for long steady stroking in the
balmy evening air. I was a king, and my hard bow seat was a throne on the
top of the world. I pointed with my paddle at the veranda.

"Frank, I feel sorry for those people," I said with the earnestness of one
who has just seen the true light. "We have everything that they have! We're
enjoying ourselves more than they are; and," I added, subconsciously
recalling my salary of $11 a week, "it isn't costing us a cent."

I believed it then and I believe it, every word of it, yet. And if you can't
believe it, take my advice and forget about canoes. Which demonstrates

that so far as I am concerned, a canoeist is unflatteringly different from other people. I'm sure you will agree when I add that I never could learn to swim.

True Yachtsmen Shine in Sartorial Splendor

Typically, the owner of a small open motorboat is a hardy, untrammeled soul who thinks of little beyond keeping his engine running well, and having fun. His favorite uniform consists of peeling sunburn, black 600-W gear grease, and a tattered pair of dungarees. If he calls his boat anything printable it is probably "motorboat."

But when he rises to the ownership of a boat with a downstairs to it, he changes psychologically. It may be only an elderly 20-footer with just enough room below deck to squeeze in a head, a galleyette, and a couple of 6-foot bench-bed-locker combinations, but to him it is no longer a motorboat but a yacht. He is not apt to call it that in public after one or two abrasive experiences but, make no mistake, in his mind it is a yacht and he is a yachtsman.

The classic yachting costume of brass-buttoned blue jacket, white flannel trousers, and a white-topped cap is seldom seen nowadays on anything much smaller than Vincent Astor's *Nourmahal* or J. P. Morgan's *Corsair,* and it would take a bold man to wear it around the Sheepshead Bay mooring areas of the T-shirt flotilla.

Our newly fledged yachtsman wants something less conspicuous, cheaper, and easier to keep clean than this fancy-pants classic garb. So, often enough, his thoughts turn to the United States Navy uniform—not the seaman's blouse and bellbottoms but the chaste blue-black serge of the commissioned officer.

There are more Navy uniforms around than you might think. At least one dealer in New York specializes in buying and selling Navy officers' second-hand uniforms—gold braid, brass buttons, insignia, and all. It is also possible to find a variety of white-topped, black-visored caps with enough flash of gold on them to deceive the casual eye. If our budding yachtsman eliminates no more "Navy" from the uniform than is necessary to save him from the cops ("impersonating a United States military officer"), he can be so impressive as to draw salutes.

And he will have plenty of company, for wherever the boating fraternity gathers, there is a chance of seeing some character arrayed in what only close inspection will reveal is not a Navy captain's uniform. And he may even be accompanied by a spouse rigged out in an even closer imitation of a Wave officer's dress uniform. But that's all old stuff, really, and only a pale imitation of the real thing.

Let me introduce you to Colonel and Admiral James G. Fisk Jr., architect of the abortive Gold Corner, the collapse of which created the Black Friday stock market panic of 1869. Jubilee Jim Fisk, a big, portly, handlebar-mustached, handsome man who adored a good time, became colonel of the Ninth New York Infantry Regiment by giving it a liberal injection of his own money. And he became admiral of the Fall River Line of passenger steamships plying Long Island Sound between New York, Fall River, and Newport by becoming owner of the line and appointing himself to admiral's rank.

Jim built up this one-horse affair also by the liberal injection of money—lavishly decorated staterooms and saloons, luxury cuisine, uniformed crews, huge bass-voiced steam whistles, and a magnificent brass band to play the boats away from their Hudson River pier.

Since the line had no military status whatever, Jubilee Jim was on his own so far as personal decoration was concerned. He made himself a rich spectacle with a fore-and-aft cocked hat, an admiral's uniform gold-braided to the elbow, and a Navy boat cloak thrown back to reveal his gold epaulettes, the gold-corded aiguillettes draped across his bosom, and the gold sword belt, with sword, girt about his ample waist.

It was his custom to go every afternoon to the Fall River Line offices, put on his regalia, and then, while the brass band was playing the passengers aboard, take up his position near the gangplank and start volleying nautical orders, which the well-trained crew neither needed nor heeded.

To assist him in these duties Jim was apt to bring along his lady friend, Josie Mansfield, a jealous suitor of whom was soon to shoot and kill Jubilee Jim as he left Miss Mansfield's palatial quarters in the Broadway Central Hotel. Josie had a phony sailor suit of her own, a navy-blue costume that she had designed herself, with brass buttons, gold epaulettes, and a feminine adaptation of a Navy officer's cap of that day. She was the first Wave in American history, or, at least, the first imitation one.

In the Mold of Sea Heroes

Just before the boat's gangplank came in, Jim would ascend to the ship's bridge and make a big production out of ordering the lines cast off.

Then, while the band blared in a frenzy and the deep-toned steam whistle shook the waterfront with its reverberations, Jim would put a long brass telescope under his arm and assume a classic naval pose combining the best of Columbus, Magellan, Sir Francis Drake, John Paul Jones, and David Farragut while the boat backed out of her slip and started downriver.

After a mile or so, she would turn around the Battery, the point of Manhattan, and enter the East River, which isn't a river at all but the extension of Long Island Sound and which ran past what were in those days the backyards of New York's slums. Here a tug would be lying to take the admiral off, and his coach would be waiting at the foot of Wall Street to convey him back to the Fall River Line building to change his clothes.

Those were the days, gentlemen—the days when yachting was yachting, men were men, and fun was really fun. I still maintain that today is just a cheap imitation of a glorious yesterday.

Bathrobes are Professional

The indoor track and field season has tapped a well of nostalgia in the bosom of Mr. Sparse Grey Hackle—a bosom which, it might be mentioned, has grown in amplitude in the years since he personally abandoned foot-racing and took up the worthier, more spiritual occupations of fishing and contributing columns to the needy. He writes:

"At my first track meet in many years, I discover that you now have to have a vivid scarlet, yellow, or green sateen warm-up suit, preferably with blinding stripes, to be an athlete. The more things change, the more they are the same.

"I was a cinder-path fashion plate myself, in 1909. Although my running pants were only an inch long in the inseam, they were split at the front of the thighs so as not to shorten my stride and were bound, top, bottom, sides, and along the splits, with 1-inch scarlet ribbon. My gray shirt was mostly armholes. The long tongues of bright yellow chamois 'pushers' which I wore in my spiked shoes flopped dramatically over my toes.

"When not performing, I wore a loudly figured scarlet and gray bathrobe. As every woman knows, cold breezes blow up under skirts; pants would have been more practicable. But pants were amateur; bathrobes were professional.

There Were Girls in the Stands

"In one pocket I had a pair of cork grips to squeeze while running; it was well known that this engendered more speed. In the other was a bottle of home-made rubdown with which I ostentatiously annointed my muscles in order to dishearten the opposition. Parenthetically, that rubdown, which was mostly turpentine, won me my novice race.

"One broiling day in August 1911 at the Corkmen's P.B.&P. Association games at Wakefield Oval, I applied this embrocation so copiously that my legs were dotted with little white blisters and seemed to be on fire. I ran 600 yards at unprecedented speed just to create a cooling breeze. Winning was a cinch; my only trouble was standing still long enough to collect my prize.

"As a member of the Commercial High School track squad, not the team, I rated no decoration. However, I discovered that years earlier the student body had been liberal in voting monograms for minor sports, with identifying initials such a 'T.T.' for track team and 'R.T.' for rifle team. When I took this information to the faculty adviser he was by turns incredulous, dismayed, and incoherent. But I won my point.

"First time I appeared with an 18-inch monogram on my anterior facade the entire track team, who had won their monograms with much sweat and toil, challenged me belligerently. They squawked long and loud when I pointed out among the convolutions a minute 'D.T.,' signifying that Our Hero was captain of the debating team. But they weren't the ones I was trying to impress; there were girls in the grandstand."

(Red Smith's column, February 17, 1953.)

Mr. Hackle's Rising Gorge

The intelligence may come as a surprise to certain followers of the dry-fly faith who have seen their parishioner, Mr. Sparse Grey Hackle, wading a) waist-high in the Junction Pool on the Beaverkill, or b) ears-deep through spaghetti and meatballs in the Anglers' Club, but in the days of his innocence, the man ran.

That is to say, the boy ran. The man, growing in grace and wisdom, eventually ceased to exhibit himself unclad in public and turned in his spiked slippers as down payment on hobnailed wading brogues. Nevertheless, a misspent life inevitably leaves a mark. To this day, Mr. Hackle's gorge rises whenever there is a reference to track and field performers which he deems less than reverent.

Even some slight impertinence with regard to the track man's taste in toggery brings him panting pell-mell to the defense of the lingerie set. The following letter is an example. It was inspired by a reference here to Roscoe Browne, the half-miler, who is practically a Ph.D. in private life and practically naked in public.

Assorted Fashion Notes

"Recently," Mr. Hackle writes on a typewriter that must have been showing its keys like teeth, "I saw a sportswriter attired in a pair of slacks with bar-rail knees in them, a horse-blanket tweed coat that needed a shave as much as he did, a shirt and necktie that looked like an explosion in a ketchup factory, a hat turned up one side, and a dark brown hangover with fiery spots before the eyes.

"In one of your favorite restaurants there is a waiter who never needs a menu: You just look at the front of his monkey suit and you can see what is on the bill-of-fare today, together with a résumé of the menus for a week past.

"And this morning I saw a newspaper man's offspring (female) wearing Hopalong Cassidy dungarees, a Daniel Boone fringed buckskin windbreaker, and a Confederate forage cap, and carrying a pair of Sonja Henie white shoes and skates.

"To none of these weird sights do you ever advert in print. So how about laying off the underdrawers brigade? Matter of fact, unless times have changed there are lots of funnier costumes to be seen at track meets than those worn by the contestants—and I do not refer to the raiment of the lady spectators.

The Waxworks Couchant

"In my day the Amateur Athletics Union ran heavily to full evening dress. The Beau Brummel of the clan was one Herman Obertubessing, who, as I recall, was built like a combination of Herman Hickman and me and who invariably turned out for the big Madison Square Garden meets in open-faced suit, cast-iron shirt, diamond studs, high poke collar with overflowing chops, and a silk top hat.

"I particularly recall the time a Canadian walker named Golden, or Golding, walked a mile in about half the time it had always required before. He went around the track as if he were on roller skates and quickly had all the officials in a frenzy.

"A record obviously was falling—but was it legal? The technical difference between walking and running seems to depend on whether the heel or toe touches the floor first and leaves it last. Something called 'lifting' produces illegal speed, and the only way to detect 'lifting' is to get down and see whether daylight shows first under the heel or the toe.

"So along with a splendid athletic performance, we enjoyed the spectacle of numerous portly, full-dress-suited, top-hatted officials down on their hands and knees with their scarlet faces and gleaming corporations against the floor, risking apoplexy and sacroiliac displacement in order to preserve the purity of the record book.

"That would have been worthy of your portable; the pallid lingerie of the sweating contestants is not.

Doctors Who Don't Cure

"P.S.—As regards doctors of philosophy, I am told that a certain atomic scientist, friend of a friend of mine, moved into a new apartment. The janitor showed the greatest interest in the family's advent and mentioned to the scientist's wife his pride at having a 'doctor' in the building.

"Alarmed at the prospect of having her spouse turned out some night on a medical emergency call, she hastened to impress on the janitor that her husband was not, as the saying goes, 'the kind of doctor does you any good.'

"'He is a doctor of philosophy,' she informed him.

"The janitor considered this during a moment's silence.

"'Well,' he said brightly, 'I guess that's the coming thing.'"

(Red Smith's column, February 13, 1952.)

Trout on a Fly

J ust as shoemakers' children never have shoes, fly tyers never have flies of their own and rod makers always lack a rod to fish with. Everett Garrison was, in his time, the best fly rod maker in the world, the Stradivarius in an art as difficult as violin making. So when we went fishing on Chestnut Hollow Brook in the Catskills he had a rod made up of joints from several old ones, flies borrowed from me, his old work pants, and no rubber boots—he forgot them. We bought an old pair of boots from a farmer and I helped him rig up, hung his landing net around his neck on its elastic cord, and put him in the stream.

He's a good fisherman. Before long he found himself hooked into a fish that was obviously a big one. He finally played it to a standstill, brought it up to him, and reached for his landing net, which was dangling in front of him.

Pants in those days had buttons down the front so the wearer could get into them and out of them. But Garry had gotten into and out of those pants so often that the buttonholes were worn and the bottom button refused to stay buttoned. Now, when he wanted to use the net, he found it was tangled around the bottom button.

He tried frantically to free it, but you just can't get a string off from around a button. The fish was reviving and something had to be done. Garry did it. He squatted in the water until the seat of his pants was immersed and the top of the net was under water. Then he leaned far back, led the fish over the net, dropped his rod into the stream, and seized the top of the netting to keep the fish from escaping.

That did it; over he went, backward into the stream but still holding onto the net. He got soaked right up to the chin. But when we weighed the trout, it went just under three pounds, a fine fish indeed in our waters.

The next day, Garry bought himself a pair of work pants with a zipper on the front. But we agreed that that was one trout who really had been caught on a fly.

The Angler Breeched

A lady's nightgown may be romantic, but a gentleman's pajamas are merely ludicrous. That is the best example I can cite of the curious fact that some garments are inherently comical while others of the same general sort are not. Thus, the fisherman's battered hat is merely disreputable; his coat of many pockets, incomprehensible; and his heavy brogans, functional. But his waders are just plain ridiculous. There are waders which are more or less sightly, because they have been custom-cut with such skill that every surface and seam is shaped to the contours of the wearer, but most waders are a matter of straight lines and plenty of slack, having been hewn out rather than cut, and they cannot help but excite the mirth of any observer who is not a fisherman.

The history of waders reflects the public's lack of regard for them. In the days of the brook trout, the rubber boot sufficed to wade the small cold streams in which the square-tail lurked. The rubber boot was something a farmer could understand; he had a pair himself. But who in the world could conceive of a pair of rubber pants with feet in them, like children's nightdrawers—who but an Englishman! So the first and for many years the only waders in this country were imported from England by a handful of wealthy, sophisticated city anglers. Small wonder that in the old days a fisherman in waders was such an astonishing and mirth-provoking sight that spectators haw-hawed loudly and crowds of small boys sat by the hour on bridge or bank waiting for the dude to fall in. When Fred White chose "O. U. Waders" for one of his noms de plume in *The Anglers' Club Bulletin,* he was harking back to a time when every urchin greeted him with that paraphrase of the then-popular "Oh, you kid."

Further evidence appears in a line of calendar art that has been published for generations, the work of a father and son each named Henry Hintermeister. The characters in all the paintings are largely the same: The hero is a sort of angling Richard Harding Davis, ruddy, handsome, and with a hearty enjoyment of his friends' troubles; he wears a high white collar and smokes a cigar. Members of the supporting cast are all dressed more or less alike in old business clothes. Then there are the local characters—small boy, farmer, constable. And there is the butt of every scene, the comical chap, the fall guy—short, fat, clumsy, perspiring, and always in trouble. He is the one who buys the country boy's trout, is caught poaching by the sheriff, and falls in while his friends laugh. And he is the only one in any of the pictures who wears waders; the other fishermen are all equipped with manly American rubber boots.

Besides being ridiculous, waders are treacherous, demanding, aggravating, uncomfortable, troublesome, and expensive, and I have small regard for them. However, I must make an exception for one pair that had quite a history. One day my wife came across an apparently brand-new pair of English waders in one of the junk stores called thrift shops.

"What are those?" demanded the deceitful minx, who at that moment had a pair of custom-cut Cordings of her own.

"I don't know; something for fishing," replied the volunteer clerk.

"My husband fishes. . . . How much are they?"

"Two dollars."

"Oh, that's too much," exclaimed my wife, who comes from New England. "I'll give you a dollar."

The waders had belonged, I found later, to a local man of means who had outfitted for salmon, tried it once, and given it up. As my wife had shrewdly surmised, the waders fitted me, and I wore them for two years. Then World War II came along and a young friend of mine, Ray Dierks, became a ski trooper and went to training camp in Colorado, where he found fishing. He wrote to me for flies and leaders, and lamented his lack of waders in the cold water, so I shipped him the dollar waders to wear

inside his GI shoes, and he had a lot of fun until one day he encountered
the colonel.

"Waders!" exclaimed the brass in pleased surprise. *"I wonder if they'd
fit me?"*

So poor Ray was ranked out of his waders; but the colonel was a sport
and used them only half the time, and he had a jeep with which they
fished farther and better waters, so it came out about even. When Ray was
transferred, the waders came back to me, but the next spring I got word
that Scotty Conover, who came up from Virginia each year for a month
on the Beaverkill, was marooned at the Brooklyn Fly Fishers by the disin-
tegration of his waders. Once more the dollar waders went forth and provided a good fellow with sport.

They came back but not to stay. More men than I can recall borrowed
them in such rapid succession that they never had a chance to cool off.
Then the war ended and I got my waders back. And they still had some
two years' wear in them before they came to their end like the One Hoss
Shay, all at once, when I slipped, made a long stretch, and split them from
belt to ankle. It was the best buck my wife ever spent.

When I said that most waders do not have the shape of a man, I do not
mean that they cannot be mistaken for one. In fact, I have in mind two
instances of just that thing happening. In the first, my friend Eddie and I
were coming home from fishing on a motorcycle, in the sidecar of which
I had a pair of Navy submarine-type waders—boot feet, with a pair of
blue mackintosh trousers, which were worn outside them. (Don't ask me
why; that's the way I got them from the surplus store.) As we dropped
down the Monticello Hill, an oncoming car broke out of line and ran into
us, ditching the motorcycle and sending Eddie and me flying over the
handlebars. People came running, not to us but to the overturned sidecar.

"My God, there's a man under there!" exclaimed the first to arrive.

That was news to me, and I walked over groggily to look. It certainly
seemed like it, for those trousered waders, the legs horribly twisted as if
the bones in them had been shattered, protruded from beneath the side-

car. It embarrassed me to tell the onlookers the truth, and somehow they seemed a bit indignant at having been deceived.

The other instance was told to me by a plumber, who declared it had given him the worst scare of his life. He had been summoned by telephone to go up into the organ loft of a church to make some repairs. Imagine his feelings when, as he mounted the stairs, the first thing he saw by the eerie light of one dim bulb was the feet and legs of a man dangling six inches above the floor.

"I thought the dominie had hung himself," he confessed, but it was just a pair of boot-foot waders. Incidentally, it may be useful to remember that some Baptist clergymen use waders professionally. When waders disappeared from tackle stores during the last war, Dana Lamb, one of my more resourceful friends, obtained a splendid pair of boot-foot Hodgmans, in a neat clerical black, by canvassing the religious supply houses on Barclay Street, New York.

A few of our tribulations with waders arise from our own lack of judgment, and this is particularly so in the matter of filling waders with water to test them for leaks. Anyone who tries it will quickly discover that not only does water weigh sixty-four pounds to the cubic foot but it is completely limp unless frozen. A pair of waders full of water weighs twice as much as an ordinary man can lift and is as difficult to handle as an armful of tapioca pudding.

The only time I tried it I used considerable forethought although not nearly enough. I put a sawhorse beside the basement laundry tubs so I could use the hose to fill the waders, which were set astride the sawhorse. And I put hooks in the ceiling, from which cords ran to the suspender buttons to hold the waders upright. It worked like a charm. In no time at all I was able to mark the leaks in this "man" who sat so firmly astride his wooden horse and looked so much like me when I neglect my diet. Then I emptied the waders.

Who has not looked back at some catastrophe and shuddered at the stupidity and mental blindness that drove him into it? My silly solution of the problem was to loosen the cords while I held the man upright, and then pick him up and empty him into the tubs.

Who was that wretched creature that crept like a drowned rat up the basement stairs to evoke the remonstrances of his wife and the mirth of his offspring? And who labored for a week to get the dampness out of the cellar while his tools rusted merrily on the workbench? Who but the author!

The water test is a handy one, but the way to use it is to fill only one leg of the waders and check it, then turn the water into the other leg, and finally into the seat. Even so, it's a two-man job.

The worst of the long list of wader woes that I ever heard of happened not to me but to an able and devoted angler, C. Otto von Kienbusch.

Like the mayfly, Otto spends eleven months of the year in a stone-bound crevice at the bottom of the stream which is New York City, dreaming of his springtime metamorphosis. But when June comes he rises to the surface, casts off his nymphal shuck, and then on shining gauzy wings flies off to Canada for a month of dry-fly salmon fishing on his miles of the Patapedia. Just as the mayfly cannot eat after its metamorphosis, so the angler cannot buy tackle once he has spread his wings, so all must be in order beforehand—and if you know Otto, you know it is.

Last winter, that his wings might be even shinier and his flight stronger, Otto decided to fit himself with those expensive, magnificently custom-tailored waders that take four months to get from England and are worth it. With thoughts of the future Junes on the Patapedia, he bought the apotheosis of all waders, the extra-heavy kind guaranteed for ten years.

June approached and Otto began to stir about the stream bottom and make his preparations for flight. All must be anticipated, all made perfect. Judge then of his consternation when one suspender button on the waders was discovered to be ever-so-slightly loose. A lackey bore them to the tailor. Time passed. The battery of new rods, the jeweled reels, the freshly imported lines, the gaudy flies, the tons of gadgets were ready—all but the waders that would make their use possible. Finally, a week before departure time, they came and Otto unpacked them.

Bessie McCoy might have sung "The Yama Yama Man" in them, those faintly indecent drawers. The Fisk Rubber "Time to Re-Tire" boy in his childish nightdrawers, now presumably grown to manhood, might have been at home in them. Adorned with ribbons, they might have set a new style in undies. But Otto will never, never cast the light fly to the silver salmon in them, for the tailor had had them dry-cleaned, thus removing every vestige of rubber from their fabric. And then had pressed them in neat creases.

Memory on Wheels

R emarks by President Eisenhower about physical fitness in America have prompted Mr. Sparse Grey Hackle, angler and scholar, to offer advice to sportswriters contemplating a tour of the baseball training camps. Only a churl would keep the advice for himself alone.

"I suggest," Mr. Hackle writes, "that you go South by bicycle. Besides publicizing the most practical, useful, and enjoyable contraption ever invented, you would reduce that Artist & Writers chest and make yourself fit—for your pants-band, that is. You could count on doing 100 miles a day (after a while—say, three years). I know it can be done because I watched the last of the 'Century Runs' stream off the Brooklyn ferry and head for Long Island back in 1903. They were starting to do 100 miles a day under controlled pace.

"I can imagine you among them, bulging your muscles and stroking your mustache at the girls, striding beside your Racing Special Lightweight Pierce Arrow with the 105 road sprocket (60 for girls, 85 for men, and anything over 100 for show-offs) and the racing handlebars that brought your back horizontal.

"For you were a 'scorcher,' a road menace, and a horse-scarer in your tight jersey with the 4-inch sash spreading your club's name across your facade, your tight peaked cap (worn backward when scorching), your tight knickers, and long black stockings.

On Pleasure Bent

"How proudly you strode, all 40 of you, in your heelless, lowcut cycling

236

shoes reinforced for toe-clips. For you all had toe-clips, a ruddy nuisance intended to keep your feet from slipping off the pedals in a sprint. Some of you even had little straps on the pedals to secure your feet in the toe-clips.

"A fall with your feet so secured produced an interesting situation, but of course you never, never fell, unless a dog got in the way or a boy stuck a stick in your spokes. Dogs you handled with a water pistol full of ammonia or a .22-caliber Velo Dog Pistol, but there was no defense against boys. There was retribution, though; I still remember a hearty boot in the pants from an enraged cyclist who couldn't take a joke.

"Besides toe-clips, you had on your nickel-plated beauty a Troxel Racing Saddle—leather-covered wood without padding or springs, which were for girls. You had a Dietz oil lamp on the spring bracket; the trademark was a scorcher bent into a D with the slogan ON PLEASURE BENT. You had a tire pump and a tool bag clipped to your 'Diamond frame,' and on the forks you had 'coasters,' brackets to rest your feet on when coasting.

"I had coasters on my Iver Johnson. With my feet up I couldn't reach the racing handlebar grips, but I could grasp the handlebar at the middle and twiddle it to steer. Injudicious coasting and twiddling on a precipitous mountain road behind Nyack, New York, helped me set a distance record for motorless flight that stood for years.

Foamy Remembrance

"You smoked cigarettes to impress the girls but you didn't drink much. I reckon bicycling will never be popular among sportswriters, because the bike is the greatest aid to temperance ever invented. We used to watch the sweaty Century-Runners troop into Kirschhubers or The Bedford Rest, order nickel schooners, and perform the now-forgotten rite of blowing off the foam.

"One schooner was okay, but not two, for the beer was strong and the schooners big enough to bathe an infant in. Watching a red-faced, glassy-eyed cyclist with a belly full of beer and 75 miles of cramp in his legs, trying to mount and catch up with the gang, was more interesting than sitting in the gallery of Corse Peyton's ten-twent'-thirt' stock-company theaters.

The Terror of Highway 301

"So go ahead and bicycle down South, sir. Motorists will honk, dogs will bark, old men will cheer, and the girls will not merely smile—they'll laugh.

"You will arrive strong, slim, and drier than the inside of a lime kiln, and you'll have something to write about after you have exhausted the meager news resources of the ball-camps."

(Red Smith's column, month and day unknown, 1957.)

Letter to Al Severeid

April 14, 1978

. . . It's so simple, when you know how! Marvin Hedge, back when he held the national title and record in distance fly casting, stood with me on the corner of Cedar Street and Broadway, in the heart of the financial district and taught me how to remedy a defect in my casting that simply prevented me from getting either distance or control, and that both Ray Bergman and John Alden Knight had failed to detect.

. . . I invited Hedge up to 120 Broadway. I walked out . . . with Hedge afterward and as we stood on the corner I mentioned my failing. Hedge took out a piece of common white cotton string, the thicker kind which we called butcher string. . . .

Hedge explained that when he was on shipboard, for instance, or some other place where he could not cast with his tournament rig, he could keep in practice by holding a length of common soft cotton string in his hand and casting with it (without a rod, of course). If your timing is right, you can lay out a surprising length of cast and turn over the end neatly (where your fly would be). I have seen an exhibition caster take a heavy salmon flyline in his hand and cast 100 feet with it at one of the Sportsmen's Shows. . . .

Hedge handed me the string and said, "Make a cast." I did, and he made me repeat it several times. "You're snatching at your backcast—rushing your backcast. You're not allowing the line time enough to straighten out fully behind you."

Five minutes of his time rescued me from years of frustration because of my casting limitations. I never became a long shooter—60 feet is a long ways from home plate, for me. But I could cast as far as I could depend on hitting a fish if it did rise to my fly, and I could control my line.

Small Rods

T rout fishermen hibernate with one eye open and one ear cocked. . . .
And so it happens that when, on Wednesday, I referred to the new-
type fly rods measuring seven feet in length and weighing two and one-
quarter ounces, and conservatively stated that these rods would handle
forty feet or more of line, a famous Darien fly-casting, worm-dunking
trout fisherman stirred in his burrow, seized pen in hand, and dashed off
the following classic.

Writes Sparse Grey Hackle:

"The same day you described that wonderful seven-foot rod, I received
a belated gift from Everett Garrison of a six-foot, nine-inch rod of his own
make. Having tried it out, I make bold to give you the horselaugh.

"If you think it wonderful for a seven-foot rod to cast forty feet, let me
tell you that I can take a standard 'D' taper fly line in my powerful left
hand and cast thirty-five measured feet, without any rod whatsoever. I can
do it anytime, anywhere there is room and no wind, and for money, mar-
bles, or chalk. Marvin Hedge, the casting champ, can cast sixty-five feet
the same way.

"This two-ounce beauty of mine cast an 'D' line over fifty feet, when I
had to quit as I was getting into the bushes. At that distance, it had a lot
left and I have no hesitation in saying it will go sixty feet. In the hands of
a man like Hedge, with a properly balanced line, I would bet that it, or
any top-notch seven-foot rod, will cast eighty feet.

"The small rod is the most difficult to make because a thousandth of
an inch means so much more on a small section than a large one. Few
makers have the tapers, the wood, and the skill to make a fine one. But

when you get one it is, to my mind, the acme in fishing rods. It will cast as far as the ordinary man fishes, and with such ease and convenience that its use is delightful. As to handling fish, it will break a 3X leader, and you can't use more power than that. It will fish in little brooks where no large rod will work, and cover plenty of larger water if you don't let the prospect scare you. Its only disadvantage is that it affords less control over the line after it is on the water, because of its shortness.

"If anybody doubts that my new rod is a real fishing rod, let him come up on the roof of 120 Broadway with me and it."

(Donald Stillman's "Rod and Gun," January 8, 1938.)

Letter to Hoagy Carmichael Jr.

August 8, 1977

This is to thank you very much indeed for the Garrison book. I am astounded at the job you have done, and utterly delighted to see so accurate and complete exposition of rod design, and the related fields of wood selection and the technique (in fullest detail) of construction.

. . . I think you can take my opinion rather seriously, because I was familiar with much of Garry's methods, both intellectual and manual, for many years, almost from his beginning. As a matter of fact, the discussion of 5-strip vs 6-strip rods . . . was written by me.

. . . Field & Stream, apparently getting some needling from 6-strip rodmakers, out of a clear sky sent Garry a check for $50 (good money in those days) and a request for a comparison of the 5-strip and 6-strip designs. Garry prepared a fine blast, including some of his fine mechanical drawings. . . . F&S wrote and thanked him, and said they were returning the article to be translated into English!!

Garry hollered for me, and grumbled that the whole thing was absolutely clear and plain. I've always been mechanically minded, and used to hang out with gunsmiths (I knew both Adolph Neidner and Harry Pope) and rodmakers, along with mechanical engineers and the like of that—for some years I was an industrial reporter for the Wall St. Journal. Garry was indignant when I told him I couldn't understand his article either. "What don't you understand?" he demanded. "Well, for one thing, this statement . . ." and I read it. He was outraged. "Why of course, because the resilience of a section increases as the cube of its diameter; any goddam fool knows that!"

"Well," I said, "this one doesn't. Now explain this so I can understand it." And finally he grumpily did. And I rewrote the piece from his explanation. I can still recognize a few of my own phrases. And F&S took and printed my version. I had my chest a bit far out for a few years after this happened, until one day I found a clipping I had saved from F&S, and made the mistake of reading it. You know, I'm not so goddam sure I made the thing any clearer than Garry's original effort!

. . . I don't doubt that Garry calculated his tapers as you expound in detail; but I'll tell you there was a little know-how, common sense and compromise in his original "212" 8-footer. John Alden Knight told me, while he still had the famous 8-footer Garry gave him, that he had suggested some slight modifications in Garry's design which made it a much more useful rod, and I believed him then and still do. Jack was a one-time tournament caster with an arm like a blacksmith, and he had at one time briefly manufactured a custom rod under the name "Delaware" with the assistance of someone who had at one time worked for Leonard. . . .

Anyway, Jack Knight knew a hell of a lot about rods and casting, and he publicized (and secured many orders for) the Garrison 8-footer. One of his stunts was to fish at the "Fisherman's Paradise" at Bellefonte, Pa. and spread the word that at noontime he would go up on the dam and cast 100 feet with an 8-foot rod. He could do it, too, even though Garry's design is not (and wasn't intended to be) a terrific long shooter.

Hiram Hawes was one of the best tournament casters (along with Eddie Mills) of his time, and he made superb rods; I have a 7½-footer of his . . . it was of old-fashioned wet-fly action, very delicate but utterly superb. It had the first hallmark of a really fine flyrod—it would straighten out all the line it would throw and turn over the fly (assuming a properly balanced line and leader) with incredible delicacy and precision. I found the action a bit slow for my Garrison-accustomed hand, so after long thought I got Garry to cut it down (it was in three joints) to seven feet, and it is a real poem; I wish I could still fish, so I could use it on appropriate water. It is in mint condition, with the old original Hawes ferrules. Hawes (and his son Merritt) and Jim Payne made the best ferrules anyone ever produced, although I always thought Jim's ferrules were perceptibly longer than was necessary. The fit on those ferrules was incredibly good—not confined to a little cone-shape at the top that soon wears loose; they were fitted full length, and smooth as silk.

Father of the Fly Rod

The true purpose of a fly rod is to prevent its bearer from being arrested for vagrancy, for the delight of trout fishing is not the full creel but things seen and people met. A roughly dressed man idling with a rod in his hand is an angler; without it he is a vagabond.

And yet a fine fly rod is a magnificent thing, a strain of music made visible, a living part of the hand that holds it. Many an angler becomes so enchanted with the casting of a perfect rod that he resents interruption by trout.

The fly rod is, in fact, a sort of miracle. A typical 8-footer contains only 2-and-a-fraction ounces of bamboo, but it can throw a fly 100 feet or kill a 20-pound salmon and after a quarter of a million casts still be a good rod.

The miracle is a modern one, for although fly rods of a sort are older than recorded history, the first that was anything more than a limber stick was made only about 75 years ago. Many men contributed to the development of the fly rod, but the man who took the last great steps in creating the fly rod that we know today was an American. He made the American fly rod the world's standard. And from the remote community of Bangor, Maine, this American's name went around the world until it was recognized wherever flies were cast for trout. But only his name; even in his own country the man himself is almost unknown.

The man was Hiram L. Leonard, who not only achieved genius in several fields but was one of the most colorful and individualistic characters in the history of American angling.

He was born in Maine but grew up near Honesdale, Pennsylvania. By the time he was 20 he was "in charge of the machinery" of a coal-mining company. Then he went to Bangor, Maine, and was, successively, a taxidermist, a gunsmith, a professional market hunter and fur trader, and a taxidermist again, before he took up rod making.

Henry David Thoreau met him in 1857, when he was a hunter, and described him in *Canoeing in the Wilderness* as a handsome man of good height but not apparently robust, of gentlemanly address and faultless grooming. He was a spiritualist, a vegetarian who abhorred liquor and detested tobacco. He was a good musician, playing the flute and bass viol, and held the entertaining belief that a man could not make a good fishing rod unless he loved music and could play at least one instrument.

Leonard set foot on the path to fame when a Boston sporting-goods house, Bradford & Anthony, was so impressed with the workmanship of a wooden rod that he had made for his own use that they started him making split-bamboo rods for them. This type was becoming popular and the firm was having trouble getting well-made rods.

That was in 1871, when Leonard was 40 years old. From the start, he had more work than he could handle, even though he soon hired Fred Thomas to help him and, subsequently, Ed Payne, Billy Edwards, and two of his cousins, Hiram and Loman Hawes, whom he brought up from Honesdale. Incidentally, all of those names—Thomas, Payne, Edwards, and Hawes—were given to famous brands of fine fly rods in after years.

Fly rods had been made of strips split from a stalk of bamboo, planed to a fit, and glued together to form a rod joint well over 100 years before Leonard ever saw one. But they were so badly designed and made that none of them could cast 70 feet, a distance to which a man can throw a line with his bare hand if he knows how. It was the nature of Leonard's art that he converted those old switches into the modern miracle through three subsidiary miracles of his own—engineering design, craftsmanship, and a new secret material.

He was the first man to make, in 1871 or 1872, a six-strip rod instead of the four-strip construction previously used. Anyone who can calculate things like longitudinal shear and bent-beam stresses can prove by immutable mathematical principles that the six-strip rod of hexagonal cross-section is inherently the best. I can't. But it is.

Leonard was also the first to use compound tapers of calculated design. And what that amounts to is this: Tapers are vital in implements that deliver a stroke—golf clubs, racing oars, polo mallets, horsewhips, and the like—because such implements increase their effectiveness by bending at the start of the stoke and straightening at the finish. Shaping the shaft with varying tapers at different points permits the force of the stroke to be controlled, timed, and directed.

Leonard's second contribution was a perfection of workmanship never previously approached. He was a superb craftsman, with genius in his hands, and could make the good rods that he did, at the start, with simple hand tools. But he never could have kept up with his orders by such methods, even though he had hired and trained help. So he designed some tools of his own.

Chief of the several machines which he invented was the "beveler," which Leonard had in use certainly in 1877 and probably in 1876. It cut the triangular, tapered strips, six of which go into each section of a rod. It cut—and still cuts, for makers of Leonard, Thomas, and Payne rods, and maybe others, still use the beveler unchanged today—the strip complete with all the varying compound tapers on its outer surface. The beveler produced glue joints so closely fitted as to be invisible under a 20-power microscope and dimensions accurate to within a few thousandths of an inch at any point on the rod.

In an age of industrial secrecy Leonard was notable for his secretiveness. He realized that he had the rod-making world by the tail and took steps to maintain his hold. The beveler was always kept in a locked room and only he and his nephew Rube Leonard operated it. If Fred Thomas had not hung around and peeked until he found out how it worked, he and Payne and Edwards and Hawes would not have been able to make the rods they did when they quit the Leonard plant. To this day, according to my information, the beveler at the Leonard plant is kept in a locked room, and only one man knows how to run it.

Leonard was, if possible, even more secretive about his third contribution to the modern fly rod—the use of Tonkin cane as a rod-making material.

Tonkin (a misnomer), the bamboo used for fly rods today, is a thick-walled and heavy-fibered cane found in China which, weight for weight, is unequaled for elasticity and resilience by any other material.

William Mitchell, a celebrated rod maker of the Civil War period, stated in the 1880s that he had made a rod of "Chinese cane" in 1869, but apparently it made no impression on him.

But Mrs. Hiram Hawes, H. L. Leonard's daughter, recalls that in 1877 Loman Hawes got hold of an umbrella, down in Bangor, that had bamboo ribs and knew that it must be something other than Calcutta, the Indian cane which up until that time had been used for fly rods. Calcutta would not have stood such treatment. He and Leonard—or maybe just Leonard—found out that the stuff was Tonkin and located a source of supply (it has always been the monopoly of a few British dealers in Hong Kong).

With it Leonard's nephew Rube increased the title-winning distance cast from 80 feet in 1882 to 102 feet in 1888. (Today's record: 194 feet.)

In 1877 Leonard lost control of his name and business by going into partnership with a Boston man named Kidder and forming the H. L. Leonard Rod Co., to which he gave the exclusive right to his name and services in a cast-iron contract. A year later Kidder sold out his interest to William Mills & Son of New York, who had recently become the sole agents for the Leonard rod.

The Mills firm wanted Leonard closer to New York, so in 1881 he moved his plant to Central Valley, New York, where it still is. About 1906 there was a big all-around row of some sort, with the result that Leonard sold his interest in the H. L. Leonard Rod Co. to the Mills firm, and all his key workmen—Thomas, Payne, Edwards, and the Hawes brothers—quit and started rod businesses of their own. Thereafter Leonard had little to do with the firm. He died in 1907 at the age of 76.

There is only one more thing to note about Leonard. He never taught anyone, even his own nephews, anything about the calculation of rod tapers. After his death there was no one in the world for a good many years who could calculate the design of a fly rod as Leonard had, on an engineering basis. It took years of fumbling experiment, suggestions from customers, and the imaginative thinking of a few advanced amateurs like the late Robert W. Crompton of Minneapolis before the custom industry began making good rods again.

It is probable that the total output of strictly first-class custom fly rods since Hiram L. Leonard made the first one is today not greatly in excess of 100,000 and that the current output is nearer 2,500 rods a year than 5,000. As to price, Leonard's first rods sold for $35 in a time when workmen supported their families on $1 a day. The price of a first-class custom trout rod today is from $100 to $150, depending on the maker.

And what of the future? Glass rods are the thing today, and they are marvelously practical although even the best falls far short of perfection. As a man who is considered a judge of rods said to me recently:

"You can get from any sports shop for about $7.50 a glass rod that is just as good as any of them except that it needs a few more guides. You can fish with it all day, lick the cows out of the way, and knock down a few apples, and when you are through, give it to the farm boy whose father let you fish and he will be in ecstasies. It wouldn't suit you or me, but it is a perfectly good rod for an awful lot of fishermen who don't know any better and don't want to."

It seems more likely that progress toward that exquisite, marvelous non-existent treasure, the perfect fly rod, will come from the experimentation of one or two custom-rod makers like Garrison and Stoner, who carry on the Leonard tradition.

Is it worth the agony? Yes, if there continue to be others like me. Logically, I should stick to a glass rod, since I am convinced that the intangibles which surround fishing are so much more important than the fishing itself. I can't cast well, and I can't tell a good rod from a bad one. Still and all, my wife and I have 8 or 10 custom rods, including a Payne and 4 Garrisons that we would not part with. And I would cheerfully go to the

loan sharks for money to pay $300 apiece, even more, for three Garrisons
that I know of if the owners (none of whom fishes any longer) would
change their minds and sell them.

A Drink of Water

No one raised as I was in Greater New York has any real awareness of drinking water until he gets beyond access to the pure, bountiful, never-failing supply which blesses that city. So when the New York militia division went to Texas on the Mexican Border Patrol, we were shocked and dismayed to find that not only was the water saturated with earth chemicals—Epsom salts, as a matter of fact—so that it was well-nigh undrinkable, but it was so scarce that on occasion it was an article of purchase and sale.

Small wonder that when the Sixty-Ninth Infantry, the Fighting Irish, marched to Laguna Seca and found a native Texan waiting there to sell them water at ten cents a canteenful because the windmill well-pump was "broken," they chased him into the brush with fixed bayonets, cut him out of harness and drove away his mules, confiscated his water, smashed the barrels, and burned the wagon. To men who as boys had followed the universal New York custom of ringing the nearest doorbell and asking for a drink of water when they were thirsty, it was revolting that there should be a price on water.

We learned about water, down there. We learned after a mass epidemic of bellyaches not to ice it. We learned that water from a mile of piping laid above ground, exposed to a 130-degree sun temperature, would quench thirst better than if it was cold. We learned to drink soldierly from a canteen by admitting air from the side of the mouth, and to drink at the trot without knocking out our front teeth by propping the thumb firmly against the chin for a steady-rest. We even enjoyed learning those things because we were very young.

Some of us learned to husband our water by drinking sparingly on the march, but the rookies didn't, so Davy Baldwin and I, caisson corporals of the fifth and sixth sections, were worried for our men when orders came for a thirty-mile march to the artillery target range at Monte Cristo Ranch, for we knew it would be a dry march. We agreed to carry two extra canteens apiece for our men but to drink none ourselves, to set a good example. Instead, we would chew tobacco. We had learned that deplorable habit from being around horses, for smoking is properly a deadly sin anywhere around a stable or even an outdoor picket line.

We made the march, as I recall, in some twelve hours, every step of the way at a walk through rolling clouds of alkali dust so dense one could not see the gun carriage ahead. Each man had his quart canteen and there was half a cup of cold coffee at the noon halt. But that afternoon our drivers were in distress, and it was well that we had an extra pint of water per man to dole out to them. Davy and I chewed stoically; and when camp was made we each rode four horses bareback into the hurly-burly around the watering tank just to show how tough we were. As I said, we were young. Then we came to the best drink I ever had.

You can grow anything in that country if you have water, and Sterling's Ranch had some seven-hundred-foot wells. Sterling raised citrus fruit in a small way, and that afternoon he had a whole barrel of fresh-fruit limeade in a shady spot, selling it for a nickel a pint-canteen cupful. Still sitting our water-bloated and weary horses, Davy and I blew the dust off our lips, licked away the mud, raised our cups to each other, and then dumped them down our throats with a single motion. It merely tasted cool. The second cup went down right after it, again with a single lift. It tasted cool and wet. We grinned at each other across the third cup and poured it down the hatch to join the others, and for the first time we tasted the flavor of limes. Then with our fourth cup in hand we booted our weary horses out of the way and sipped the delightful draft—four gulps instead of one. It is inconceivable to me now that a skinny young man of 147 pounds could drink two measured quarts of liquid in five minutes, but I did and no bellyache either. Must have been the tobacco that saved me. Or maybe I was just young.

Because of what the army taught me, I am no friend of surface water; I won't drink from any stream that has any human habitation on its watershed. And I'm suspicious of rural wells. A farm well is usually at the lowest point in the landscape, but surprisingly often the privy is on the highest, and sometimes so is the barnyard manure pile. Just the smell of some of those old wells is enough to convince you that there is something in them besides water. If I have to use such water, I boil or chlorinate it. Even the sparkling spring deserves to have its antecedents considered. One of my friends got typhoid from a lovely sparkling spring which, tests with soluble dyes later proved, flowed right through the mountain from a polluted area in the next valley. If all this sounds old-maidish and timid, I will remind you that I have not yet had typhoid.

But when you go into the deep woods, you come to the very best kind of drinking that there is. And you enjoy it all the more because nothing builds up a deep, insistent thirst like carrying a heavy pack through close, unstirring second growth on a broiling, humid August day. Your clothes become cemented to you, the packstraps emboss your tender skin, the hot touch of the pack itself raises prickly heat on your back, and your glasses slide around on your streaming face.

Then, just as your knees start trembling and you begin to see little black spirals before your eyes, you come to an icy trickle, bubbling and murmuring over bright pebbles. You discard your reeking hat and foggy glasses, drop to your knees and then to all fours, and you lower yourself, pack and all, onto your belly, and drink like a horse.

I use that simile because a horse really enjoys his water. He can be dainty enough when he is not very thirsty, shoving floating dust aside with his muzzle and playing with the water. But a horse that has walked thirty miles under a blazing Texas sun shoves his long face in right up to the eyes, and you can see gulps of water as big as oranges chasing each other down his throat. When he has to come up for air he snorts and shakes his head and throws water all around, then resumes drinking until he sloshes and gurgles internally. Then he turns away, luxuriously chewing his last mouthful of water and letting it run out of his mouth and down his chin.

So you drink like a horse, cooling your face in the water, until you come up gasping and snorting. As you lie there flat on your belly you put your hands and wrists into the icy flow and not until they begin aching do you climb to your feet, a new man.

The prettiest drinking place that I remember was on Finch & Pryne's timber reserves in the Adirondacks, on which we were trespassing to fish the Rock River, long ago. This was the deep cathedral woods. Right beside our camp was a tiny spring. Water seeped from under the dead leaves, trickled over a mossy stone, and fell from the emerald fringe, a drop at a time, into a pebbly basin that held just enough to fill a coffeepot or a very thirsty fisherman. As it fell, each drop sounded a different note, so that the spring continually played a chime of little silver bells. One scarcely noticed it by day, but in the stillness of the night the wood sprites played faint elfin tunes on it, ineffably sweet and clear. No wonder the bucks came down in the moonlight to cut up their stamping ground with their hooves, and the beavers worked on their dam so close we could hear the falling of trees and the slapping of broad tails. It was an enchanted place.

But the saddest drinking place I remember was on Ed Hewitt's Neversink. He had five princely miles of that river, the most wildly beautiful stream I ever saw. It was brilliantly clear. ("The water is lucent as air," Theodore Gordon wrote.) It ran over white and granite stones through a narrow forested valley, a place of rugged bristling steeps, moss-hung rock faces, brawling rapids, and deep blue pools. So wild it seemed that one expected any moment to see the painted, feathered head of a Mohawk rise stealthily among the alders. On a bench extending into the largest of the valley meadows stood an old farmhouse, which Ed called The Camp, and here his "rods," who rented annual fishing privileges, used to gather after the day's fishing was over for unforgettable nights of fun and companionship. It was the last of the Golden Age.

Then New York City took most of Hewitt's stream for a reservoir and came in with bulldozers to remove every tree and bush and blade of grass right up to the projected waterline of the reservoir, and even to alter the contours of the valley, leaving a wasteland of desecrated, barren ground.

It was 110 degrees by the thermometer on Ed Hewitt's mountain-top porch that August afternoon when I walked down the breakneck trail into the valley to see what the bulldozers had done. In the biblical phrase, it was the abomination of desolation. The river was shrunken, the pools bulldozed into narrow channels among bare, rough stones and sterile dirt that held the heat like the lining of a blast furnace. As I climbed up onto what was left of the elevated spur of land, I couldn't even be sure just where The Camp had been.

Then I heard running water. The bulldozers had leveled The Camp and filled in the foundation, all but one corner, and in that was the spring which the original builder had taken pains to include in his cellar. I climbed down into the crevice and found protruding from the foundation wall a pipe from which poured a strong, lively stream, clear as air and cold as ice, the only living thing in that valley of silent ruin. Beside it was a champagne bottle—what other fishing camp boasted champagne?—and I chilled the hick green glass before I filled it.

Then I had a drink better than any champagne, a drink from the old Camp spring—a drink all alone save for the friendly and approving spirits of as fair a company of good angling companions as ever existed. I raised the bottle high and toasted the good old days on their behalf.

Then I climbed out and went up the river, past the Camp Pool and Molly's Pool and the Shop Pool; the Flat Pool, the Long Pool, York's Ford, the Island Pool—or rather, the places where they had been—and up to the Little Bend and the Big Bend. As I walked, salty drops ran down my face; but they were just perspiration. Just perspiration.

Epilogue

There comes a time in a day's trout fishing when, standing in the ever-pushing water, you become aware of how tired you are. The dull ache at the back of your neck, your belt leaning heavy on your hip bones, toes cold and numb in the end of your brogues, fingers cramped, and eyes tired. Climb out, with your legs and feet as weighted as in a nightmare escape, and walk into the woods until the sound of the stream becomes background. There you will find a round carpet of pine needles, deep and sun warmed, and a good broad trunk to ease between your shoulder blades. Now tobacco smoke pulled deep into your lungs, warmth coming through on your stretched-out calves, and quiet. If you wait long enough the quiet will pass and all the woods noises, stilled by your lumbering passage, will begin again. A chickadee will surely come close and stand upside down on a twig for you, and you will hear delicate foot rustlings like the fast sliver of a needle through dark cloth with the pause for slow-drawn thread.

The Works of Sparse Grey Hackle

My sincerest thanks to Kenneth Callahan and Judith Bowman, both booksellers extraordinaire, for their enormously generous help in tracking down material that would otherwise have disappeared, forgotten and lost. It is not the fault of either Ms. Bowman or Mr. Callahan that this is an incomplete list of all the works of Sparse. I was unable to track some publications down, some had no indices going that far back, and some material has simply been forgotten in the passage of time.

Books

Darbee, Harry and Austin M. Francis. *Catskill Flytier: My Life, Times and Techniques.* Introduction by Sparse Grey Hackle. Philadelphia: J. B. Lippincott Company, 1977.

Fox, Charles K. *Advanced Bait Casting.* Preface by Sparse Grey Hackle. New York: G. P. Putnam's Sons, 1950.

Hidy, V. S. *The Pleasures of Fly Fishing.* Foreword by Sparse Grey Hackle. New York: Winchester Press, 1972.

LaBranche, George M. L. *The Dry Fly and Fast Water & The Salmon and the Dry Fly.* Reprint from 1914, also 1924, 1942. Introduction by Sparse Grey Hackle. New York: Scribner, 1951.

Melner, Samuel and Hermann Kessler. *Great Fishing Tackle Catalogs of the Golden Age.* Introduction and Commentary by Alfred W. Miller. New York: Lyons & Burford, 1972.

Miller, A. W. "Helpfulness," "It Worked—Both Ways," "Warning," "Dr. Tinckerberry's Accident," "Fishing," "Boys," "Hooked, Played and Landed." In *The Outdoor Trail of Don Stillman.* Ed. by Don Stillman. Harrisburg, Pa.: Stackpole, 1952.

———. "Nocturne." In *A Treasury of Fishing Stories.* Ed. by Charles E. Goodspeed. New York: A. S. Barnes and Company, Inc., 1960.

———. "Who Is Sparse Grey Hackle?" In *The Gordon Garland.* Ed. by Arnold Gingrich. New York: The Theodore Gordon Flyfishers, 1965. (See also *American Trout Fishing* listing below.)

———. "Who Is Sparse Grey Hackle?" In *American Trout Fishing: Theodore Gordon and a Company of Anglers.* Ed. by Arnold Gingrich. New York: Knopf, 1966. (Trade edition of *The Gordon Garland.*)

———. *Fishless Days, Angling Nights.* New York: Crown Publishers, 1971.

_____. *Sparse Grey Hackle: His Life, His Stories, and His Angling Memories.* Ed. Austin M. Francis. Epilogues by Patricia Miller Sherwood and Nick Lyons. New York: The Anglers' Club of New York, 1993.

Slaymaker, S. R. II. *Simplified Fly Fishing.* Introduction by Alfred W. Miller. New York: Harper & Row Publishers, 1969.

Sparse Grey Hackle. "The Indomitable." In *Angler's Choice.* Ed. by Howard T. Walden. New York: Macmillan, 1947.

_____. *Fishless Days.* New York: The Anglers' Club of New York, 1954.

_____. "Murder." In *The Fireside Book of Fishing: A Selection of the Great Literature on Angling.* Ed. by Raymond R. Camp. New York: Simon and Schuster, 1959.

_____. "The Perfect Angler." In *The Wonderful Words of Sport: An Anthology.* New York: Time, Inc., 1967.

_____. "Murder." In *Fisherman's Bounty.* Ed. by Nick Lyons. New York: Simon & Schuster, Inc., 1970.

_____. "The Perfect Angler." In *The Armchair Angler.* Ed. by Terry Brykcznski, David Reuther, and John Thorn. New York: Charles Scribner's Sons, 1986.

_____. "The Father of the Fly Rod." In *The Flyfisher's Reader.* Ed. by Leonard M. Wright Jr. New York: Simon & Schuster, Inc., 1990.

_____. "The Pennsylvania Boys." In *Limestone Legends.* Ed. by Norm Shires and Jim Gilford. Mechanicsburg, Pa.: Stackpole Books, 1997.

Walden, Howard T. II. *The Last Pool: Upstream and Down & Big Stony.* Introduction by Sparse Grey Hackle. New York: Crown Publishers, 1972.

Periodicals

Fly Fisherman. Harrisburg, Pa.: Cowles Enthusiast Media

Sparse Grey Hackle. "The Angler Breeched." Vol. 3, No. 1, pp 12–13.

_____. "Nice Work If You Can Get It." Vol. 3, No. 2, pp. 26–28.

_____. "Only Yesterday." Vol. 4, No. 2, pp. 22–29.

_____. "Roy Steenrod: The Legend and the Legacy." Vol. 9, No. 1, pp. 20–23.

Harper's Magazine

Sparse Grey Hackle. "Traditions." 249:6, August 1974.

The Ledger. Brooklyn, N.Y.: Students of The Commercial High School
Miller, Alfred W. "Reuben Comes to Town." (Date unknown—circa 1909.)

The New York Times, New York
Sparse Grey Hackle. "So Beware; So Beware." Boat Section, January 15, 1967.

_____. "Avast: Don't Rock the Status Symbol." Boat Section, April 30, 1967.

_____. "It's All in the Mind." Boat Section, February 9, 1968.

_____. "Sports Canoeists of Old Days Daring Breed of Adventurers." Boat Section, February 11, 1968.

_____. "Ingenuity to the Fore." Boat Section, March 31, 1968.

_____. "True Yachtsmen Shine in Sartorial Splendor." Boat Section, April 28, 1968.

_____. "A Beauty in the Boat; Storm Signals Fly with a Woman Aboard, One 'Joik' Sadly Learns." Boat Section, January 26, 1969.

_____. "Of Bottoms and Boats." Boat Section, March 30, 1969.

_____. "Houseboats . . . Bah!" Boat Section, April 27, 1969.

_____. "Bargain Buy in Sports." Boat Section, January 25, 1970.

_____. "Forgotten Knowledge." Boat Section, date unknown.

Outdoor Life. New York: Popular Science Publishing Co., Inc.
Miller, Alfred W. "That Fall Guy." 116:60–1, December 1955.

Pennsylvania Angler. Harrisburg, Pa.: Pennsylvania Fish & Boat Commission
Sparse Grey Hackle. "Starvation Pond." July 1955.

Sports Illustrated. New York: Time-Life
Sparse Grey Hackle. "Note for Next January." In "Events & Discoveries." January 27, 1956, pp. 13–14.

_____. "Father of the Fly Rod." June 4, 1956, pp. 79–81.

_____. "Me and Those Canoes." September 2, 1957, pp. 45–46.

_____. "Penn's Creek." April 7, 1958, pp. 38–?

_____. "The Perfect Angler." April 6, 1959, pp. 83–86.

_____. "The Forgotten Fun of Driving." February 1, 1960, pp. 58–64.